Queer Georgians

A hidden history of lovers, lawbreakers and homemakers

ANTHONY DELANEY

doubleday

TRANSWORLD PUBLISHERS

UK | USA | Canada | Ireland | Australia
India | New Zealand | South Africa

Transworld is part of the Penguin Random House group of companies
whose addresses can be found at global.penguinrandomhouse.com.

Penguin Random House UK, One Embassy Gardens,
8 Viaduct Gardens, London SW11 7BW

penguin.co.uk

First published in Great Britain in 2025 by Doubleday
an imprint of Transworld Publishers

001

Copyright © Anthony Delaney 2025

The moral right of the author has been asserted

Every effort has been made to obtain the necessary permissions with
reference to copyright material, both illustrative and quoted. We apologize
for any omissions in this respect and will be pleased to make the
appropriate acknowledgements in any future edition.

As of the time of initial publication, the URLs displayed in this book link or refer to
existing websites on the Internet. Transworld Publishers is not responsible for, and
should not be deemed to endorse or recommend, any website other than its own or
any content available on the Internet (including without limitation at any website,
blog page, information page) that is not created by Transworld Publishers.

Penguin Random House values and supports copyright. Copyright fuels creativity, encourages diverse
voices, promotes freedom of expression and supports a vibrant culture. Thank you for purchasing an
authorized edition of this book and for respecting intellectual property laws by not reproducing,
scanning or distributing any part of it by any means without permission. You are supporting authors
and enabling Penguin Random House to continue to publish books for everyone. No part of this
book may be used or reproduced in any manner for the purpose of training artificial intelligence
technologies or systems. In accordance with Article 4(3) of the DSM Directive 2019/790,
Penguin Random House expressly reserves this work from the text and data mining exception.

Typeset in 12.5/15.75 Dante MT Pro by Jouve (UK), Milton Keynes
Printed and bound in Great Britain by Clays Ltd, Elcograf S.p.A.

The authorized representative in the EEA is Penguin Random House Ireland,
Morrison Chambers, 32 Nassau Street, Dublin D02 YH68.

A CIP catalogue record for this book is available from the British Library

ISBNs:
9781529927689 (cased)
9781529927702 (tpb)

For
Paul O'Grady
(1955–2023)
Hellraiser, trailblazer, history-maker, friend.

Contents

AUTHOR'S NOTE	xi
PROLOGUE	1

CHAPTER ONE
A House on Field Lane ... 13

CHAPTER TWO
The Deadly Nevergreen ... 31

CHAPTER THREE
Sedition and Defamation Display'd ... 55

CHAPTER FOUR
No. 31 Great Burlington Street ... 79

CHAPTER FIVE
Our Little Community ... 101

CHAPTER SIX
The Speculation ... 119

CHAPTER SEVEN
That Feverish Dream Called Youth ... 155

CHAPTER EIGHT
Inflammable Materials ... 173

Contents

CHAPTER NINE
Geranium Sylvaticum — 201

CHAPTER TEN
A (Not So) Singular Case — 235

CHAPTER ELEVEN
The Amalgamationist — 253

EPILOGUE — 273

NOTES — 287

SELECT BIBLIOGRAPHY — 311

ACKNOWLEDGEMENTS — 321

PICTURE ACKNOWLEDGEMENTS — 325

INDEX — 328

*'Well, well, it looks like we've got help
with the washing up.'*

Lily Savage, 30 January 1987,
as police officers raided the
Royal Vauxhall Tavern, London.

Author's Note

THE PERIOD EXPLORED IN this book (1714–1837) is foreshadowed by the introduction of the Marriage Duty Act (1695), which imposed punitive measures on bachelors who did not wish to, or could not, marry. It incorporates the continuation of the Buggery Act (1533), which sought to punish all sex acts beyond the procreative, but particularly targeted men who had sex with other men. This period also includes other pivotal moments in the history of gender and sexuality such as the raid on Margaret Clap's molly house (1726), the introduction of Hardwicke's Marriage Act (1753), and the raid at the White Swan on Vere Street (1810), a proto-gay bar. This book, therefore, looks at a time of significant 'heteroregulation' in Britain and beyond.

I coined the term 'heteroregulation' in its current context whilst writing my PhD to be used as an alternative to 'heteronormative'.[1] I reject the linguistic implication that there is a 'normal' (hetero) sexuality, counter to which others might be judged 'abnormal' and legislated against accordingly. There is nothing 'normal' about the heteronormative. Indeed, the term 'heterosexual' once implied an 'abnormal or perverted appetite toward the opposite sex', or a 'morbid sexual passion for one of the opposite sex'.[2] Instead, 'heteroregulated' better describes the deliberate social, cultural and legislative acts that were calculated to control and admonish minority groups across several centuries. That regulation continues today.

In its determined opposition to this regulation *Queer Georgians* is queer in focus and broadly adheres to the scholar Eve Kosofsky Sedgwick's use of the term in *Tendencies* (1993). She argued that queer history is 'the open mesh of possibilities, gaps, overlaps, dissonances and resonances, lapses and excesses of meaning when the constituent elements of anyone's gender, of anyone's sexuality aren't made (or *can't be* made) to signify monolithically'.[3]

There will be some who argue that applying the word 'queer' to the past is anachronistic. It is, but that's how historians communicate their findings. The word 'family' does not mean exactly the same thing now as it did in the seventeenth and eighteenth centuries, but experts talk freely about the history of the eighteenth-century family. I hear no objection when historians write about 'heterosexual men' in the seventeenth century; heterosexuality is seen as the normative positioning, an identity that needs no definition. Meanwhile, historians of gender and sexuality are tying themselves in knots trying to define and justify their use of the word 'queer'. If we readily accept these anachronistic tendencies because they are the easiest way in which we might discuss a specific experience or idea in the past, then we must grant the same grace to the study of queer lives.

That said, beyond 'queer' I have largely refrained from applying modern identity categories to the histories that follow. Indeed, I suggest it is *heteroregulation*, not *queerness*, that has seen the formalization of various gender non-conforming identity categories in our own time. Once rigidly categorized, identity markers can be used to fracture and divide so that the most vulnerable

Author's Note

amongst us might be more stringently regulated. The Georgians had no need for such categories and markers, however, and so they are largely dispensed with here. In a similar vein, I refer to my protagonists throughout using the pronouns they used for themselves. Sometimes, tantalizingly, this changed depending on the day. The Chevalier d'Éon, for instance, refers to herself as 'she' approximately 55 per cent of the time, and 'he' 45 per cent of the time. I have followed his example.

Throughout this book you will encounter words and descriptions of people in the eighteenth and nineteenth centuries that sit uncomfortably with modern sensibilities. They are included here, however, as a marker of the time in which they were written or said.

Modern monetary values are provided alongside their eighteenth- and nineteenth-century equivalents to give an indication of spending power. These equivalents have been calculated using the Bank of England Inflation Calculator.

Prologue

WE HAVE NO HISTORY. The queers, I mean. That's what they say, anyway. Sure, there was the upheaval of the Stonewall riots in New York and the administrative quagmire that was the Wolfenden Report in the United Kingdom, but these are very *modern* concerns. Not *real* history. These things are, some argue, the result of a liberal bias, fuelled by an elite mainstream media which has been morally corrupted by 'the gay agenda'. Besides, how can anyone write a history of Georgian queerness when homosexuality wasn't even 'invented' until the latter half of the nineteenth century?

On 6 May 1868, the Hungarian journalist Károly Mária Kertbeny drafted a letter to Karl Heinrich Ulrichs, a German lawyer and activist who campaigned for the rights of same-sex-attracted men. In his letter, Kertbeny attempted to categorize sexual experience, rather than sexual identity, and so left us with the first recorded occurrence of the word *homosexual*. From there, *homosexual* and its derivatives took on several profound medical, legal, social and cultural meanings.

Perhaps, then, there really is no legitimate way of writing about queer histories prior to 1868? What words would we use when our ancestors didn't have the same language by which to understand themselves? Certainly, the vast majority of LGBTQIA+ history pays homage to our twentieth-century forebears. By then, the queer archive had been preserved in a more deliberate and transparent fashion. But queer histories run much deeper than this and significantly predate the invention of homosexuality in 1868. As such, though it is true to say that the language used by our queer ancestors to describe their gender identities and sexual experiences may differ from our own, they are no less queer for that.

So why do the queer *Georgians* deserve special attention? And why do they demand that attention now? As a historian I spend a lot of time in various archives, poring over details of broken hearts that have long since stopped beating, or imagining the frustrations of a writer whose ink I find splodged unceremoniously across her delicately crafted correspondence. My research interests have predominantly been drawn to the 'long eighteenth century', often referred to as the Georgian period in Britain and its colonial territories.[1] Despite huge popular focus on the tempestuous Tudors and Stuarts (1485–1714) and the dour Victorians (1837–1901), the Georgian period was foundational to the ways in which we understand the world today. Not to mention altogether more thrilling than either, and more than just a little bit camp.

The Georgians were asking many of the same questions about gender, sex and sexuality that we are today: What makes a man? What is a woman? What exactly was the 'Third Sex'? And what did that mean for the other two sexes? Although few attempted to answer these questions definitively, there are clues to their attitudes, ideas and personal experiences littered throughout various primary-source documents if you know where to look. The first of these appeared to me in the homely form of a 'cotquean'.

I initially encountered the term whilst in the information-gathering stages of my PhD. In the brilliant *Behind Closed Doors* (2009), historian Amanda Vickery briefly mentioned this type of gender non-conforming man in her exploration of 'The Trials of Domestic Dependence':

> Conduct books prated that the management of all things interior fell to the mistress. In popular culture men who meddled with domesticities were disparaged as 'cotqueans', while ballads sniggered at the chaos unleashed by interfering husbands.[2]

And that, essentially, was that. Despite my best efforts, I could find no other substantial reference to the cotquean, who seemed to me a potentially queer figure, in any history books. So I set about gathering as much new evidence as I could to help uncover this forgotten history.

Over the next three years I discovered that the word 'cotquean' comes to us from early modern French, 'quean' meaning woman (a sense that has recently been repurposed, viz. 'Yasss Qween!') and 'cot' or 'cote' denoting house or hut.[3] Though the word 'cotquean' has fallen out of use today, it was widely known in the eighteenth century. Everyone from hawkers to duchesses would have used it and understood the cotquean to be 'a man who busies himself with women's affairs'.[4] Amongst his other 'feminine' domestic traits, such as sewing, interior decoration and hosting, the cotquean was reportedly 'endowed with the Gift of tossing of Pancakes, and had a wonderful Knack at tempering the Materials of a Bag-pudding'.[5]

However, because of his domesticated ways this effeminate man was to be excluded, some contemporaries believed, from two important institutions: politics and marriage.[6] Further, in a

Prologue

striking section from an anonymous eighteenth-century pamphlet snappily entitled *Satan's Harvest Home* (1749), it was stated that the cotquean was explicitly understood by Georgians as a man who had sex with other men.[7] Here I had encountered a male 'type' who was blatantly linked to same-sex activity in the pre-modern past. The cotquean was, as I had suspected all along, very queer indeed.

Forgotten details such as this show us that gender, sex and same-sex desire was a much more complex and deep-rooted historical experience than many experts have previously imagined. Naturally, this discovery then posed another pressing question: if the cotquean had been forgotten or, indeed, deliberately obscured from our history, what else had we missed? What other parts of the queer past had been taken from us, misinterpreted, or lay safely secreted between the pages of a dusty old diary, waiting to be rediscovered? And so I dug deeper, read between the lines, and eventually set about reclaiming a lost history.

As the years went by, a motley crew of politicians, sex workers, aristocrats, milkmen, landowners, spies and labourers emerged from their archival obscurity to occupy my every thought and (I hope) to enliven these pages. They are the queer Georgians, and it is my privilege to introduce some of them to you across the next eleven chapters.

Our narrative begins with a Londoner in 1726 and ends with a New Yorker in 1837. In Chapters One and Two, a milkman named Gabriel Lawrence pulls back the curtain on a secretive gathering of men overseen by the indomitable Margaret 'Mother' Clap. Here be the London mollies, a riotous group of working-class men who were attracted to other men. However, these mollies had caught the attention of London's moralizing class, and the relative safety of their underground network was about to come

Prologue

crumbling down around them. Inevitably there was heartbreak in what followed, and together we will track the 'sodomites' route' through the disease-ridden and corrupt Newgate Prison before finding ourselves underneath 'the three-legged mare' of the gallows at Tyburn. Despite this, something altogether more defiant emerges from the violent chaos that Gabriel Lawrence found himself caught up in. This is also a history of a queer community forged with safety, succour, security and sex in mind.

Chapters Three and Four tell a love story. They examine the shared history of John, Lord Hervey and Stephen (Ste) Fox, whose relationship blossomed in the years following Gabriel Lawrence's demise. As members of the aristocracy, their London was very different to the one Gabriel and his queer comrades knew. For Hervey and Fox, one of their main objectives was setting up home together, despite the conventions of the day. However, because men like them were the very types who helped shape Britain's laws and social customs, we will see how their elite status granted them the requisite privileges by which they might circumvent traditional domestic regulation. This, however, did not necessarily protect them from the attentions of their political enemies, who wished to expose their intimacies and bring them down.

Chapter Five introduces readers to John Chute and Francis Whithed, better known to their extensive coterie of effeminate bachelor friends as The Chuteheds. Once squirrelled comfortably away behind the red-brick façade of Chute's impressive country pile, The Vyne, it quickly becomes apparent that ideas of a 'queer community' are archivally discernible at least as far back as the eighteenth century. Within these communities, as this group of devoted (and sometimes gloriously bitchy) friends demonstrates, a clearer sense of queer identity emerged. Unfortunately, as we shall discover, the queerer elements of these gender non-conforming identities inspired a targeted proto-homophobic violence that will feel all too familiar to some readers today.

On the surface of it, Chapter Six is a rollicking Georgian adventure story that stretches the length and breadth of Europe. When examined more closely, though, it serves as a timely reminder of the importance of observing several coexisting and sometimes tension-filled subtleties when we talk about gender and sexuality, especially when those experiences are grounded in the past. As an influential courtier and spy, the Chevalier d'Éon experienced the might of royal power in both Britain and France. Yet he was also forced to drag himself through various dilapidated hovels before ending his days in penury. This remarkable gender-bending history has, in recent years, marked her out as a brilliantly defiant trans ancestor. However, to my surprise, I discovered that the Chevalier's archive does not support this twenty-first-century interpretation. What I uncovered instead is a new, complex and yet profoundly queer interpretation of a life that deserves greater clarity and nuance in its telling. From this reinterpretation a new history emerges that aims to acknowledge the historical legacy of a much-overlooked section of the modern LGBTQIA+ community.

I count Lady Eleanor Butler and Miss Sarah Ponsonby as my direct ancestors. Not because we're blood kin but because, like them, I am a queer person originally from County Kilkenny in Ireland. Sometimes, when I'm home and walking along the high street or the parade, I think of them both traipsing the same lanes and alleyways as me, albeit centuries apart. So, in preparation for the research that went on to inform Chapter Seven, I was utterly charmed to follow in their footsteps, making my way from the port in Waterford, across the Irish Sea, and eventually to an impressive cottage in the small Welsh town of Llangollen. Eleanor and Sarah became famous as the Ladies of Llangollen, attracting the attention of other same-sex-attracted women, poets and royalty alike. It is a wonderful story, and their life in Wales is well documented; less so their desperate start. I have combed the archives at the National Library of Ireland to reconstruct, in detail, their Irish adventures. For it was in Kilkenny that the true drama played out, leading Eleanor and Sarah to defy their families and abscond together. You will not find a tranquil history of an all-female rural idyll here. Instead, you'll encounter a vigorous, determined tale of joyous defiance full of runnings away, disguises, midnight flits, yapping dogs, racing carriages and a crafty maidservant who was ferocious with a candlestick when backed into a corner. Very much my kind of history.

Chapter Eight charts a series of 'sodomitical' scandals that unfolded between William Beckford, 'England's wealthiest son', and William 'Kitty' Courtenay, the 9th Earl of Devon. Initially both men were discovered together in a compromising situation in what has become known as the infamous 'Powderham Scandal'. However, in light of new evidence, I propose that there was no such thing as the *Powderham* Scandal at all. This chapter also charts the various ways in which archives are tampered with in an attempt to deliberately erase the queer past.

I toyed with the idea of leaving Anne Lister out of this book. 'What more is there to say?' I thought. She has secured her place in queer history (and legend). She has achieved icon status and has even had her own TV show, for goodness' sake! But when her history intersected with that of Lady Eleanor and Sarah in Llangollen, I found myself lost in the pages of her diaries once more, but this time from an altogether different perspective. Lister led a remarkable life, and we are forever indebted to her for the wealth of material with which she furnished the queer archive. But the more I read and re-read, the more it seemed clear to me that Lister was far from the 'queero' (queer hero) we invented following

Prologue

Sally Wainwright's *Gentleman Jack* (BBC/HBO). Instead what I encountered was a female patriarch who was at times abusive and manipulative and often cruel. And so hurried emails were dashed off to Alex, my editor, admitting that although I'd initially wanted to exclude her, the project felt incomplete without her. Thankfully, he agreed. Her inclusion serves as a reminder that queer people in the past might have been brilliant, accomplished and noteworthy but also altogether flawed. Naturally, we feel less comfortable addressing some of these trickier examples, but it is unfair to expect those who came before us to embody modern ideals. Anne Lister was extraordinarily bold in her same-sex desire but she was also a product of her time, and that, as we shall discover, often led to some downright brutal actions.

The working-class labourer George Wilson assumes the penultimate position in Chapter Ten. Through him we uncover largely forgotten details about the lives of people who transed their gender identities. I also address the idea of queer emigration in the early nineteenth century, the first time (as far as I am aware) that the topic has been considered this far back. By comparing the cases of Kitty Courtenay and George Wilson we begin to uncover the hint of a pattern in queer travel, from Europe towards America – New York, to be precise. There, on the streets of the Lower East Side, Wilson embraced the traditional elements of immigrant working-class life. That is until he was discovered by a policeman, three sheets to the wind, on a street corner in a well-to-do neighbourhood. What happened next confused and confounded authorities before Wilson silently slipped back into obscurity, where he felt most comfortable. Sometimes, for the people who lived them, their histories served them best when they remained hidden.

Finally, in Chapter Eleven, we meet the person who has stayed with me long after I'd left the letters, paintings and newspaper articles, the sketches and stately homes behind: Mary Jones, also known as Peter Sewally. Jones's history guides us down the less salubrious alleyways of New York City, not far from Wilson's neighbourhood. It was there, alongside other sex workers, that she doggedly carved out a place for herself– no mean feat for a Black working-class sex worker who frequently transed her gender identity. Public reaction to Mary ranged from admiration and acceptance to fear and repulsion. She was even called a 'monster' by contemporaries because she dared to follow her own path, messy and winding as it might have been. There is a misconception still, I think, that to 'make history' one needs to disrupt or reshape it in some global way. But Mary Jones puts to rest this misconception and demonstrates that sometimes just getting back up when you're so often told to stay down is all it takes to change the world.

What follows is a contested history. A history that is too dangerous, in some quarters, to take up space on library shelves or to be used as a point of historical reference in the classroom. It is the culmination of over five years spent teasing apart details discovered in various repositories across Britain, Ireland, Europe more generally and the United States. I make no apologies for what I found there. Rest assured, however, that I have interrogated my source material in the most robust manner possible throughout, as any historian would. As a result, not every case study I investigated met the burden of proof I set for inclusion. The history of the supposedly queer American Army general and Founding Father Friedrich Wilhelm August Heinrich Ferdinand von Steuben provides a cautionary example.

Numerous secondary sources, for example, will tell you that von Steuben was 'openly gay'.[8] In a 2023 graphic novel, *Washington's Gay General: The Legends and Loves of Baron von Steuben*, Josh Trujillo and Levi Hastings state that their work is a biography of,

Prologue

amongst other things, 'a flamboyant homosexual . . . in an era when the term didn't even exist'.[9] They dedicate their book 'to the countless historians, queers, and allies throughout history who selflessly work to document, preserve, and share our incomplete story'. I second that dedication and acknowledge the incomplete nature of the historiographical work. But, after careful analysis, I have found no conclusive evidence that von Steuben helps us to complete it.

In support of the 'von Steuben was gay' theory, the journalist Erin Blakemore has argued that a party thrown by von Steuben shortly after he arrived at Valley Forge, to which none should be admitted that had on a 'whole pair of breeches', was sexually charged. Senator William North's admission that 'We love him [von Steuben] . . . and he deserves it for he loves us tenderly' has also been put forward as proof of an unconventional three-way relationship between himself, Benjamin Walker and their former general. Others claim that von Steuben lived with North and Walker after the American Revolutionary War had ended. To help tally with the supposed queerness of this arrangement, all three men are seen to live under one roof (which they did not), and their wives are often missing from the narrative altogether. Whilst I fully appreciate the impetus to reclaim the queer past, these historical insinuations demonstrate a lack of the broader contextual knowledge required to interrogate the specific subtleties of same-sex desire, army life and friendship between men in the long eighteenth century. With this knowledge to hand, von Steuben's apparent queerness quickly falls away.

For instance, at the point in the Revolutionary War when von Steuben's trouserless army party was held, the Continental Army, historians agree, was without discipline, food, hope and, crucially, uniforms. Those lucky enough to have any clothing at all paraded in rags. Von Steuben's request that soldiers attend his party trouserless was not an opportunity for him to admire their shapely legs, merely a light-hearted acknowledgement of the terrible conditions he found them in. It was nothing more than an attempt to lift spirits before bringing the men in line and organizing them towards victory. With, may I add, decent uniforms.

Additionally, in the context of the late eighteenth century, men openly declared their love for one another, as North did in his letter, without the slightest implication of same-sex desire. Indeed, men linked arms in the street, even exchanged kisses without a hint of flirtation. Further, that von Steuben's inner circle later wished to accommodate their former general and respected friend in their individual homes when he had fallen on hard times is not in the least bit unusual.

The truth is that such historical forays, however well intentioned, distract from our purpose. The von Steuben archive offers no concrete evidence whatsoever that von Steuben was what we would term queer. New evidence may well come to light which could convince me otherwise, and I'd caveat my conclusion by saying that this in no way means that he was *not* same-sex-attracted. It simply means that I have seen no convincing archival material to support the claim that he was; this therefore excluded him from the purview of this book. I say this not to frustrate those who may once have advocated the importance of having identified a gay Founding Father, only to reassure sceptical readers that care and consideration have been applied to each of the following chapters.

As a direct result of its queerness, then, this book is an open invitation to discover a history previously obscured, a history that belongs to and has shaped *all* of us, even if we are not part of the queer community. For some of you, many of the histories that follow will feel instinctively personal. If that's the case, I am glad

Prologue

this book found you. I hope the adventures that follow make you punch the air in silent triumph, and mourn for what they (and we) have lost. I hope these accounts help to better root you in our once-hidden histories and direct you, more joyously and defiantly, towards a better future.

With that, let us begin.

CHAPTER ONE

A House on Field Lane

ONE SUNDAY NIGHT, FEBRUARY 1726. It had just passed nine o'clock as Gabriel Lawrence made his way purposefully towards Field Lane in Holborn. The winter darkness had transformed familiar London streets into something altogether more perilous, despite the intermittent grid of oil lamps. Flames, feeble and odorous, struggled to light the clogged arteries of the great city. Once night descended, even the savvy Londoner was forced to navigate an assault course of stinking waste (animal, vegetable and human), abandoned mounds of building rubble, and a rogue's gallery of thieves, vagabonds and the desperate. Lawrence was keen to reach his destination.

As he walked apace, street musicians lifted their fiddles to offer a bawdy song, their bows slashing back and forth by their necks. The music they made underscored the continuous din from nearby alehouses, taverns and coffee houses; laughter, screams and shouts burst through doors left momentarily ajar – the strident, stinking symphony of the nocturnal city. Eighteenth-century London was never quiet. It remained a 'prodigious and noisy' place, 'where repose and silence dare scarce shew their heads in the darkest night'.[1]

Forty-three-year-old Lawrence, jostling through the crowds, likely cast a distrustful eye towards the sky as he walked. The capital had temporarily emerged from a dramatic deluge that had soaked its people for some months. It had been bitterly cold too, unseasonably so, even for an English winter. Now that the rain had abated, Londoners squinted through a distorted haze of windows, wondering if they might soon be granted the welcome ease of spring.

Gabriel Lawrence was a milkman.[2] For Lawrence, this meant early starts and heavy loads. Lawrence's customers will have had some extra money in their purses as milk was less an everyday commodity in the eighteenth century than it is today; it was not a staple of the average Londoner's diet. Gabriel Lawrence, therefore, will have spent his working days in middling and upper-class neighbourhoods where his product was more likely to sell. For now, though, the working day was behind him, and he sought comfort and camaraderie from an establishment run by Margaret Clap which was located on Field Lane.

Mark Partridge would be there, no doubt, for he was a regular in Clap's exclusive coterie. He and Lawrence had recently had a messy spat which resulted in Lawrence losing his temper and, in the heat of the moment, calling Partridge a 'vile Dog, a blowing up Bitch and other ill Names'.[3] Lawrence had suspected Partridge of being loose-lipped about the closely guarded secrets of their hidden fraternity. Lawrence was concerned that Partridge, a sex worker whose knowledge was for sale in addition to his services, had divulged the sites of their meetings to those who were legally and morally opposed to them, those who wished to see them hang. Despite Lawrence's suspicions, Partridge had somehow managed to reassure his friend that their secrets remained safe, and the two men had affectionately reconciled. So on that particular night it is safe to assume that Lawrence would have counted Partridge's company as good as any other.

A House on Field Lane

More tantalizing a prospect for Lawrence, the records show, was the possibility of his meeting again with one Martin Mackintosh, an orange-seller in Covent Garden. Amongst this particular group of friends Mackintosh went by the mouth-watering pseudonym 'Orange Deb'. It was not unusual for these men to be given female nicknames or 'maiden names' that indicated something about their lives, personalities or professions and confirmed their place within this exclusive club. Martin/Deb's associates included 'Dip-Candle Mary', a candle-maker, the 'Duchess of Camomile', a resident of Camomile Street, 'Old Fish Hannah', a fish-seller, and 'Susan Guzzle', the origin of whose maiden name remains unclear (though I encourage you to use your imagination). When last they met, we know that Lawrence and Orange Deb, being 'very fond [of] one another', had 'hugged and kissed and employed their Hands in [as some saw it] a very vile Manner'.[4]

As Lawrence turned right, with his back to the City, he finally found himself on Field Lane, 'a narrow and dismal alley, leading to Saffron Hill'.[5] In his *Survey of the Cities of London and Westminster* (1720) the clergyman, historian and biographer John Strype described Field Lane in rather uninviting terms; it was 'narrow and mean, full of Butchers and Tripe Dressers, because the Ditch runs at the back of their Slaughter houses, and carries away the filth'. The locality was 'of small account . . . and [was] pestered with small and ordinary alleys and courts taken up by the meaner sort of people; others are', he observed, 'nasty and inconsiderable'.[6]

However unpleasant, Field Lane was Gabriel Lawrence's desired destination. As he pushed open the heavy wooden door to the premises, unseen observers silently confirmed that this man 'belonged' to the house: he was one of the regulars. Lawrence then slipped inside, allowing the door to close behind him. In that moment, unbeknownst to himself, he had sealed his fate.

Queer Georgians

Figure 1. Field Lane on John Rocque's 1746 map of London: 'A Plan of the Cities of London and Westminster, and Borough of Southwark', John Pine & John Tinney, 1746.

We know that Margaret Clap was married to a man named John Clap. However, historians disagree as to the exact nature of their business. Some say they kept a 'public' house, others a coffee house, others a tavern, others still an alehouse of some sort. Some experts believe that the husband-and-wife entrepreneurs may have divided their labour; that John ran a tavern and Margaret a coffee house. Most likely, Clap's was all of these things in various measures and, due to the diversity of their services, it was a relatively busy little spot. Contemporary accounts tell us that

> Mrs Clap's House was next to the Bunch of Grapes in Field-lane, Holbourn . . . and for the better Conveniency of her

Customers, she had provided Beds in every Room in her House. She usually had 30 or 40 of such Persons there every Night, but more especially on a Sunday.[7]

Margaret Clap, rather than her husband John, has been largely credited with the successful running of their business. This falls in line with what we know about working-class women at this time as, contrary to popular opinion, they made a significant contribution to the eighteenth-century workforce. Many of the jobs these women undertook in the 1720s were associated with childcare, intimate care, housekeeping and the domestic sphere. This was hard and often undervalued work. Other women oversaw inns, lodging houses or coffee houses in an attempt to secure their financial future. Women often procured the licence for such businesses in their husband's name.[8] Margaret Clap had secured her house on Field Lane in this way and, like many of her contemporaries, she succeeded through a combination of necessity and economic aptitude.

Mrs Clap, discerning businesswoman that she was, had courted a loyal and distinct customer base. This included men like Gabriel Lawrence, Mark Partridge and Orange Deb. But if Mrs Clap's clientele were loyal to her, they were no more loyal than she was to them. If any of her most frequent patrons, like a certain Mr Derwin, found themselves in a scrape with the authorities, then Mrs Clap was happy to bear witness, under oath, to their good character. Indeed, she had recently given evidence to a judge, Sir George Martins (a former Lord Mayor of London, no less), on behalf of the said Mr Derwin, who was accused, some gossiped, of committing sodomy with a linkboy.[9] Mrs Clap later 'boasted that what she had said before Sir George, in Derwin's Favour, was a great Means of bringing him off [acquitting him]'.[10] It was in this way that her customers came to refer to her as 'Mother Clap'.

This practice of naming influential, non-kin elders 'mother' persists in the queer community today.[11]

Mother Clap's belonged to a wider network of inns, taverns and coffee houses which formed a dynamic social patchwork across eighteenth-century London. At the upper end of the social scale, 'principal' inns provided not only an opportunity for men and women to eat, drink and chat together in a polite setting, they also acted as the location for some legal proceedings and public meetings. At the less salubrious end of the scale, Gabriel Lawrence would not have expected to meet members of the nobility or even the respectable middling classes at Mother Clap's. Field Lane's reputation tells us all we need to know about the general class of punter to be found there. It is sometimes said that eighteenth-century inns and taverns were social melting pots, catering for those at the very top alongside the unfortunate creatures at the very bottom of society. In general, however, there is little support for this. Some establishments linked to theatres may have boasted a socially diverse customer profile, but most social spaces reinforced hierarchy; a social space for everybody, and everybody in their social space.

Once inside an establishment, regardless of its class strata, a customer became part of an ever-rotating, highly entertaining and politically engaged affair. The appeal of establishments like Mother Clap's was manifold and included the opportunity to get away from home for a bit, friendship, a place of rest, a place to eat, warmth and an opportunity to learn and share news and gossip. It comes as no surprise, then, that coffee houses, taverns and inns grew in popularity at this time. Evidently, in no small part due to this popularity, the Claps seem to have managed to piece together a reasonable living for themselves on Field Lane. But despite its familial character and the relative success of their establishment, all was not well at Mother Clap's.

We don't know specifically what it was that alerted the authorities to her premises in the lead-up to February 1726. Her business, whilst popular, was likely unlicensed. In this, though, Clap's would not have been unusual; many of the 'lower sort' of coffee houses, inns and taverns were. By the beginning of the eighteenth century, efforts were being made to regulate their activities, though unlicensed premises continued to flourish so it seems unlikely that this was the cause. More probable is that Mother Clap had come to the attention of local moralists and lawmakers because her patrons, without exception, were suspected sodomites. As witnesses at the time would come to testify, 'Mrs Clap's House was notorious for being a Molly-House.'

In 1709 the writer Ned Ward described the London fraternity of mollies thus:

> THERE are a particular Gang of *Sodomitical* Wretches, in this Town, who call themselves the *Mollies*, and are so far degenerated from all masculine Deportment, or manly Exercises, that they rather fancy themselves Women, imitating all the little Vanities that custom has reconciled to the Female Sex, affecting to speak, Walk, Tattle, Curtsy, Cry, Scold, and to mimic all Manner of Effeminacy . . .[12]

Contrary to Ward's claims, most mollies did not fancy themselves as women, despite their gender non-conformity. What is irrefutably clear from Ward's description, however, is that our queer eighteenth-century ancestors were recognized as part of a distinct social group that met together in 'safe spaces' like Margaret Clap's.

To many in the eighteenth century like Ward, mollies were a disgrace to men and masculinity. Their marked femininity, noticeable in their gossiping, chatter and manner, set them apart from others of their sex. Ward condemned the effeminate manners of the mollies, implying not only that they betrayed their own sex but that they mocked 'the fairer sex' in imitating them. Unlike the cotquean, who was a distinctly private, domestic and often rural type, the molly might be found in more public, urban spaces. To Ward and his ilk, mollies were a clear and present threat to traditional manhood and the family. But Ward went further and made it clear that mollies were not just effeminate men; they were specifically men who had sex with other men:

> No sooner had they ended their Feast, and run through all the Ceremonies of their Theatrical way of Gossiping, but, having washed away, with Wine, all fear of Shame, as well as the Checks of Modesty, then they began to enter upon their Beastly Obscenities, and to take those infamous Liberties with one another, that no Man, who is not sunk into a State of Devilism, can think on without Blushing, or mention without a Christian Abhorrence of all such Heathenish Brutalities.[13]

By abandoning his 'natural' attraction to women, the molly threatened to topple the social order.

Mollies were not exclusively found at molly houses like Mother Clap's, however. There were public sites where they 'cruised' for 'trade' too, particularly in Covent Garden, at London Bridge and along a path in Moorfields which became known as 'The Sodomites' Walk'. They also frequented the same social hotspots as everybody else. One disgruntled onlooker, having spotted 'Pretty Fellows' at a popular coffee house in the West End, picked up his pen in disgust and wrote to *The Tatler* on 6 June 1709:

> Some of them I have heard calling to one another as I have sat at *White's* and *St. James's*, by the Names of Betty, Nelly, and so forth. You see them accost each other with effeminate Airs:

They have their Signs and Tokens like Free-Masons: They rail at Womenkind; receive Visits on their Beds in Gowns, and do a Thousand other unintelligible Prettinesses that I cannot tell what so makes of. I therefore heartily desire you would exclude all this Sort of Animals.[14]

Though not quite reaching the loftier social heights of White's chocolate house, Ned Ward would have recognized Mother Clap's house as one which 'bore the public Character of a Place of Entertainment for Sodomites'. For Clap and her customers, therefore, these were high-stakes gatherings.

The 1533 Buggery Act had been introduced under Henry VIII 'for the punishment of the vice of Buggery'. Through this Act, Parliament had sought to regulate anal sex and bestiality in the civil rather than ecclesiastical courts, as had previously been the case. Sodomy now became a capital offence in England and remained so until 1861. The last recorded execution under this Act took place in 1835, over 300 years after its introduction. So in 1726, even entering Mother Clap's house could cost you your life. Given the social, cultural and legal ramifications of male same-sex desire at this time, Clap's was, therefore, a site of unseen revolt.

In spaces such as Clap's, the simple act of intimacy, the insistence on carving out joy for oneself and the quiet defiance of living with authenticity constituted a radical act. If Gabriel Lawrence had thrown his arms round Mark Partridge to greet him that night, or had he placed a rough, flirtatious kiss on Orange Deb's cheek, he undertook an act of resistance. At Clap's trust was begrudgingly granted, and not guaranteed indefinitely. Mother Clap's clientele was, on the whole, made up of regulars who would have been familiar to her and to one another. Her establishment did not accommodate the weary stranger looking for a place to rest his head. Unknown men, even when attending with regular punters, were viewed with suspicion and it could take some time for them to be welcomed into the fold. The last thing Clap and her house wanted was to be secretly infiltrated by the Society for the Reformation of Manners.

By 1726, the Society for the Reformation of Manners was firmly entrenched in a battle for the very soul of the nation. The Society's various pious members, spread across multiple stand-alone societies, felt that, due to man's sinful ways, God lay forgotten and biblical disaster slumbered round each and every corner. 'Have we not brought forth *Apples of Sodom*,' they lamented melodramatically. Faced with such moral corruption, the Society knew that action must be taken. 'God expects from us all a *National Reformation* before his *Anger* be pacified,' its leaders, like the Reverend Josiah Woodward, observed. The Society stood ready to shape this spiritual overhaul. Society members committed to combatting '*Swearing, Cursing, Drunkenness, Revilings* [sic], *Lasciviousness, Whoredoms, Riot, Gluttony, Blasphemies, Gamestring* [betting on card games], and such-like Wickednesses'. Sexual immorality was thought to be at the root of many of these particular evils, and as a result sex workers, brothel-keepers and sodomites became targets for the Society's reforming zeal.

All citizens had a part to play in bringing about this reformation of manners, for it benefited all citizens. The Society's appeals for information or help that could curb immoral behaviour extended to '*every* private Christian [who] *may become* a public Blessing *to the Nation*'.[15] This commitment to its cause meant that by 1738 the Society had racked up more than 100,000 accusations, involving about 14 per cent of the population of London.

A key tactic used by the Society in order to uncover vice, particularly at molly houses, was the use of 'Under-Agents to the *Reforming-Society*': spies, essentially.[16] Wretchedly, unbeknownst to Mother Clap, Gabriel Lawrence and the other men gathered at Clap's that night, two spies from the Society already formed part of their band of brothers. Samuel Stephens and Joseph Sellers had gained entry by promising payments to Mark Partridge, the young sex worker Lawrence had suspected of betraying them some weeks before. Whatever instinct or information Lawrence had been acting on when he lost his patience with Partridge had, sadly, been correct. Partridge had betrayed his friends, and by February 1726 Stephens and Sellers believed that they had all the information they required to bring down Mother Clap's house of Sodom, brick by brick.

On that Sunday night, as Gabriel Lawrence settled jovially amongst his friends, Stephens and Sellers watched on, preparing to spring their trap. Outside, acting on their intelligence, two reforming constables, Messrs Williams and Willis, had positioned themselves on Field Lane. A squadron of other constables and numerous key members of the Society used the shadows to provide cover. These invisible adversaries had been arranged to cut off all possible escape routes when the mollies inside were ambushed.

Whether Stephens and Sellers within or Williams and Willis without made the first move in the early hours of the next morning is undocumented. Either way, upon realizing they had been betrayed the mollies ran for their lives. Although the accomplices of the Society hidden along Field Lane attempted to block their escape, some of the luckier men managed to evade capture and absconded across the cobbles.

Nonetheless, approximately forty men, including the milkman Gabriel Lawrence, were rounded up that night, alongside the dynamic Mother Clap. The captured men will no doubt have been concerned for their mothers, their fathers, their wives, their children and the consequences their discovery would have for them, as well as thinking on which of their friends present that night had escaped to safety. They themselves would now be delivered to London's notorious 'prototype of hell', as magistrate and novelist Henry Fielding called Newgate Prison. There they would await their fate.

Little is written about the months Gabriel Lawrence and the other men captured at Mother Clap's spent at Newgate whilst they awaited trial. Experts have, understandably, focused more on the salacious details that emerged regarding molly house culture as a result of the raid. The subsequent trials, which we will examine in the following chapter, have also proved too rich a source for most to ignore. However, it is important for us to understand the system of incarceration for same-sex-attracted men specifically. Here, for the first time, I have pieced together this lacuna in queer history.[17]

Immediately following their capture, Lawrence and the other men were dragged before a local justice of the peace (JP) to be processed. This could have taken place at the JP's home or in a nearby inn or tavern. Processing up to forty men in one go would have required focus, stamina and legal rigour. One of the determining factors in establishing that the crime of sodomy had been committed was, of course, that the men accused were caught in the sex act. However, as none of the men captured that night were discovered with their breeches down (though some of their breeches were reportedly unbuttoned), many of them were released during processing.

For those retained, the JP had to determine whether the witness testimony against them was enough to facilitate a trial. Testimony tested, the accused were then selected to pass through to the next stages of regulation, the issuing of fines and incarceration. We can't be sure how many men continued through the system at this point, though it was significantly fewer than the forty or so that had been swept up initially. What we do know is that Gabriel Lawrence and Margaret Clap were amongst those unhappy few. Having been processed, Lawrence was then led to 'the heinous gaol of Newgate' alongside his remaining friends. He would have been well aware of its wretched reputation. Not only was it a filthy, overcrowded, lice-infested place, but it also housed the city's most dangerous and hardened criminals.

Archaeological excavations have revealed that some form of prison had stood on this site since Roman times: Newgate's roots of restraint ran deep. The prison, as it stood before Lawrence, however, had been reconstructed in 1672 following the Great Fire of London in 1666. The rebuilt Newgate occupied a relatively small site of twenty-six yards by sixteen yards but loomed five storeys overhead. Had Lawrence looked up he would have seen four distinct niches spaced across the face of the building. Each niche contained a full-length figure carved from stone which represented Peace, Security, Plenty and Liberty to those without its walls. For those inside, these four principles were either temporarily suspended or lost forever.[18]

Beneath the mouth of Newgate 'the lodge' awaited Lawrence and the others. The first thing that struck new arrivals was the smell, an acrid assault on the nostrils, a tangy mix of sour milk and faeces. As the prisoners' eyes gradually adjusted to the dim candlelit interior they would have been able to identify its source: an open sewer cutting through the chamber, carrying the waste of the inmates into the River Fleet beyond. No doubt the grim reality of what lay in store now started to dawn on them. Incidentally, this chamber, where newly arrived men and women were first introduced to Newgate, was also the condemned cell; it was one of the last places those sentenced to hang at Tyburn would have seen.

Soon two 'truncheon officers' took hold of Lawrence and pinioned him to a nearby wall. It wasn't unusual for two other officers to rifle through the inmates' pockets at this point, extracting whatever they deemed valuable. Lawrence was then handed over to two resident convicts. These men would have 'hovered about him like so many Crows about [a] piece of Carrion' and demanded '2s 6d of garnish money, otherwise they strip the poor Wretch if he [has] not the wherewithal to pay it'.[19] Garnish money was taken from a new prisoner, either as the gaoler's fee or as money with which to 'garnish' the other prisoners with drink. The primary-source material does not tell us if Lawrence managed to obtain the money before he was escorted to Newgate, though as it was roughly equal to a day's wages it would not have been beyond his means.

A rusty collar of iron was then bound round his neck, cutting into his flesh. His wrists were similarly restrained with manacles, and shackles were added to his ankles. Later, when Lawrence had been assigned his quarters, these restraints could be attached to fixtures on the floor or embedded in the walls, keeping him in line in this 'Place of Terrors', as former prisoner Batty Langley called it.[20]

Once they were bound in fetters, new inmates were then admitted to either the Master's or Common Side of the gaol. Within these divisions, further distinction was made between inmates who were debtors or felons. Simply put, a debtor owed money that could not be paid, and a felon was thought to have committed a serious crime against another person or against property. It was at this point that Mother Clap was separated from her customers as Newgate accommodated men and women separately. Had one been assigned to the Master's Side, one could have afforded to pay for a reasonably comfortable stay at the gaol, which might have included decent meals, comfortable surroundings and even a somewhat jovial social life. Unsurprisingly, given his social status, it was not within Lawrence's means to occupy the Master's quarters. Instead he was assigned to the Common Side of the prison.

Batty Langley tells us that Lawrence's particular patch was 'a most Terrible Wicked and Dreadful Place'. The Common Side was further divided into three separate areas: the Stone Hold, the Lower Ward and the Middle Ward. The Stone Hold, as Langley elaborated, was a 'stinking, dark and dismal place' situated entirely underground. Prisoners assigned to the Lower Ward had it slightly better and 'lye upon ragged Blankets . . . The Lice crackling under their Feet, make such a Noise as walking on Shells which were strewed over Garden Walks.'[21] It is most likely, however, that upon his induction into this 'abode of misery and despair, a hell such as Dante might have conceived', Lawrence was housed in the Middle Ward, where common felons who had paid their dues were held. This ward 'is also very Dark, but not so cold as the foregoing, the Floor thereof being Oaken Plank, on which however, the Felons lie without any sort of Bed'.[22] What makes it more likely still that Lawrence was held on this ward is that adjacent to the Middle Ward was what was referred to as the 'Buggering Hold'.

The 'Right Villainous' John Hall, another Newgate prisoner, tells us that he did not know where the Buggering Hold got its name, but surmises that 'some coffined there may [be] or have been addicted to Sodomy . . . But what Degree of Latitude this Chamber is situated in I cannot positively demonstrate, unless it lies 90 Degrees beyond the Arctic Pole; for instead of being dark here but half the Year, it is dark all the Year round.'[23] This was the never-ending dark that became 'home' to Gabriel Lawrence after he was incarcerated.

Once he adjusted to his shackles and the cold and the dark of the Buggering Hold, Lawrence would have to fall in line with the routines of daily prison life at Newgate. At 7 a.m. prisoners, had they managed to temporarily escape into sleep, were woken by the clanging of the prison bell. Those prisoners who were docile, fearful and worn down enough compliantly rose to another doleful day. They then emptied their chamber pots before being counted and made their clanking, stumbling way to breakfast. A typical morning meal at Newgate might have consisted of a porridge or gruel-type concoction, or a small portion of rye bread.

Once they had managed to eat, Lawrence and the others would have been left to their own devices until the afternoon, when the common felons would be treated to their main meal of the day. This consisted of bread and water, but once a week they might be afforded meat. After this, inmates were once again left to do with their time as they wished before they were directed back to their wards at 10 p.m. to sleep once more.

At the time Lawrence was incarcerated there were thirteen Common Wards and four Masters' Wards at Newgate. The prison had been rebuilt to house about 150 inmates, but at any one time it wasn't unusual for at least 250 people to be crammed together, especially in the Common Wards. Amidst this overcrowding, lice and fleas quickly spread the dreaded typhus. An infested prisoner first developed chills and a fever, accompanied by a pounding headache. Their breathing then became shallow and rapid as aches and pains spread through every muscle. Soon an itchy rash confirmed their worst fears – that 'gaol fever', as they called it, was upon them. Coughing, nausea and vomiting ensued until the inmate, now emaciated to skin and bone, expired. So prevalent was typhus at Newgate that in 1726, the year Lawrence was incarcerated, twenty-one prisoners lost their lives at Tyburn, their necks broken by the noose, whilst eighty-three died of gaol fever. This was a place of nightmares, a place more terribly tangible than the white-hot flames of Hell.

With each crunch of the lice underfoot and each icy gale that blew through the Buggering Hold, Gabriel Lawrence's trial drew ever closer. As the stench, rancour and rigours of Newgate persisted, the Old Bailey, the world-famous courthouse, remained a beacon of hope, a chance for him to plead his case and win his freedom once more. It would be the fight of his life.

CHAPTER TWO

The Deadly Nevergreen

HISTORY IS A DETERMINED thing; even on the darkest of nights it continues to evolve. So as Gabriel Lawrence languished in the hold at Newgate, the whirligig of early Georgian life (and death) continued apace. Days trundled into weeks, and weeks lapsed into months. Charwomen darted between lodging houses, laundered linen, dusted desks and readied grates for warming fires. On the streets of London, old and infirm crossing-sweepers provided a percussive accompaniment to the persistent rainfall, which dampened overcoats and soaked the shoes of those lucky enough to have them. That spring the downpour was so persistent that the Thames reached its highest level in forty years.

By now, news of the captured mollies had spread throughout England. 'One Whittle, a Victualler in Pall-Mall, is committed to the Gatehouse, Westminster, by five Justices, being charged with Sodomy,' reported *The Weekly Journal* on 26 February 1726. On 9 April the *Ipswich Journal* recorded that 'one Gabriel Lawrence was lately committed to Newgate . . . for Sodomy'. Days later, on 12 April, it commented that 'Indictments were also found against William Gent, alias Mademoiselle Gent, and

John Whale, alias Margaret, alias Peggy Whale, for Sodomitical Practices'. The Society for the Reformation of Manners' determined plan was coming together. It was one thing, however, that Gabriel Lawrence and his friends had been committed to their respective gaols, quite another to ensure that they received the ultimate punishment according to English law: death. Hearsay would not send Lawrence and his coterie to the gallows; the burden of proof in sodomy cases was too high. Instead, a turncoat witness who might repent his own sexual proclivities and provide enough information to damn the others was required to shore up the case against them. Mr Thomas Newton proved himself just the man.

Newton had first come to the attention of the constables in the closing days of February, almost immediately after the raid on Mother Clap's. He had initially been sent to the constables, Williams and Willis, on Clap's behalf, entrusted with an amount of money that was intended to facilitate her release on bail. Williams and Willis, however, were not interested in discussing the innkeeper's bail conditions and instead presented Newton with a proposition. They informed him that they knew him for a sodomite. They were aware, too, that Newton was familiar with Clap, her establishment, Lawrence and the others in custody. They suggested, therefore, that Newton might attest to what exactly went on at Clap's on Field Lane at the forthcoming trial.

At thirty, Thomas Newton could hardly have been called green. He will have understood the implications of the offer Williams and Willis made. In return for immunity, he would act as a witness for the prosecution. He would divulge the names of frequent visitors to Clap's house, tell the constables what went on there, and eventually testify to all of this in court. Refusal meant arrest and possible hanging. The constables may have offered him some financial reward for his co-operation too, aware that money in the pockets of the poor was no small matter.

Newton may have needed some time to think on their offer, or initially refused it, for he left the constables without having agreed to a deal. A few days later, as misfortune would have it, he himself was 'taken up' on suspicion of sodomy. Once incarcerated, he invoked the offer Williams and Willis had made in order to secure his release, cementing their pact. Then, at the beginning of March, Newton was 'set at Liberty'. The very next day, and on several occasions thereafter, he sat down with the constables at the house of Sir John Fryer, the Lord Mayor of London, and 'made voluntary Information' that would determine the course of the impending trials.

In 1726 the Old Bailey stood adjacent to Newgate Prison. The Justice Hall or Sessions House, as it was sometimes known, lay beyond what had formerly been the western wall of the City of London. The courthouse took its name from the street on which it stands, the trajectory of which marks the line of the original City wall or 'bailey'. The grand building that the Central Criminal Court occupies today is the result of several reconstructions undertaken between 1673 and 1913. The 1726 Old Bailey would have looked remarkably different. The courthouse had been rebuilt in 1673 following the Great Fire and by 1720 it stood as 'a fair and stately building', according to the ever-observant John Strype. 'The court-room,' Strype continued, was approached

> by stone steps from the ground, with rails and banisters, enclosed from the yard before it; and the bail-dock, which fronts the court where the prisoners are kept until brought to their trials, is also enclosed. Over the court-room is a stately dining room, sustained by ten stone pillars, and over

it a platform, headed with rails and banisters. There be five lodging-rooms, and other conveniences, on either side the court. It standeth backwards, so it hath no front toward the street; only the gateway leadeth into the yard before the house, which is spacious.[1]

Perhaps the most striking feature of the Old Bailey that Gabriel Lawrence would step into was the open façade which exposed the wooden interior to the elements. A portion of wall had been deliberately omitted from this side of the building to encourage the circulation of fresh air through the courtroom, which was particularly important in the event that a prisoner from Newgate might be displaying any of the ghastly symptoms of gaol fever. These measures were known to fall short on occasion, though. For example, the spread of typhus from the prison to the courtroom

Figure 2. Justice Hall in the Old Bailey, c.1723, showing the open courtroom. The bail dock stands behind the central gates beyond the high walls capped with spear-like heads.

put an end to the life of a later Lord Mayor, Sir Samuel Pennant, and at least five other individuals at one trial in 1750.[2]

On the day of his trial, Wednesday, 20 April 1726, Gabriel Lawrence made the short journey, in fetters, from Newgate to the courthouse. Sessions at the Old Bailey were held eight times each year, usually from January to June, in August, October and again in December, so multiple cases were heard on each trial day. As a defendant in a felony case Lawrence was not offered, nor would he have expected, any kind of formal legal defence before or on the day of his trial. Instead, in preparation for his appearance before the judge, it is likely he spent hours in Newgate 'in mock Tryals, and instructing . . . [other prisoners] in cross Questions, to confound Witnesses; and all the Stratagems and Evasions that can be of Service, to elude the Charge that shall be made against them'.[3] In this way, the early Georgian courthouse was a 'contest of citizen equals'.[4] In the absence of barristers, judges undertook any necessary cross-examination as they saw fit. As questioning proceeded, jurors were entirely free to interject with questions or points of clarification as and when they arose. As such, these proceedings might best be described as 'managed mayhem', structured around procedure and precedence but fizzing with caprice.

Following a trial for the theft of clothing and the neglect of a child, in which the defendants were found not guilty, Lawrence was ushered from the outdoor bail dock, through the Sessions House Yard and up the stone steps into the courtroom. The Justice Hall was fittingly imposing in its austerity. Lawrence was placed at the bar or in the dock, a simple lectern in the centre of the room. Around him, panels of darkened wood creaked and yawned back into repose as jurors, positioned either side of the courtroom, shifted in their seats. Because of the notoriety of Clap's sodomites, the jurors will have been waiting for the first of their trials and it is unlikely they approached the matter impartially.

Directly in front of him Lawrence could see the witness box and the judges, who were elevated above him. Below the judges an industrious bench of clerks, men of law and stenographers stretched their fingers and prepared fresh sheets of paper in anticipation of furiously scrawling an account of the proceedings as they unfolded. These recorded *Proceedings*, part of the Old Bailey archive, inform much of what we know about working-class queer Georgian men today.

His back to the elements now, Lawrence may have felt the swell of the crowd in the Sessions House Yard as they moved closer in anticipation, eager to grasp at any wisp of scurrilous detail. As he settled in place, a brilliant, continuous stream of light struck Lawrence's face. A reflector had been placed above the bench where the judges sat, strategically positioned so as to focus the external light on the face of the accused. His face thus illuminated, those gathered in the courtroom could better determine the authenticity of his defence.

Accounting for jury deliberations and the announcement of the verdict, Lawrence could have anticipated his trial lasting no longer than thirty minutes. What followed next, to a modern reader, will seem extraordinarily concise, particularly since a life was at stake. Gabriel Lawrence, the court heard, 'was indicted for feloniously committing with Thomas Newton, aged 30 Years, the heinous and detestable Sin of Sodomy'. Newton was then instructed to take the stand. He swore that

> At the End of last *June*, one *Peter Bavidge* (who is not yet taken) and ____ *Eccleston* (who died last Week in *Newgate*) carried me to the House of *Margaret Clap* . . . and there I first became acquainted with the Prisoner.[5]

Having briefly described his impressions of Mother Clap's molly house, Newton testified that he had first met Gabriel Lawrence there on 20 July 1725. Newton continued, 'I was conducted up one pair of Stairs, and by the Persuasions of *Bavidge* (who was present all the Time) I suffered the Prisoner to commit the said Crime.' Newton was keen to have those assembled understand that he had reformed his ways, even if Lawrence had not:

> He, and one *Daniel*, have attempted the same since that Time, but I refused, though they buss'd [kissed] me, and stroked me over the Face, and said I was a very pretty Fellow.

And that – apart from an account of how he had come to the attention of the constables Williams and Willis – was that. It was not much, but if the jury believed him it would be enough.

Samuel Stephens then took the stand. Stephens was one of the undercover operatives acting on behalf of the Society for the Reformation of Manners who had infiltrated Clap's, posing as a harmless patron. He spoke as follows:

> Mrs *Clap's* House was notorious for being a Molly-House. – In order to detect some that frequented it, I have been there several Times, and seen 20 or 30 of 'em together, making Love, as they called it, in a very indecent Manner. Then they used to go out by Pairs, into another Room, and at their return, they would tell what they had been doing together, which they called marrying.

Joseph Sellers, Stephens's accomplice, confirmed Stephens's testimony. The judge then turned to Lawrence for his version of events.

Lawrence had, in fact, formulated a defence. He had called numerous witnesses to testify to his good name in the hope that he might be spared. Lawrence 'acknowledged that he had been several Times at *Clap*'s House, but never knew that it was a Rendezvous for such Persons'. If he offered any further testimony, it was not recorded. Instead, the *Proceedings* tell us, he began calling his witnesses. The first, Henry Hoxan, took the stand and testified:

> I have kept the Prisoner Company, and served him with Milk these 18 Years, for he is a Milk Man, and I am a Cow-Keeper, I have been with him at the *Oxfordshire* Feast, and there we have both got drunk, and come Home together in a Coach, and yet he never offered any such thing to me.

Samuel Pullen, another cow-keeper, corroborated Hoxan's testimony, adding that he had 'never heard such Things of him [Lawrence] before'. Lawrence's reputation, it seemed, was impeccable. And it was just as well, for as Margaret Chapman, a friend of Lawrence's, forcefully attested, 'I have known him seven Years. He has often been at my House, and, if I had suspected any such Stories of him, he should never have darkened my Doors, I'll assure ye.'

Members of Lawrence's extended family appeared for him too. His father-in-law, Thomas Fuller, stated that Lawrence had 'married my Daughter, 18 Years ago; She has been dead these 7 Years. And he had a Girl by her, that is 13 Years old.' Fuller's testimony was vital. Though Lawrence was a widower, he had married a woman and had a child with her. The implication was that he could not have performed the role of the family man *and* been a sodomite. To the mind of an early-eighteenth-century juror, perhaps Lawrence had to be one or the other, and there was a daughter to prove he was the former.

A final piece of testimony came from Lawrence's brother-in-law, Charles Bell, who declared: 'He married my Wife's Sister. I never heard the like before of the Prisoner; but, as for the Evidence, *Newton* . . . bears a vile Character.' With that the testimony ended, and Gabriel Lawrence's fate hung in the balance.

It is not known how long the jury deliberated; probably only a few minutes. Doubtless they had the shock of Newton's testimony still ringing in their ears. It is less likely, in the wake of such salacious details, that they gave the same consideration to the testimony delivered by Lawrence's witnesses, Henry Hoxan and Samuel Pullen. Unlikely too that the jury gave much thought to Lawrence arriving at Margaret Chapman's door, a welcome guest, and the hours he had whiled away at her hearth. Had the testimony of Fuller and Bell left a deeper impression? There had been a wife, had there not? And there was a child, a girl of thirteen? Whether these brilliantly unremarkable details seeped into the jury's deliberations is impossible to tell. Whatever the case may be, they felt justified in determining the outcome of Gabriel Lawrence's life with just two recorded words: 'Guilty. Death.'[6]

Following Lawrence's guilty verdict, a slew of other men who had been taken on the night of the raid or had thereafter been associated with Mother Clap's molly house were similarly arraigned. William Griffin, who had been lodging with another man, Thomas Phillips, 'near two Years in *Clap*'s House' was next up. Phillips had wisely 'absconded' following the raid, but Griffin had been captured. Thomas Newton once more struck the fatal blow. Newton testified that on 10 May he 'went upstairs, while the Prisoner [Griffin] was a Bed, and there he committed the Act with me'. As before, Griffin's verdict was handed down in gravely elementary terms: 'Guilty. Death.'

George Kedger testified that Edward 'Ned' Courtney, who like Newton had turned witness for the Crown, had blackmailed him when he refused to pay Courtney for sex. Kedger said that Courtney had declared: 'What . . . am I not handsome enough for ye?' Courtney, Kedger swore, was known to live in a 'very poor and ragged Condition' owing to the precarity of his life as a sex worker. Kedger advised the younger man to 'leave off that wicked Course of Life', but Courtney wouldn't listen. 'If I would not help him to some [money],' Kedger went on, 'he would swear my Life away.' By now the jury had a developed predilection for a hanging: '[They] found [Kedger] Guilty. Death.'

However, Courtney failed to convince the jury to hang George Whytle, who ran an 'Ale-House, the Royal-Oak, [at] the Corner of St. George's-Square in Pall-Mall'. Courtney asserted that Whytle

> keeps a back Room for the Mollies to drink in, and a private Room betwixt that and the Kitchen, there is a Bed in it, for the Use of the Company, when they have a Mind to be married, and for that Reason, they call that Room, The Chapel.

Whytle, in his defence, 'first objected against the Credit of Courtney's Evidence, he being a scandalous Fellow, and had been thrice in Bridewell [Prison]'. Whytle continued:

> I had a Wife, she has been dead these 2 Years. I had 2 Children by her, one of them is dead, but the other is here in Court, a Girl of 13 Years old. I was upon the Point of visiting another Widow, upon the Account of Marriage, just before this Misfortune broke.[7]

In sodomy cases marriage was currency, and the pre-modern household was thought to be 'linked to other households in a chain of credit'.[8] The more one complied with regulated expectations, the more 'credit' one amassed. Maybe Lawrence and Whytle had compared defence notes in Newgate and sought to use the credit marriage and fatherhood afforded them in an attempt to save their reputations and their lives. Whereas Newton had proved too 'credible' a witness in Lawrence's case, Courtney did not hold the same sway in Whytle's and the jury acquitted him.

Once a small number of other unrelated cases had been heard, all prisoners convicted of capital crimes, including Gabriel Lawrence, were then addressed together and their sentences pronounced:

> O yes! O yes! O yes! My Lords, the Kings Justices, strictly charge and command all manner of persons to keep silence while sentence of death is passing on the prisoners at the bar, on pain of imprisonment... The law is that thou shall return from hence, to the Place whence thou camest, and from thence to the Place of Execution, where thou shalt hang by the Neck, till the body be dead! dead! dead! and the Lord have Mercy upon thy Soul.[9]

Lawrence was then escorted in shackles back to Newgate, this time to the condemned cell. There, in his earthly limbo, surrounded by his fellow condemned, he would await the next hanging day.

The condemned cell, stinking, dismal and located close to the prison gate, consisted of a stone floor and a basic wooden shelf which acted as a communal bed for the condemned prisoners. It also contained a narrow window which taunted them with a sliver of the outside world. As condemned prisoners, Lawrence and the others were now allowed visitors who might speak with them through a wooden partition between their cell and the prison lodge. We do not know if any visitors came to see Gabriel Lawrence. However, whilst hope of his being freed had dwindled, all was not completely lost. He might yet be handed a reprieve, should Thomas Newton have perjured himself during the trial, say. Alone together, the mollies in the condemned cell once more awaited their fate.

As the weeks passed, Lawrence anticipated the arrival of the 'Dead Warrant', the final list of the condemned. If your name was on that list, barring your dramatic escape, you would hang, but the warrant also served as a confirmation of who was no longer sentenced to death. When it arrived, George Kedger had indeed been reprieved. During the course of the trial and in the weeks that followed, Ned Courtney had proved himself an unscrupulous witness and the judges were no longer content to let a man hang on the basis of his testimony. Kedger was a free man once more. Thomas Newton, however, had been more convincing. Etched on the warrant, black ink bleeding into the heavy weave of the paper, Gabriel Lawrence's name appeared as plain as day. All hope was lost now; the noose anticipated his neck.

James Guthrie was formally appointed Ordinary at Newgate Prison on 19 February 1733, though he had carried out those duties since September 1725. As Chaplain of the gaol he tended to the spiritual needs of the condemned prisoners, but one of his other main activities was to publish an account of the prisoners in his care in the final days and weeks of their lives. The *Ordinary's Accounts*, as they were inventively titled, were designed to act as a moral deterrent to those who read them, reducing crime and, in turn, keeping others from the noose. However, the *Accounts* also appealed directly to the growing appetite for true-crime stories across Georgian Britain. Printed between 1676 and 1772 and priced between 3d and 6d, these publications could earn the Ordinary up to £200 (£33,000) of additional income. With such sums up for grabs it is no wonder Guthrie wished to publish printed details of Gabriel Lawrence's final days.

Guthrie's *Accounts* tell us that Lawrence 'was a Papist, and did not make many particular Confessions to me'. English Catholics, particularly in the first half of the eighteenth century, were depicted in contemporary prints and pamphlets as dishonest and corrupt by nature, and Guthrie would have been acutely aware of this when he made note of Lawrence's religion. However, whilst contemporary writing recounts the ways in which Catholics were reputedly excluded from English society, Guthrie noted that Lawrence 'kept the Chapel with the rest, for the most part . . . made frequent Responses with the rest, and said the Lord's Prayer and creed after me'. Guthrie also noted that Lawrence 'was always very Grave'. His reputation in tatters, and seemingly having accepted his fate, Lawrence left one final statement with Guthrie in an attempt to secure his legacy. 'He said that Newton had perjur'd himself, and that in all he had never been guilty of that detestable Sin, but that he liv'd many Years with a Wife, who had born several Children, kept a good sober House; and this he desir'd me to Publish.'

Late on Wednesday, 8 May 1726 Guthrie preached the 'condemned sermon' in the chapel at Newgate to Lawrence and his comrades. Also in attendance were a significant number of 'strangers' who had crossed the gaoler's palm to gawk at the final torturous hours of those scheduled to swing. Then, back in the condemned cell, 'dismal Cries and Lamentations' rose up amongst the prisoners as, beyond its walls, the sexton of St Sepulchre's rang his midnight bell. As the bell tolled, the sexton bellowed his customary grisly incantation, the same one he delivered each night before a hanging:

> All you that in the condemned Holds do lie,
> Prepare you, for to Morrow you shall die;
> Watch, and pray, the Hour's drawing near,
> That you before th'Almighty must appear:

> Examine well your selves, in time repent,
> That you may not t'eternal Flames be sent;
> And when St Pulcher's Bell, to Morrow tolls,
> The Lord above have Mercy on your Souls.

Scarcely a shred of sleep can have been expected that night. Early next morning, Lawrence joined Guthrie and the others once again in the chapel for further prayers in preparation for the journey ahead.

Thursday, 9 May 1726. Despite the early hour, the streets around Newgate were abuzz. Before the sun had risen a crowd had gathered outside the gaol. The monotonous toil of workaday life had been set aside, for that day was a hanging day and citizens were therefore granted a brief hiatus and encouraged to gather along the well-worn route towards the western boundary of the City of Westminster. Tyburn lay some three miles hence and many of those gathered had decided to walk the distance together. Given the spectacle that would soon unfold, the atmosphere around the gaol was neither sombre nor grave. Instead, an intoxicating vitality ran through the crowd. Whispers gathered, eyes trained on the prison. A pre-dawn mummer played mezzo-piano.

At 9 a.m. the gates opened. The prisoners were walked through the stone hall, through the gateway, and then to the horse-drawn carts in which they were to travel. Amongst the crowd one can imagine Death, shrouded and covert, taking stock of the prisoners, preparing to meet them face to face. Then the pushing started, the crowd on tiptoes straining to catch a glimpse of the condemned.

That day was no ordinary hanging. Amongst the condemned was Mrs Catherine Hayes, widow and murderess, who oversaw the beheading of her husband, John. There too was her lover and accomplice, Thomas Billings. This infamous pair had disposed of Mr Hayes's mangled head in the Thames. Thomas Wood, her second extramarital paramour and co-conspirator, had already expired in Newgate of gaol fever. Hayes and Billings would have been known to the crowd as their likenesses had appeared in newspapers and prints for weeks.

That morning, Mrs Hayes carried a prayer book, eyes fixed to the ground. Having been found guilty of petty treason, she was to be partially hanged until unconscious before being burnt alive. But the hangman would miscalculate, and she would be awake as the flames began to lick, her screams loud enough to raise the dead. But in that moment, she just held her book tight. Here too, of course, were the mollies, whose house on Field Lane had lately been raided and their deplorable sins unveiled. With such notorious necks for the noose, no wonder so many Londoners gathered excitedly together.

Then the Newgate irons were struck from the prisoners. Their hands were tied in front of them with rope. The undersheriff stepped forward, as was customary, and instructed that the prisoners be passed into his custody. In return, he handed the gaoler a receipt for each man and woman's body, the value of their lives having already drained from their limbs.

Another man stepped forward then, solemn and deliberate in his steps. He approached each prisoner and placed a noose round their necks. Faces peered from every upper floor in the vicinity; window space had been sold to punters on account of it being a hanging day. The condemned were then put in the horse-drawn carts that would transport them to Tyburn. At this, an almost instant cacophony of 'howling . . . scolding and quarrelling' erupted from the assemblage. 'Seas of Beer . . . are swilled; [accompanied by] the never ceasing Outcries for more.' Hawkers shouted above the din, selling cautionary ballads or the final words of the condemned (which had not yet been uttered, but that hardly mattered). It was at this point, contemporary chroniclers tell us, that church bells all along the route began a sudden and continuous collective peal, scattering pigeons in fright to circle overhead.

> The Traders, who vent it among the Mob on these Occasions, are commonly the worst of both Sexes ... most of them weather-beaten Fellows, that have mis-spent their Youth. Here stands an old Sloven, in a Wig actually putrefied, squeezed up in a Corner, and recommends a Dram of [gin] to the Goers-by: There another in Rags with several Bottles in a Basket, stirs about with it, where the Throng is the thinnest, and tears his Throat with crying his Commodity.[10]

The driver alerted his mule; the procession began. The horse-drawn carts moved slowly into action and the crowd followed close by. 'At last, out they set; and with them a Torrent of Mob bursts through the Gate.'[11] The procession passed through St Giles's, St Andrew's and Holborn before taking the Tyburn Road to the gallows, making sure to visit the most populated districts as it went.

Due to the unpredictability of the mob, the condemned carts were escorted through the streets by a retinue of armed law enforcement. James Guthrie will either have accompanied Lawrence and the others in their carts, dispensing moral direction as they travelled, or tended to the mob, demonstrating the fate that awaited them should they similarly transgress.

The journey to Tyburn was littered with numerous ceremonial stops; the first of these was a short halt outside nearby St Sepulchre's. The sexton who the night before had extolled the condemned to consider, confess and repent their sins in preparation for death took his place on the churchyard wall. With an apparent flair for the ominous, he delivered another warning:

> All good people pray heartily unto God for this poor Sinner who is now going to his death, for whom this great bell doth toll. You that are condemned to die, repent with lamentable tears; Ask mercy of the Lord for the salvation of your own soul, through the merits, death and passion of Jesus Christ, who now sits [at] the right hand of God, to make intercession for as many as not return to him.
> Lord have mercy upon you!
> Christ have mercy upon you!
> Lord have mercy upon you!
> Christ have mercy upon you!

Once the sexton had completed his cries for mercy, a clutch of young girls flung nosegays and blew kisses towards the cart, sending the condemned on their way once more.

Thereafter it was customary for the prisoners to stop at as many as half a dozen taverns, 'impatient that they fill themselves full of liquor', no doubt to 'stifle their Fear'. Bernard de Mandeville, the Anglo-Dutch philosopher, observed that the consumption of alcohol 'seems to be contrived on Purpose, to take off and divert the Thoughts of the Condemned from the only Thing that should employ them'.[12] James Boswell, the noted Scottish diarist, lawyer and biographer, admitted later in the century:

> I must confess that I myself am never absent from a public execution ... when I first attended them I was shocked to the greatest degree. I was in a manner convulsed with pity and terror, and for several days, but especially the night after, I was in a very dismal situation. Still, however I persisted in attending

them and by degrees my sensibility abated; so that I can now see one with great composure . . . the curiosity which compels people to be present at such affecting scenes is certainly a proof of sensibility, not callousness. For it is observed that the greatest proportion of spectators is composed of women.[13]

Executions were public events, meant to be attended by all sections of society, high and low. As Dr Johnson observed to Boswell, the self-confessed gallows connoisseur, 'Sir, executions are intended to draw spectators. If they do not draw spectators they do not answer their purpose.'

All these interruptions considered, then, it might have taken anything up to three hours for the procession to finally arrive at Tyburn, at the intersection of Oxford Street and Edgware Road, where the Marble Arch stands today. The Tyburn gallows was a triangular configuration of three sturdy pillars of lumber approximately ten feet high, connected across the top by beams from which the bodies hanged. The set-up had been perfected in the late sixteenth century following the use of a series of temporary gallows on the same spot. This meant that numerous hangings could be carried out simultaneously, as opposed to one at a time, which had been the case previously. From the horizontal beams up to twenty-four men and women could swing, and with as many as twelve hanging days each year the bodies soon mounted up. The poet and satirist John Taylor tells us as much:

> I Have heard sundry men oft times dispute
> Of trees, that in one year will twice bear fruit.
> But if a man note Tyburn, [t]'will appear,
> That that's a tree that bears twelve times a year . . .
> It bears no leaf, no bloom, or no bud,
> The rain that makes it fructify is blood.

By the time Gabriel Lawrence arrived at the site of the scaffold the crowd could have swelled to as much as 100,000 people owing to the celebrity status of the murderess Catherine Hayes and the notoriety Lawrence and his coterie had gained. On a hanging day a view of the scaffold was a lucrative commodity; some people purchased window space, whilst a temporary bank of seating had been set up on either side of the gallows, and hawkers sold room on the backs of their carts as impromptu viewing platforms to those who could not stretch to the price of a seated spot.

As the condemned neared the scaffold the enormous crowd pressed ever forward and, according to eyewitness accounts, shoved and jostled beneath the gallows. As a result, some of the supporting timbers began to sway and move. Suddenly, under this extraordinary pressure, three sections of the gallows gave way, crushing and injuring sections of the crowd beneath. The Ordinary, James Guthrie, spent this time consoling Gabriel Lawrence, William Griffin, Catherine Hayes, Thomas Billings and the other condemned as they lived out their final moments amidst the chaos. As repairs to the scaffolding were carried out, hymns were sung, final prayers offered up and the Apostolic Creed spoken.

Once order had been restored and the injured parties removed, family members were then allowed to speak to the prisoners. We do not know who, if anyone, appeared for Lawrence. It is possible his father-in-law, Thomas Fuller, attended. Perhaps his brother-in-law, Charles Bell, accompanied him to the gallows too; both had been willing to appear at the Old Bailey on his behalf, after all. Anonymous amongst the gathered crowd, friends from Clap's who had not been discovered may well have stood in silent solidarity as they watched him take his final journey. It is also unknown whether Lawrence's thirteen-year-old daughter attended her father that day, to see him on his way. Having already lost her mother, the young girl would soon be orphaned and then apprenticed, if she was lucky. Her father may very well have asked her to stay away, preserving her from his final ghastly moments. And so Gabriel Lawrence, the London milkman, the widower, the father, the neighbour, the friend, the molly, took his final steps.

Along with the others, Lawrence was moved on the horse-drawn cart, beneath the gallows. The crowd would have expected the condemned, once positioned, to deliver a dying speech. For the most part the final words of those who were about to die were nothing out of the ordinary. Whether innocent or guilty, they voiced an acceptance of their fate and appealed to God for forgiveness. They invariably asked that He might receive them in the life to follow. Lawrence's 'dying words' were recorded and printed for distribution. However, it is worth noting that these supposed speeches were often printed in advance of the condemned having ever reached Tyburn and were, in many respects, works of fiction. This is certainly the case when it comes to *The Last Speech Of Mr Gabriel Lawrence* (1726), for it contains numerous inaccuracies and omissions. To begin with, 'Gabriel' admits he is a sodomite, but we know from James Guthrie's account that he never did. The speech also claims that Lawrence was a Protestant, which Guthrie told us he was not. In essence, *The Last Speech* was written and distributed as an 'admission' of Lawrence's unusual 'Course of Sin, a Crime not only against the Divine, but human Nature in general'. It describes how unhappy Lawrence was due to his same-sex attraction and never mentions his wife or his child. What his final words actually were we will never know.

He will have publicly forgiven the hangman, Richard Arnet, as was the custom, and possibly tipped him to ensure his body was handled mercifully after he had been cut down. Lawrence will then have joined with the thousands gathered in reciting Psalm 51: 'Have mercy upon me, O God, according to thy loving kindness: according unto the multitude of thy tender mercies blot out my transgressions.' Finally it was time. Arnet tightened the noose round Gabriel Lawrence's neck then fastened the other end to 'the fatal tree' above. He placed a cap over Lawrence's head, took his place by the mule that had led the cart beneath the gallows and gave the signal. With that, the cart moved away. Gabriel Lawrence dropped downwards before being violently caught by the rope, suspended above the ground. There he squirmed with the others as the crowds looked on, hanging amongst the freshest fruit newly matured on 'the Deadly Nevergreen'.

And what of Mother Clap? Often, when historians have undertaken the histories of same-sex-attracted men, women have been noticeably absent despite the pivotal roles they played in their lives. On 11 July 1726 Margaret Clap's case was heard at the Old Bailey. Clap was tried for keeping a disorderly house or 'keeping a brothel'. It is worth noting that there is no archival record of Clap having procured sex for her customers, though certainly male sex workers frequented and operated within her establishment. Samuel Stephens, the undercover operative, testified that he had visited Clap's house on '*Sunday* Night, the 14th *November* last' to gather intelligence. Stephens likely shocked those in the courtroom by declaring:

> Sometimes they'd [the mollies] sit in one another's Laps, use their Hands indecently[,] Dance and make Curtsies, and mimic the Language of Women. *O fire sir!—Pray Sir!—Dear Sir! Lord, how can ye serve me so! Ah ye little dear Toad!* Then they'd hug, and play, and toy, and go out by Couples into [a] Room on the same Floor, to be married, as they called it.[14]

This vilification inadvertently alerts us to something far more enlightening. Running counter to the tale of spies, raids, cruelty, gaol time, typhus and hangings, Stephens's recorded statements also remind us that, prior to their being 'taken up', the lives of the mollies were full of camaraderie, sexual intimacy, dance, skits, jokes and a vicious sense of fun.

Stephens's testimony reveals that Margaret was 'present all the Time, except when she went out to fetch Liquors'. Likely she secured these refreshments from the Bunch of Grapes next door and resold them at her own establishment for a profit as the merrymaking continued. Clap knew her customers, and she knew that to provide a space uniquely for them was good business. That is not to say that Clap was solely profit-driven. She enjoyed the company of the mollies she catered to: 'The Company talked all manner of gross and vile Obscenity in the Prisoner's hearing, and she appeared to be wonderfully pleased with it.'

Following Stephens's testimony, which was corroborated by Sellers, Clap's own defence reads suspiciously briefly. 'I hope it will be considered that I am a Woman,' she is recorded as having said, 'and therefore it cannot be thought that I would ever be concerned in such Practices.' Given everything we know of the formidable Margaret Clap, it is unlikely that she had not prepared a more robust defence than that. But maybe Newgate had worn her down? Or, more likely still, she *had* said more, but the court stenographer thought it unnecessary to record it. Although women made up 40 per cent of defendants between 1694 and 1740, female testimony at the Old Bailey is significantly truncated or omitted altogether from the *Proceedings*. The evidence presented by Stephens and Sellers, however, was deemed to be 'full and positive' and 'the Jury found her Guilty'. Margaret Clap was sentenced 'to stand in the Pillory in Smithfield, pay a Fine of 20 Marks, and suffer two Years Imprisonment'.

Pillorying involved placing the criminal in stocks, usually secured round their hands and neck, but sometimes their ankles, in a public square or near where their crime had been committed. Those pilloried were jocularly known as 'stoop nappers' or 'overseers of the new pavement'. The ordeal highlighted the fact that the restrained person had broken a social contract and damaged their reputation. The pillory could be a brutal place, and accounts from the eighteenth century tell us that

> the low populace ... pelts the prisoner with mud, rotten apples, dead cats and dogs, and that with such gusto and enjoyment that sufferers in some cases have been removed in a very exhausted condition.[15]

After this harsh, violent humiliation the prisoner was expected to repent and, having faced public condemnation, might eventually see their reputation restored.

For Clap, however, the experience proved particularly ferocious. She was pilloried at Smithfield, a busy eighteenth-century thoroughfare, at the end of July 1726. *The London Journal* reported that 'The Populace treated her with so much Severity that she fell once off of the Pillory, and fainted upon it several times.' *The Weekly Journal: or The British Gazetteer* of the same date tells us what then became of Margaret Clap. 'Being unable to bear the Salutes of the Rabble, she swooned away twice, and was carried off in Convulsion Fits to Newgate.' It is not known what happened to her after this, for she disappears from the record.

As we leave Clap and Lawrence, it might be tempting to conclude that their histories are overwhelmingly melancholy and lead, tragically and inevitably, from Field Lane to the scaffold and the pillory. After all, many of the documents consulted across these two opening chapters are court proceedings and damning newspaper reports. Such accounts were never intended to provide a basis through which historians might piece together an account of the queer past, but as a record of the ways in which it might be totally obliterated. However, between the catastrophic lines of Samuel Stephens's testimony and Joseph Seller's depositions, if one listens closely enough one cannot help but discern the low rumbling of revelries from inside Margaret Clap's molly house prior to the raid in 1726. To be a molly in the eighteenth century was a perilous thing, as Gabriel Lawrence and his friends knew only too well; but it was also a life worth pursuing, even in the face of such danger. In that way, their defiance is greater than their demise. That is our inheritance. We will remember them in what is yet to come.

CHAPTER THREE

Sedition and Defamation Display'd

JANUARY 25 1731. It was four o'clock on an icy afternoon in Green Park, London. The Whig politician John, Lord Hervey, a winter weasel of a man, stood in hushed conversation with the austere-looking Henry Fox. Fox dispensed steady counsel, though he was mightily concerned as to what might happen next. Fox had not expected his friend to react so decidedly to the accusations laid out against him in a recent scurrilous pamphlet. There, in black and white, the anonymous author had accused Hervey of being a sodomite. Though the author of the pamphlet had been anonymous, Hervey had determined the man behind the accusation. This man, Hervey's one-time friend, would have to be held to account. And so Hervey and Henry Fox carried out the final checks to sword and sheath in preparation for a retaliatory duel. Gentlemanly honour, above all else, must be preserved.

Concurrently, William Pulteney, a fellow Whig linked to an opposing faction within the party, walked purposefully out of his London house into his back garden. This was Hervey's opponent and the person who had 'outed' him. Like Hervey, he was accompanied by a second man. Once Pulteney and his friend reached the end of the garden, they unlocked a wooden door that gave on to Green Park and walked in the direction of the other two men.

All four then stood face to face. Hervey indicated a pocket in his waistcoat and informed Pulteney that it contained a letter. The letter confirmed it was Hervey who had challenged Pulteney to the duel. This would ensure Pulteney's inculpability should Hervey perish during their fight. Formalities observed, and despite the cold, the duellists then stripped down to their shirts, drew their swords and assumed their positions. Soon, following the clash of blades, blood would be spilt across the crystalline winter grass.

John (Jack) Hervey was born in Jermyn Street, London, on 16 October 1696 to the 1st Earl of Bristol and his second wife Elizabeth Felton. Jack was one of eighteen children (the fifth child, the second son) born to the earl across both his marriages. Tragically, only twelve lived beyond childhood, roughly in line with infant mortality rates between 1618 and 1749. Jack, though precocious, was himself a sickly child and there were times when it was not at all certain that he would survive. It is unclear exactly what ailed him. Some historians have speculated that he had epilepsy, others have posthumously diagnosed him with some form of autoimmune disease. Whatever the case, his ill-health remained with him throughout his life.

Unlike his older brother, Carr, Jack was educated at home by a series of private tutors until he was fifteen. As a result, he formed a particularly strong bond with his father, though his attachment to his mother was strained. Later, Hervey would lament that the 'vehemence of My Lady Bristol's Temper' had often been the cause of tensions at Ickworth, their family seat in Suffolk. Domestic tensions aside, once his health improved in his teenage years, young Hervey did go on to observe most of the social milestones that marked him out as an English gentleman. At the age of sixteen, for instance, he entered Westminster School, and a year later Clare College, Cambridge before graduating in 1715 with an MA. Hervey then embarked upon the Grand Tour, the customary coming-of-age tour of Europe undertaken by young noblemen.

From the late sixteenth century, any young man worth his salt enjoyed the supervised adventures of a Grand Tour. This trip, the culmination of a classical education, might follow various routes but often included stops in the Low Countries, Paris, Venice and Florence. Invariably it ended in Rome. Young gentlemen were accompanied by a tutor or 'cicerone' throughout and were expected to return bearing the spoils of their travels: sculpture, portraits and other treasures that would be displayed in their English houses as a sign of their mature masculinity, taste and refinement. The sites and monuments encountered on the tour left a significant mark on English tastes which, in turn, transformed the English architectural style, with Italian Palladianism becoming an aesthetic benchmark for elite building in the first half of the eighteenth century. The Palladian style celebrated strict proportion, symmetry and classical form in its execution. It spoke to simple grandeur, coveting restraint and control. This architectural style was wholeheartedly embraced and disseminated by the likes of Lord Burlington and his companion William Kent, though Jack himself could be critical of their designs. Despite his intermittent Palladian misgivings Jack adored life in Europe, and when the time came for him to return to England the rural niceties of Suffolk paled in comparison to his continental romps.

Following his return, Jack's life initially unfolded much as you might expect. He met and married Mary Lepell on 21 April 1720. Children would soon follow, eight in total. However, on 15 November 1723 Jack's fortunes took an unexpected turn. On that day his older half-brother and Member of Parliament for Bury St Edmunds, Carr, Lord Hervey, 'drowned in drink' and died, making

Jack Baron Hervey of Ickworth and heir to his father's earldom and estates. Hervey was elected MP for Bury St Edmunds in place of his brother on 2 April 1725. John, now Lord Hervey, was the epitome of landed respectability. Less conventional, however, was Hervey's gender non-conformity.

Like many other aristocratic gentlemen in the early Georgian period, Hervey had taken up the French habit of wearing white powder on his face, a mark of style and status that detractors interpreted as overly effeminate. That criticism, in itself, was not singular and might have been applied to many a well-to-do fop. But it was something far more innate that set Hervey apart.

Lady Mary Wortley Montagu was one of Hervey's best friends, or worst enemies, depending on what had last transpired between them. Born in 1689, she was witty and brilliant, learned and erudite. Her carefully crafted words and her pockmarked face singled her out as one of the most enduring characters of the age. Remarkably, she was also responsible for first introducing a process of inoculation against smallpox to England when she deliberately infected her own three-year-old child with a tiny amount of the disease in 1721. Despite the successful outcome of her scientific endeavours, people at the time dismissed her discoveries as the dangerous actions of an 'ignorant woman'.

However, it is not Lady Mary's scientific innovation that links her so steadfastly to Hervey. Instead, her astute understanding of sex and gender has bound them together in a timeless alliance. Lady Mary did not obsess over Hervey's dress or his powdered face like the others; rather, she identified Hervey's effeminacy as being something far more foundational to his personhood. In fact, she is reported to have famously remarked, 'The world consists of men, women, and Herveys' when summing him up.[1] Hervey, in Lady Mary's eyes, was neither male nor female. According to her, he belonged to a category beyond these binaries.

Figure 3. John Fayram, 'The Right Honourable The Lord Hervey, PC', c.1737.

In the eighteenth century, members of the 'Third Sex' were generally men who did not comply with ideals of everyday masculinity. This third category of gender identity was often used in conjunction with, or in substitution for, molly, sodomite, cotquean or 'hermaphrodite'. But whilst Hervey's gender non-conformity was simply noted by Lady Mary it could be exploited by his political enemies, as we shall soon discover. To others, though, Hervey's gender performance inspired confidence, warmth, intimacy and, in the case of Henry Fox's older brother, Ste, a deep affection and love.

Stephen (Ste) Fox was born on 12 September 1704. He was educated at Eton and Christ Church, Oxford. When he was twelve he inherited his father's estate, including the family seat at Redlynch,

Figure 4. Detail: Ste Fox from William Hogarth, 'The Hervey Conversation Piece', c.1738–40.

Somerset. This was worth the very comfortable sum of £5,000 (£935,000) a year. As he matured, Ste undertook improvements to the house and gardens at Redlynch, cultivating a rustic, rural oasis. Though he loved Redlynch dearly and hated being away from it, in 1721 (as Lord and Lady Hervey were starting their family in Suffolk) Ste embarked upon a Grand Tour before returning to be elected MP for Shaftesbury in 1726. Owing to his new parliamentary obligations, Fox begrudgingly took lodgings in St James's Street, London. As with Hervey before him, all seemed to be ticking along more or less as one might have expected. All that, however, was about to change.

Jack was first introduced to Ste in the spring of 1727 by Fox's younger brother, Henry (Hervey's wingman in the wintry duel). He was instantly taken with the elder Fox's delicate features, his slight frame and his exquisite, pensive face. This connection, luckily, was not one-sided. Despite his bucolic contentment, Fox's infatuation with Hervey found him drawn to London more and more. His presence in London was, Hervey revealed, very welcome. On 1 June 1727, Hervey wrote to Fox with all the giddy abandon of an infatuated teenager:

> I won't tell you how I feel every time I go through St James's Street [where Fox lived] because I don't love writing unintelligibly; & the more faithful the description was, the farther one of your temper & way of thinking would be from comprehending what it meant. I might as well talk to a blind man of Colours, an Atheist of Devotion, or an Eunuch of f———'.[2]

Hervey flirted with Fox, teasing him that he was so level-headed that he couldn't possibly be thinking of Hervey as much as Hervey was thinking of him. In this, he attempted to draw the other man out. To test if he felt the same. Hervey need not have worried. What followed over the next decade was an imperfect love story for the ages played out in stolen weekends, long periods away from England together and in their letters to one another. Like all the very best love stories, however, it also ends in heartbreak. But before all of that, let us begin with what they wrote.

The Hervey–Fox literary flirtations were written just one year after Gabriel Lawrence had been hanged at Tyburn. The execution of Clap's clientele made such a significant cultural impact that it is almost impossible to think news of these events would not have reached both Hervey and Fox when they occurred. Maybe Hervey had even attended the execution, watching from one of the specially erected stands as Lawrence's final moments played out. Whether he had been there or not, there is no doubt that Hervey would have been acutely aware that he must not betray himself in his letters to his lover, despite his excitement. They must censor their written emotions, lest they be discovered and lose their lives. This proved to be an ongoing source of frustration for the men when they were apart. On one occasion, after Fox sought reassurances of Hervey's affections, Hervey comforted his companion: 'If it were possible for me to write to you, my dear Ste., with the same security that I speak to you . . . you should have no opportunity to complain of my silence.' However, he also warned Fox that he must temper his frustrations for he was not free to profess his love in letter-writing as Fox might have wished. To do so, he observed, 'would be dangerous to me'.[3] He was right to be cautious.

Despite the frequency and importance of written communication at this time, neither the writer nor the intended reader could expect letters to remain wholly private.[4] They might be intercepted or accidentally left unattended for prying eyes to pore over. Therefore, if one of Hervey's overly effusive letters happened to fall into the wrong hands, and there was a decent chance it might, all would be lost. When they were together, however, caution was cast to the wind and love blissfully bloomed.

It was to Fox, for instance, that Hervey turned when his beloved sister Elizabeth suddenly died, retreating with him to Redlynch and forsaking his family and duties at Ickworth. There, Hervey tells us, Fox 'loved me too well' and did 'all in his power to alleviate the weight of it [the bereavement]'. That autumn, Hervey and Fox went to Bath together, before returning once more to Redlynch at the start of November 1727. This greedy communion granted the men an opportunity to indulge the all-consuming nature of their romance. These intimacies became a 'Honey-moon' of sorts, as Samuel Johnson defined it, the early stages 'after marriage where there is nothing but tenderness and pleasure'.[5] And, it seems, there was much pleasure to be had.

Hervey tells us that Fox had 'left such [physical] remembrances behind you that I assure you . . . you are not in the least Danger of being forgotten'. Had Fox left bruises on Hervey following a particularly vigorous round of intimacies? If so, Hervey did not resent them. Instead, he coquettishly revelled in their presence. 'The favours that I have received at Your Honour's Hands,' he teased, 'are of such a Nature . . . that 'tis impossible for me to look on a Leg or an Arm without having my memory refreshed.' He joked: 'I have some thoughts of exposing the marks of your pollisonerie [lewdness] to move Compassion . . .'[6] The men became inseparable. 'I hear you in the deadest Silence,' Hervey pined, '& see you in the deepest Darkness . . . I look upon you as my Dwelling.'[7] Yet all this was still not enough. They craved even more time together. Essentially, they began to plan for a life which they could live as a married couple might, despite the heteroregulation that prohibited such unions.

Hervey and Fox had each undertaken Grand Tours as younger men, as we have noted, so it must have come as a surprise to many when, in July 1728, they suddenly left for Ostend, together with a small party including the Duke and Duchess of Richmond on their impressive yacht the *William & Mary*. Hervey's doctor had strictly opposed the trip following his patient's recent bouts of recurrent ill-health. But nobody could have been more surprised or frustrated at the prospect of this second Tour than Mary Lepell, Lady Hervey.

Since her husband had met Ste Fox the previous year she had hardly clapped eyes on him. Now, left with an amiable but ageing father-in-law and a bullish mother-in-law, she must have felt utterly discarded and distraught. Not so long ago she had been one of the fairest young ladies at court, batting away suitors; now she was confined to a damp, discarded corner of an old house at Ickworth with children to raise. This was not what pretty Mary's life might have looked like. But it was exactly what contemporary commentators had warned prospective brides they might experience if they found themselves hitched to a gender non-conforming man.[8]

Mary Lepell, known as Molly, was born in the month of September, but whilst her tombstone tells us she entered this world on 26 September 1700, her baptism register gives her date of birth as 16 September 1699. Her arrival, whenever it occurred, was the result of a union between Miss Mary Brooke, an English heiress, and the German-born Brigadier-General Nicholas Wedig Lepell. Driven by curiosity, Molly acquired a level of education that placed her intellectually beyond most of her female contemporaries. She had a decent grasp of Latin, for example, and read widely. She was lively, engaging company too, having spent most of her formative years at court. There she learnt to negotiate the polite dynamics of elite life with aplomb. By 1715, Molly's connections and accomplishments had seen her become one of six maids of honour to the future Queen Caroline. This was a prestigious position and came with an annual salary of £200 (£33,000).

Molly's intellect, charm and beauty did not go unnoticed at court and she turned many a gentleman's head. Admirers included the much older dramatist and poet Nicholas Rowe (1674–1718), who spilt forth the following verse concerning the young Miss Lepell and the countless pursuers she deftly commanded:

> I counted o'er the long, long score
>   Of laughing Cloe's lovers;
> Which, sad to see! besides poor me,
>   Full forty-nine discovers.
> But Cupid cries, 'Her nimble eyes

> Will quickly end your sorrow:
> Fifty a day, for that's her play,
> She kills – you'll die tomorrow'.[9]

The one man she was interested in, however, was Jack Hervey. The pair first met on 28 October 1719 and their mutual attraction caught the attention of the poet John Gay, who wrote to inform his fellow poet Alexander Pope (who himself had a soft spot for Molly) of their spark:

> Now Hervey, fair of face, I mark full well,
> With thee, youth's youngest daughter, sweet Lepell.[10]

By spring the following year, Lord Bristol, Hervey's father, recorded in his diary that his 'dear & hopeful son Mr. John Hervey was married to Mrs. Mary Le Pell'. Bristol was delighted by the union, writing to his new daughter-in-law:

> My son has shown the nicest skill in choosing you . . . since in you alone he could securely promise himself not only every quality essential to his own happiness, but has also made a wise provision to entail good sense & virtue . . . on our (now) flourishing family.[11]

Initially, their marriage remained a secret, despite both families having granted their permission for it to take place. Historians have speculated that this may have granted Molly six additional months to benefit from her maid of honour payments, which she would have to forgo as a married woman. Though the definitive explanation for this secrecy remains unclear, the marriage was officially announced on 25 October 1720 and the young couple took a small house on Bond Street, less than ten minutes' walk from St James's Street. Further poetical expressions appeared commemorating their union:

> Bright Venus yet never saw bedded,
>   So perfect a beau and a belle,
> As when Hervey the handsome was wedded,
>   To the beautiful Molly L[epel]l.[12]

The Hervey marriage was fruitful, and their first child, George William Hervey, arrived on 3 August 1721. Lady Hervey then gave birth again in 1723 (Lepell), 1724 (Augustus John) and 1725 (Mary).[13]

At about this time, and despite these auspicious marital milestones, it was Lady Hervey's reputation and not her husband's that first inspired courtly gossip. In August 1725, Hervey's friend, the incorrigible Lady Mary, noted: 'Lady Hervey is more Delightful than ever, and such a Politician that if people were not blind to merit she would govern the Nation.'[14] This was a reference to Lady Hervey's intellect and charm, no doubt, but it also alluded to the gossip swirling about court that Lady Hervey had become mistress to the sixty-five-year-old King George I. Court tittle-tattle declared:

> Or were I the King of Great Britain,
> To choose a Minister well,
> And support the Throne that I sit on,
> I'd have under me Molly [Lapelle] . . .
>
> Heaven keep our good King from rising,
> But that rising who's fitter to quell,
> Than some lady with beauty surprising,
> And who should that be but [Lapelle].[15]

Despite these rumours, it is impossible to prove that Lady Hervey accommodated the carnal needs of her elderly monarch. She certainly appears to have flirted liberally with the old man on occasion, but that might simply have been to help her husband's political ambitions; remember, Molly was a canny courtier. Whatever the case, in the early years of their marriage there can be no doubt that Lord and Lady Hervey were very much working in courtly cahoots. That being the case, as things stood in 1728, with her husband off to Europe with Ste Fox, Molly must have felt that those exciting days were far behind her.

Back in Belgium, and having taken the spring water at Ostend, Hervey and Fox left the Duke and Duchess of Richmond and set out for France together. In these first weeks of travel their progress was significantly slowed as Fox was struck down with a serious chest cold and a subsequent arm infection. And so, just as Fox had tended to Hervey in London as he grieved the loss of his sister, Hervey now cared for Fox on the continent.

It was the unknown potential within this intimate caregiving abroad that made critics of the Grand Tour uneasy. If Englishmen were to spend so much time travelling and sleeping together in private quarters, caring for one another in place of women, who knows what the outcome might be? One such critic was the anonymous author of the perpetually outraged *Satan's Harvest Home*, who lamented that the Grand Tour was no less than 'the *Mother* and *Nurse* of *Sodomy*', as a result of which 'the *Master* is oftener *Intriguing* with his *Page*, than a *fair Lady*'.[16] Between their 'intriguing', once Fox had recovered sufficiently, the companions continued south to Naples in search of warmer, drier weather before returning to Rome and then moving on to Florence.

★

As her husband and Fox crossed Europe together, at Ickworth Lady Hervey felt increasingly isolated. Whilst Hervey devoted his time to caring for Fox, Lady Hervey complained that her husband had effectively abandoned her. She wrote, plainly, 'I can never get any answer from him.'[17] Resolved, on 20 September 1728 she took pen in hand and set her frustrations and jealousies aside. She wrote to Ste Fox begging him for information on her husband and his health. 'I'm afraid you'll think me very troublesome,' she confessed, 'and indeed I think myself so, but the concern I have . . . ever since I had my Lord's last letter, had got the better of every other consideration.' She wished to know 'How he looks, if he sleeps well, sweats o' nights' and asks that Fox 'be sincere in your account of my Lord' whilst stipulating, 'I beg my Lord mayn't know of this letter.'[18]

Where jealousy, resentment and hatred might otherwise have taken root, in approaching Fox directly Lady Hervey acknowledged the intimate relationship he had with her husband. Fox, in return, recognized the difficulty of her circumstance and vowed to keep her updated as they progressed on their travels. For this Lady Hervey was eternally grateful. Ultimately they developed a secret system of co-spousal caregiving which Hervey was unaware of. For example, Lady Hervey might instruct Fox:

> I beg you'll prevail on him never to walk late in the evening . . . And do me the favour as soon as you have received this, to let me have some accounts . . . How does he sleep? I wish he would live as little as possible on the vegetable part of his diet, the farrinaisous [starchy] part of it is I believe verily much better for him.[19]

Domestic details concerning Hervey's sleeping pattern and diet indicate an acknowledgement that Lady Hervey now shared some of her 'wifely' duties with Fox. 'Pray don't go out of town . . . till he is much better,' she later requested when he was ill, 'I'm very much obliged to you for the punctual performance of your promise...'[20]

Fox carried out her instructions perfectly. Having arrived in Florence, Hervey found himself ill and bedridden once again. When he finally got round to writing to his wife, his verses (in which he regularly wrote) were filled with nothing but praise for Ste's devotion:

> But sick or well, where'er I move,
> In ev'ry Hardship that I prove,
> Fidus Achates [Ste] still is near,
> And makes my Welfare all his Care.[21]

Hervey later recounted Fox's devotion in more explicit detail. He recalled that Fox had 'never left me night or day'. The men were inseparable, 'he went out with me whenever I was able to go out', Hervey continued, 'read to me at home when I had not the spirits to talk, and constantly lay in my room'.[22] Lady Hervey must have welcomed the update. She was glad to know her husband was taken care of. But somewhere along the line this arrangement must have chipped away at her heart, little by little.

Whilst they were in Florence, Hervey and Fox met and befriended the great physician Dr Antonio Cocchi. Years later Cocchi would publish a treatise, *The Grand Question, Is Marriage Fit For Literary Men?* (1769), which proposed that some men were not suited to marriage with women and that they should cultivate the great intimacies of their private lives with other men.[23] One wonders if these ideas were inspired by or perhaps even discussed in 1729 with Hervey and Fox in the Florentine heat. Certainly, Hervey had pointed to the possibility that he and Fox might continue their domestic ease when they returned to England:

> Oh! would kind Heaven, those tedious Suff'rings past,
> Permit me Ickworth, Rest, and Health at last . . .
> From Business, and the World's intrusion free,
> With Books, with Love, with Beauty, and with Thee.[24]

Hervey dreamt of Ickworth, of rest and retreat, surrounded by the simplicity and abundance of nature, whiling away the hours not with his wife but with the man to whom he addressed these lines, Ste Fox. Hervey might well think ahead to life in England, for after fifteen months in Europe together England and obligation beckoned once more. Following a visit to Paris, including a quick detour to take in the splendour of Versailles, Hervey and Fox eventually returned to London. Once back in England, Hervey was, according to his father, 'in perfect health & according to my prayers'. It was just as well, for Hervey quickly found himself reacquainted with the perils of a political life.

William Pulteney, much like Hervey, was a natural politician. Their navigations through the tricky waters of power, however, could not have been more different. By 1730 Pulteney, twelve years Hervey's senior, was a well-established MP for Hedon in Yorkshire. He was a talented classical scholar, a gifted public speaker, robust in his horsemanship and (worryingly for Hervey) a noted swordsman. Like Hervey, Pulteney also belonged to the Whig Party.

Towards the end of the previous century, England had divided into a two-party political structure. These parties were known as the Whigs and the Tories. The word Tory is Irish in origin and initially implied support for the old Stuart monarchs and a tolerance of Roman Catholicism. In 1730 the Tories formed the opposition party in George II's government. The Whigs on the other hand, having supported the ascension of the Hanoverians to the British throne, formed the government. One might expect, therefore, that Pulteney and Hervey would be natural allies and for a time they were. But politics is a tricky business, alliances ebb and flow and internal tensions often threaten to tear a party apart. For the Whigs the cracks were already well established.

In 1721 Robert Walpole had become the first de facto Prime Minister of Great Britain. Prior to this he had gathered a select group of loyalists around him to whom he had promised political office. William Pulteney had expected to be one of the chosen loyalists but was not. Instead he was granted a trifling peerage for his loyalty, which he dramatically rejected. The scorned Whig made no secret of his disappointment. On numerous occasions he took to the floor in Parliament and lambasted the 'Robinocracy' Walpole had created for himself. He was, Pulteney believed, self-motivated and only concerned with lining his own pockets whilst in power. Many Whigs were bewildered by Walpole's decision to sideline such an influential (and vociferous) party member, but Walpole would not acquiesce. When, in 1724, Walpole once again passed over Pulteney for office, Pulteney formed an unofficial but influential opposition to the Walpole administration from within the Whig Party itself. Though he started with only a few members, support for Pulteney quickly grew and appeared to threaten Walpole's grip on power. And so when Hervey returned from Europe to undertake his parliamentary duties once more, Pulteney was keen to capitalize on his friendship with the MP for Bury St Edmunds and recruit him as another opponent to Walpole.

Pulteney roguishly counselled Hervey to abandon Walpole's leadership and side with the Whig defectors. Should he oppose the prime minister, Pulteney teased, once his faction replaced him Hervey would be financially and politically rewarded. Hervey, however, was not a pontificator like Pulteney. He did not respond to bluster and display. Instead he preferred a more subtle, contemplative approach to power and was not convinced by his old friend's argument. Hervey doubted that Pulteney had the numbers to replace Walpole and so he refused to commit to the cause there and then. He would bide his time. Hervey allowed these internal tensions to spark and quench as they might, observing each faction and carefully weighing up the possibilities should he choose to align himself with either man. It soon became clear to him, though, that his best bet for political influence lay with Sir Robert Walpole and he quickly became unwavering in his support for the prime minister. Pulteney felt betrayed, and as a result their political and personal relationship began to fracture.

Whilst one friendship disintegrated, another alliance prospered. In return for his loyalty, Walpole appointed Hervey Vice-Chamberlain of the Royal Household in 1730. In his new role, Hervey deputized for the lord chamberlain and oversaw receptions for dignitaries, balls and concerts, and the more prescribed elements of royal marriages and funerals. He was also responsible for the repair and maintenance of furniture and elements of 'interior decoration' at court; a true cotquean. These responsibilities required Hervey to live in apartments at St James's Palace and, thus situated, the reign of Herveyan influence began. Remarkably, it was Hervey's perceived effeminacy that was to prove his most vital asset in the viper's nest that was court politics.

Much has been written about the restrictions imposed upon even the most privileged Georgian women when it came to the exercise of power in the long eighteenth century. Books like *The Laws Respecting Women* (1777) were adamant that women were not natural wielders of authority. However, feminist historians have since established that many Georgian women had considerable authority and influence, albeit in less overt ways. For example, today it is very well documented that Queen Caroline of Ansbach, wife to George II, was an erudite, pragmatic and gifted practitioner of what we now understand as 'soft power'. She harnessed the genuine affection between herself and her husband to influence and co-opt the king to some of her many causes. She was a formidable politician in her own right.

In the same way, I believe historians have overlooked the different ways in which gender non-conforming men, who are often said to have forfeited their masculine right to authority, could subvert political expectations too. Hervey's femininity, for example, granted him considerable ease and meaningful friendships with women throughout his life. In this way, once established at court, Hervey proceeded to cultivate a close, personal and lasting relationship with Queen Caroline. The friends cemented their alliance in the queen's private quarters, to which Hervey was guaranteed admittance. There they might be discovered exchanging whatever recent gossip had piqued their joint interest just as easily as they might be found planning their next strategic move. It was because of his unrivalled proximity to the queen that Hervey could sway his royal friend to Walpolean will. Then she, convinced by the cause and tactical as she was, would tackle the king, particularly in instances where Walpole had failed to convince him directly.

In this way, femininity was a powerful political tool during the reign of George II. However, this subtle system of effeminate clout and Hervey's 'queanly' approach to maintaining it flew in the face of heteroregulated expectations. As we have seen, neither women nor effeminate men were to be allowed near the centre of power in any real way. As such, the Walpole-Hervey-Queen-King line of influence inevitably irked plenty of powerful factions at court. None more so than Hervey's new enemy, William Pulteney. So when it came to Pulteney's attention that Hervey had played a part in publishing a rather scathing attack against him, the white over-wrist kid gloves (with a plain rounded cuff) were well and truly off.

★

In the very early days of 1731, a controversial Whig publication appeared entitled *Sedition and Defamation Display'd*. It was written (we now believe) by Sir William Yonge, otherwise charmingly referred to as 'Stinking Yonge'. Hervey was certainly involved in its publication, though more likely as a patron than an author. In *Sedition*, Pulteney, though not directly named, was easily identifiable to those in the know. He was portrayed as wilful, arrogant, resentful and disloyal to Walpole. Pulteney was outraged by this depiction and believed that Hervey had been primarily responsible for its execution. Aggrieved, Pulteney set about mounting a swift, robust response, as was customary. His reply was duly delivered to Mr Richard Franklin, a printer, on 20 January 1731 and soon found itself in coffee houses throughout the capital.

Pulteney's reply was snappily entitled *A Proper Reply to a Late Scurrilous Libel; intitled Sedition and Defamation display'd*. In it Pulteney mused on the 'unmanly' authorship of the original attack and mocked the writer of the offending pamphlet. He suggested that *Sedition* had been so poorly written that it must be the work of a mere child – likely a young girl, in fact. Pulteney, despite having no proof to substantiate his claim, then went on to reveal that the second-rate author of the original piece was, in fact, none other than Lord Hervey.

Pulteney claimed that despite the attack on his honour, he could not possibly dream of fighting Hervey in retaliation as it would be dishonourable: 'He is a *Lady* Himself,' he claimed, 'Or at least such a nice Composition of the two Sexes, that it is difficult to distinguish which is most predominant.' Here he crassly echoes Lady Mary Wortley Montagu's assertion that Hervey was perceived as belonging to a 'Third Sex'. Pulteney goes on to call Hervey a *'Hermaphrodite'* and *'a pretty, little, Master Miss'*. As Pulteney saw it, Hervey's gender non-conformity diminished his masculinity and therefore his authority. The libels in *Sedition*, so claimed Pulteney, were barely worth the attention of a 'real man' such as himself.

These attacks on Hervey were bad, though not wholly damning. Hervey might not have felt the need to offer another printed riposte had that been where it stopped, but Pulteney was not done yet. What he included next would lead directly to the duel in Green Park. 'Give me Leave to illustrate Vice,' Pulteney begged his reader, before going on to deliver the fatal blow. The vice he referred to was sodomy. And the perpetrator? Hervey himself. However, he did not act alone. Pulteney went on, 'it is well known that there must be two Parties in this Crime; the Pathick and the Agent; both equally guilty'.

Pulteney had crossed a line. Had he only accused Hervey of being a sodomite, Hervey could have turned the other cheek. But then there was talk of another party, a lover, and Hervey's friends knew Pulteney could only be referring to one man, his beloved companion Ste Fox. This would not stand: aristocratic reputations, inheritances, familial legacies were at stake. But even in the wake of such serious revelations, Hervey's subsequent actions confounded his friends. Having quickly deciphered that Pulteney was responsible for *A Proper Reply*, Hervey consulted his honour and, finding it bruised, challenged his former friend turned political enemy to a duel.

Duelling's foundational elements had been forged in medieval times, whilst the idea of engaging in one-on-one combat as a result of a personal insult had emerged in Europe during the sixteenth century. Duelling had parried its way to English shores by the 1570s and continued to grow in popularity until the early seventeenth century. By the eighteenth century, however, the purpose of the duel had morphed from being purely antagonistic to a show of courage. Now, Hervey felt compelled to deploy this most manly of responses to redress Pulteney's accusations of effeminate sodomy. Melodramatic as it was, swords must be drawn.

Having informed Ste that he intended to challenge Pulteney to a duel, he allowed heated tempers to cool for three days. Then, on that January morning, Hervey sent Ste's younger brother Henry to Pulteney with questions for him to address. The most significant inquiry aimed to ascertain if Pulteney had written *A Proper Reply*. Pulteney was obliging. He had written it, he proclaimed, but only in retaliation to what he (incorrectly) believed Hervey had published about him previously. But the details mattered little now. Confirmation obtained, following Hervey's instructions to the letter, Henry Fox then asked Pulteney to name the time and place most agreeable to face Hervey in a duel. Stumped by Hervey's unexpected move, Pulteney relinquished scheduling obligations to Fox, who named the New Walk (now Green Park)

Figure 5. Anon., 'William Pulteney fighting a duel with Lord Hervey observed by Robert Walpole', 1731.

at 4 p.m. as the place and the hour. Pulteney agreed and set to his preparations.

Once the agreed time arrived and the fragile sun was near to setting, the four men came together under the last wisps of pink in the afternoon sky. All was remarkably still given their proximity to the hustle and bustle of town. Then a clash of blades burst through the icy anticipation. It had begun.

As they parried, Hervey received several nicks to his hand. Then a more worrying wound to his side. His shirt was stained with dark blood. Pulteney, the better fighter, acquired nothing more than a single scrape to his hand. Then:

> they [both] closed in, which in all probability would have been fatal to one if not both of them but the seconds [that is Henry Fox and Pulteney's companion] by consent rushed in . . . and seized their swords, upon which Mr. Pulteney said, 'Let us [contend] no more, my Lord,' and embraced him [Hervey].[25]

The seconds had fulfilled their duties well, ensuring both men survived. The duellers could part satisfied: Hervey had defended his honour, Pulteney had fought admirably. Swords sheathed, Hervey said nothing more to his opponent, only bowed with a terrific flourish. Around them, oil burners were lit in anticipation of the encroaching dark. It was no evening to be outside. So, turning on his heels, Hervey disappeared into the flat white landscape and headed for the comfort of a nearby address, 31 Great Burlington Street.

CHAPTER FOUR

No. 31 Great Burlington Street

THE IMPRESSIVE GEORGIAN HOUSES on what is now Old Burlington Street (formerly Great Burlington Street), London were originally built as part of a larger housing development undertaken in the early eighteenth century by Richard Boyle, 3rd Earl of Burlington and 4th Earl of Cork. In Burlington's day these streets were simultaneously lined with impressive new homes for the rich and haphazard rubble from the ongoing construction work. Today only a handful of the original buildings remain. The few that do sit uncannily on the same pavement as modern car parks, galleries, office blocks and shops. Truth be known, you'd probably walk past them without noticing them at all. But next time you find yourself wandering down Old Burlington Street take a moment to stop outside one of the remaining few. No. 31, to be precise. Take in the intricate moulding that flanks the great door, the dirtied old brick and the windows that decrease in size as they near the roof. There is no blue plaque outside No. 31 to indicate its importance to the queer past, but you should know that history was made here. For it was in this building that John, Lord Hervey and his companion Ste Fox defied convention with the very simplest of acts. It was here that they made a home.

Lord Hervey had never forgotten the domestic intimacies he and Fox had enjoyed together on their European tour. He had even speculated openly with Fox about the possibility of cultivating a version of that shared domestic bliss in England: 'Why should we only see one another by visits, but never have a common home?' he asked his companion in the summer of 1730. 'Think, if you please, that it is not easy to contrive it, but take care of concluding it is impossible.'[1] No. 31 Great Burlington Street would become that possibility.

Lord Hervey purchased the lease on 31 Great Burlington Street in 1725 to replace the 'deal-box' of a house he and Lady Hervey had previously shared on Bond Street.[2] They had very quickly

Figure 6. No. 31 Old Burlington Street.

No. 31 Great Burlington Street

outgrown their original residence once their children started to arrive. Lady Hervey particularly enjoyed being in town. It gave her access to friends from her former courtly life and she was stimulated by the constant happenings of the capital city. But, as we have seen, by 1730 Hervey had taken court lodgings at St James's Palace. And whilst Lady Hervey was free to visit him there (and did), she preferred to stay in the more familiar surroundings of the house on Great Burlington Street.

Simultaneously, Ste Fox was on the hunt for a permanent London residence. He had sourced a few options, but none were quite right. There had been one particular house he had liked very much but Hervey disapproved and so, after a brief lovers' tiff, that particular residence was forgotten about. It was not that Lord Hervey was not keen for Fox to have easy access to him in London, indeed he was very keen; but he wanted his companion to find the right house. Then it occurred to him: he no longer had much need for the house on Great Burlington Street. Fox, he proposed, should take over the lease.

So on 14 November Hervey strategically assigned the lease for 31 Great Burlington Street to Ste Fox, who paid £4,000 (£690,000) for the privilege. In addition to achieving the goal of a home for the two men, this would have placed the house off-limits to Lady Hervey, except as a visitor. Fox, when in London, was now housed less than a fifteen-minute walk from the Palace, from Hervey. Tastes changed quickly in a society increasingly fixated on consumption and luxury, and to mark this new phase in its ownership it was decided that No. 31 might benefit from some refurbishment. Crucially, however, it was not Fox who approached the cabinet-makers, ordered the linen or chose the new wood panelling, as one might have expected. He was the new owner, after all. Instead, Lord Hervey took on the role of interior designer with aplomb. He may no longer have had a legal claim to the property, but he was still very much invested in domestic life at 31 Great Burlington Street.

It is worth noting that it was not unusual for elite Georgian men to refurbish or renovate their houses, particularly just before or after they had been married. Gentlemen thought it prudent to provide fashionable domestic comforts for their new brides. In turn, their wives might more comfortably oversee the day-to-day running of their households.[3] In this case, however, there was no new bride to accommodate. Nonetheless, Lord Hervey's overseeing of the work at 31 Great Burlington Street unfolded with much the same 'matrimonial' intent, to accommodate their lives *together*. The new Hervey–Fox household would provide a domestic setting for same-sex intimacy and joy beyond the coffee house, beyond the molly house, beyond the latrine or the other shadowy cruising grounds across London that the aristocracy tended to steer clear of. It dignified the significance of their relationship not only with bricks and mortar, but eventually in the mundane rhythms of a shared home life. This house afforded these two same-sex-attracted men the luxury of privacy.

Hervey wrote to Fox in December 1731 to update him on the progress of the renovations. He had busied himself picking linens, decorative items to display throughout and art to adorn the walls. He had employed skilled craftsmen, such as upholsterers and cabinet-makers, to help execute his vision. Once the pounding of hammers had subsided and the dust had been cleared away, Hervey looked around the house that they had both held legal ownership of. His home. Fox's home. He beamed in a letter to his companion:

> It is quite finished, and looks the smuggest, sprucest, cheerfullest thing I ever saw. Nothing can improve it but a piece of

moveable goods of my acquaintance [i.e. Fox], which I expect home with more impatience than I can tell you . . .[4]

This, as Hervey tells us in his own words, was to be their *home*. But it is only through Fox's presence that the house took on that noble distinction. No. 31 Great Burlington Street became the site of a comfortable coup in 1731; an elite same-sex household that has gone unremarked by previous scholars of Georgian domestic life and same-sex desire.

But if Hervey could barely contain his excitement at seeing Fox at Great Burlington Street, his wife became increasingly cast off. It had been over three years since she had occupied the primary position of affection and desire in her husband's life, and it had cost her. Her rural pickling at Ickworth continued to preserve her in the dreary everydayness of elite country life. Despondent and faced with Hervey's intermittent attentions, she once again appealed to Fox. 'I beg . . . you'll be so good to let me know how he looks . . . & what spirits he is in,' she pined. Then, in desolate anguish, she enquired, 'Is there no hopes of his making us a visit this summer . . . I can assure you the Park is in the full perfection of beauty . . .'.[5] Their separation was almost too much for her to bear.

In response, Fox dutifully arranged for himself and Hervey to see Lady Hervey at Ickworth shortly afterwards. The house at Ickworth at that time was a modest country mansion, not the spectacular triumph it is today. Both Hervey and Bristol (his father) had ambitious plans to modernize the damp 'little' dwelling throughout their lifetimes but, either because of lack of finances or time, that never came to pass. Instead, the task of modernization eventually fell to Hervey's son, Frederick, in 1795. Despite the modest nature of the old house, however, the crowning glory of Ickworth was its place in nature, its rolling parklands and its shady, mature trees. Even so, although Hervey agreed to follow Fox to Suffolk, he would only consent to staying there a few days.

Hervey's indifference towards his wife had become more apparent. It is true that he continued to write to her in his formulaic epistolary manner during this time. It is also true that he saw to his conjugal duties whenever he was forced back to Ickworth, as the Hervey offspring continued to grow in number during this time. But true intimacy was absent, as we can see in her letters to Fox. Hervey wrote to Fox from Kensington Palace on 31 August 1732 following a stay at his family seat, revealing his discomfort. 'I thought of you often at Ickworth,' he revealed, 'talked of you often, and wished for you oftener.' Hervey lamented that without Fox the Suffolk house now seemed unfamiliar. 'The place seemed disagreeably altered,' he wrote, 'as it would do with all its oaks cut down.'[6]

In Fox's absence, Hervey articulated the distinction between a *house* and a *home*. He tells us that a man may have '*a home to go to* . . . (for everybody that has a home, has not a home to go to, any more than everybody who has a home they *must* go to, have one they *would* go to)'.[7] Hervey *must*, whether he liked it or not, go home to his wife and his family at Ickworth, but in Fox and at 31 Great Burlington Street he had found the home he *would* go to.

Beyond the relative safety of his front door, however, Hervey's public reputation continued to attract unwanted attention. Following the publication of William Pulteney's *A Proper Reply* the previous year and the resulting duel, the catamite (so to speak) was out of the bag.[8] Once Pulteney's accusation of sodomy had been printed and so widely disseminated it could not be unwritten. Pulteney had succeeded in creating a public persona for Hervey: the effeminate sodomite. It was a persona another of Hervey's enemies was only too happy to exploit.

★

No. 31 Great Burlington Street

Of all the satirists in Georgian England the sharpest, and therefore the most dangerous, was Alexander Pope. A contemplative Londoner with a chip on his shoulder, Pope gave the distinct impression of a wistful half-moon, aloof but knowing. A Catholic at a time when it was still inconvenient for an Englishman to be one, Pope was born in 1688, during the political turmoil of the so-called 'Glorious Revolution'. To his great frustration, he had known the limiting impact of the Test Acts throughout his early years. These were a series of laws that dictated one's eligibility for public office and other social and financial privileges dependent on one's adherence to the established Protestant Church. These Acts had curtailed Pope's access to formal education. As a result his schooling had been conducted covertly by family members and through illegal Catholic schools in the capital. Despite these obstacles, a dogged pursuit of knowledge and an uncanny natural ability led Pope to master the classics by the time he was a teenager.

Pope had experienced multiple childhood mishaps and illness too. He recounted having once been trampled on by a cow and had, at the age of twelve, contracted Pott disease (tuberculosis of the spine). As a result, Pope only ever reached four feet six inches in height. He also struggled with debilitating headaches. All of this only served to compound his sense of 'otherness' by the time he came of age. So although by the 1730s Pope's satire and other literary works had earned him acclaim and recognition, his social and cultural exclusions had also fostered in him an unenviable ability to hate. This was to prove rather unfortunate for John, Lord Hervey.

Pope was no fan of Hervey's. In Pope's eyes, Hervey, or Sporus as he called him (a classical reference to Nero's castrated boy-husband), had many strikes against him. Hervey, for instance, had enjoyed all the trappings of privilege throughout his life, whereas Pope had had to hustle and work for any of the accolades he had gained. Hervey's beauty was often commented upon, especially when he was younger; Pope could not compete. Pope, like many men at court, had also been enamoured by the character and beauty of the then star maid of honour, Molly Lepell; Hervey had got the girl. Pope dreamt of intimate access to Lady Mary Wortley Montagu; Hervey had it. Pope had mainly (though not exclusively) aligned himself with the Tories; Hervey was a Whig. In addition to all this, Pope was vehemently against Sir Robert Walpole's 'Robinocracy'. This, despite his Tory links, had resulted in a keen (though temporary) friendship with none other than Hervey's committed enemy, William Pulteney. In their distrust and hatred of Hervey and his political prowess, both men were utterly aligned.

In January 1735, Pope published one of his most scathing satirical pieces. It was called *Epistle to Dr Arbuthnot* and was, ostensibly, a tribute to a dying friend. Despite its noble intent, however, Pope also took clear and deliberate aim at the character of Hervey, gleefully rehashing many of the outrageous effeminate tropes that his friend Pulteney had first established in his *A Proper Reply*. In no uncertain terms Pope threw literary fists, and his pummelling reminded Hervey, and the whole of London, that despite the privacy he and Ste Fox had cultivated together on Great Burlington Street their relationship was no secret at all.

'Let *Paris* tremble,' Pope declared as he launched his attack in the first edition of his poem; 'Paris' is Hervey, and Pope alludes to his 'frenchified' effeminacy in the opening description. Pope proceeded to mock Hervey for having duelled with Pulteney following the publication of, and insinuations contained in, *A Proper Reply*. Hervey's actions were a suspicious overreaction, as Pope saw it. The Hervey doth protest too much!

Pope continued to antagonize him; Hervey was 'a Bug with gilded wings' and a 'painted Child of Dirt that stinks and stings'.

Pope's Hervey possessed all the ornamentation of the pampered, effeminate elite: the powdered face, the gossipy wit, but underneath it all was little substance. He lacked the grit Pope had cultivated through his many tribulations.

Despite his dismissiveness, however, Pope acknowledged that Hervey occupied a significant position of power in Georgian political life. As long as Hervey continued to use his 'feminine wiles' to persuade the queen, and by association the king, in state matters, Pope believed the kingdom was corrupt. Hervey was outraged by these accusations. Something would have to be done.

Since demanding a sword fight had been in hindsight, too acute a reaction, Hervey shied away from conflict this time. Still, he felt he had to manage these rumours once and for all. If he and Fox had secretly co-opted elements of heteroregulated marriage to cement the early stages of their union (the 'honeymoon', the shared home, etc.), Hervey would now manipulate the institution to his own ends once more. If he was successful, he might finally distract his enemies from his intimacies with Fox and silence them once and for all. It was settled, then: his companion, Ste Fox, must take a wife.

For some years, Henry Fox, Ste's brother, had been Mrs Susannah Strangways-Horner's *inamorato*. Susannah had married the Tory politician Thomas Horner on 17 November 1713. The match had been relatively functional in practical terms, but once Susannah and Henry Fox met and fell in love the Strangways-Horners spent more and more time apart. During these separations Thomas Strangways-Horner stayed at his country seat, Mells Manor in Somerset. However, Mrs Strangways-Horner and her daughter, Elizabeth, lived with Henry in France. It was Elizabeth's marital future, however, that would necessitate a more permanent return to England.

On their return, Henry introduced Mrs Strangways-Horner to Lord Hervey so that he might help in advancing Elizabeth's cause and reputation before she entered the marriage market. Hervey facilitated an audience with his friend, Queen Caroline, as a starting point, but his marital machinations had only just begun. Despite her 'terror and awe of [Hervey's] superior understanding', as Mrs Strangways-Horner put it, she found him 'extremely good-natured and well-bred'.[9] She liked him 'exceedingly', and so she turned to Hervey for advice relating to the families that might provide a suitable husband for her daughter when the time came. Which eligible bachelors made that shortlist we do not know, but by January 1736 the trio (Hervey, Henry and Susannah) had begun to consider Henry's brother and Hervey's companion, Ste, as a serious contender. Hervey recognized that a marriage 'settlement' would establish Ste, who was now thirty-two, in the next stage of his adult life. It would also bring social, financial, dynastic and patronage advantages not available to a committed bachelor.[10] Little importance was placed on the emotional elements of the match, particularly what the thirteen-year-old Miss Horner might have thought about their plans for her future. Sadly for little Elizabeth, she was a mere chess piece in this strategic manoeuvring. Whilst in the eighteenth century it was not unheard of for children to marry (in England one could legally marry from the age of twelve), to marry at thirteen would still have raised eyebrows and been seen as distinctly old-fashioned.[11] But by matching Fox with a child, Hervey anticipated that their own same-sex union would continue; that it would grant Ste access to the patriarchal privileges that heteroregulated marriage provided and would safeguard them both against further accusations of sodomy.

For her part, Mrs Strangways-Horner then returned to her disgruntled husband in order to secure his support for her daughter to wed Ste Fox. She may not have loved the man, but for their daughter's marriage to be conducted in the most legitimate circumstances the approval of the child's father was key. Thomas was none too keen, however. It was not so much his pride that set him against the idea, rather his daughter's age that was prohibitive, as far as he was concerned. More inconvenient still, however, was his proposed son-in-law's political leanings: Ste Fox was a Whig and moved peripherally in Walpole's circle. Thomas Strangways-Horner was a Tory. The political imbalance between the families was clear. No, as far as Elizabeth's father was concerned, Ste Fox would not do at all. He wished her to marry into a good Tory family and furnished his wife with instructions to this effect. Mrs Strangways-Horner, however, had never been bound by the expectations of her husband. Ste Fox had been chosen for her daughter and it was Ste Fox she would marry.

On 15 March 1736, a small, secretive group convened at 31 Great Burlington Street in the library on the first floor. A clergyman, the Reverend Villeman, surveyed those gathered. Directly in front of him was Elizabeth, not yet five foot tall, and to her right, Ste Fox. This union was overseen by God, Villeman stated, for the 'mutual society, help, and comfort, that the one ought to have of the other, both in prosperity and adversity'.[12] The only other people in attendance were Mrs Strangways-Horner (the bride's mother), Mrs Charlotte Digby (the groom's sister) and John, Lord Hervey. The bride's father remained blissfully unaware of what was under way. And then it was done: thirteen-year-old Elizabeth Horner became Mrs Elizabeth Fox.

The service was repeated again a week later so that others might slowly be co-opted into the secret. The second service took place in the same room at No. 31 and was, once again, overseen by the Reverend Villeman. This time the female witnesses were replaced by Fox's male friends Thomas Winnington, Charles Hamilton and Lord Falkland. Hervey was in attendance once more, the master of ceremonies. Following these clandestine manoeuvres, the mismatched newly-weds were publicly declared the following week, when they were presented together at court. One can only imagine the depth of Thomas Strangways-Horner's humiliation when the news finally broke.

Hervey and Fox now hoped that they could more discreetly return to the private world they had created together on Great Burlington Street. Hervey was very aware that it was social custom, given Mrs Fox's age, that a prolonged period of celibacy would follow their marriage to allow the new bride to mature. Mrs Fox would also be expected to live in a separate household from her adult husband, overseen by her mother. The Fox–Horner union was, then, a closeting of sorts, with Hervey and Fox engaging in the 'traffic [of] women ... as exchangeable, perhaps symbolic, property for the primary purpose of cementing the bonds of men with men'.[13] In this way, despite their queerness, Hervey and Fox were still elite Englishmen. They could tap into the privileges of patriarchy when it suited them. By so doing, and with Mrs Fox out of sight, they had, they hoped, bought themselves some extra time. And so on they went, together.

Their love remained strong. On 15 October 1737, for example, over a year after the Foxes' marriage, Hervey wrote to Ste:

> I have loved you ever since I knew you, which is now many years, so much better than most people are capable of loving any thing, that for your own sake at least you would not nor could not I am sure ... be insensible of it, and consequently not desire to preserve it ...[14]

In addition to these written archival traces, it is William Hogarth's conversation piece, *Lord Hervey and His Friends*, that speaks most vividly of the enduring nature of their relationship after Fox's wedding. In fact it surreptitiously declares it.

William Hogarth, likely the most reproduced artist of the eighteenth century, was born on 10 November 1697 to a schoolmaster father, Richard Hogarth, and his wife Ann Gibbons. For historians of early Georgian England Hogarth remains one of the foremost social, political and cultural commentators of the time. Nothing of the visual cues Hogarth has left us is incidental and certain tropes return again and again in his work; fruit and fruit baskets imply children or offspring, upturned furniture hints at disharmony, and so it is with *Lord Hervey and His Friends*.

Hervey and his coterie are flanked by two distinct figures of authority: the Church in the form of the clergyman on the left, and Athena in white marble to the right, the archetype of classical wisdom and warfare. If both were meant to signify moral and legal righteousness, then the direction of their respective gazes is

Figure 7. William Hogarth, 'The Hervey Conversation Piece', c.1738–40.

telling. They avert their glances from the men at the heart of the painting, neither condemning nor condoning them.

Those gathered, from left to right, include a dubiously identified clergyman, then Ste Fox, comfortably seated. Henry Fox inserts himself between his older brother and Lord Hervey, who wears his gold key of office as Vice-Chamberlain of the Royal Household. Next, seated in red, is Charles Spencer, 3rd Duke of Marlborough, Gentleman of the King's Bedchamber, and finally Thomas Winnington, the Whig politician. The clergyman in the left of the picture has been variously identified as the Reverend John Theophilus Desaguliers, the Reverend Conyers Middleton and the Reverend Villeman, the clergyman who performed the secret marriages between Fox and his child bride. Here, then, is our assembled cast.

Hogarth, though, is not done storytelling. In his works, as we have noted, a toppled chair denotes chaos and in this painting the one our Reverend is standing on has begun to falter. If you look closely you can see that it has been disturbed by Ste Fox's walking stick, an insinuation that these men might quietly topple the established institutions of Georgian society. (Incidentally, a walking stick often carries phallic associations in Georgian art.) Another important unit of Georgian society, the family, is alluded to here as well. In the centre foreground sits a pretty basket of fruit, placed on the ground between Hervey and Fox. One might find similar fruit baskets in traditional artworks that depict a couple at the centre of the image; they are used to indicate the fruitfulness of their union, their future progeny. But in this case Hogarth places the fruit basket in the dirt. No children shall result from this same-sex union. Hogarth questions the moral nature of this group of friends in that way too. And yet, the painting still tells us something of family, does it not? It is a commissioned (let's not forget) declaration of the Hervey–Fox family: the personal, social and political legacies of their union, a 'queer family romance'.[15] If the Fox–Horner marriage was a type of 'closeting', Hogarth's depiction here is a coded 'outing'.

Raised aloft between the companions is a drawing for a new, more impressive building than their Burlington Street town house. Here is a proposed country seat, the foundations of a queer legacy. Under Hogarth's skilful direction, Lord Hervey and Ste Fox alone confront the viewer's gaze, cruising for our attention, telling us secrets only silence can tell. In this way, the painting does not depict the *possibility* of queer domesticity, as others have suggested. That had already been achieved at 31 Great Burlington Street. This is the blueprint for its proposed *progression*. The satisfied smirks on Hervey's and Fox's faces seem to say, if you know, you know.

The Hervey–Fox household had insisted on its militant mundanity, an elite same-sex household built on love. Its foundations were solid, for despite the recurrent intrusions and threats from Hervey's enemies, and the introduction of a new child bride, it appeared that nothing could breach their companionship. Nothing besides the elemental thrill of a younger, arguably more handsome face.

The Italian poet and scholar Francesco Algarotti (1712–64) was a very handsome man. Everybody agreed. He impressed everyone he met. So when, aged twenty-four, he set out for London, none other than Voltaire had handed him a letter of introduction en route, addressed to his friend (the now forty-year-old) John, Lord Hervey. Voltaire was certain that Hervey would respond to the young man's considerable charms. You see, I think, where this is going.

Hervey was, as Voltaire had predicted, smitten with the Venetian and he was not alone. He and his friend Lady Mary Wortley

Montagu (now forty-seven) repeatedly fell over one another in their attempts to impress the young man. When they were not with him they sent him fawning love letters. When they were in his presence they clung to his arm. Hervey, when not attending to his royal duties, abandoned Ste Fox and now devoted his time to Francesco instead. Even when he was in Fox's company at Redlynch, Hervey wrote to his new love interest offering, if it were needed, 'fresh proof of [his] perpetual affection'. As for Lady Mary, so besotted by young Algarotti was she that she threatened to kill herself in his absence. 'I haven't the vanity to dare hope I please you,' she lamented, 'I have no purpose except to satisfy myself by telling you that I love you.'[16]

Their competing affections made the once-close friends squabble and snipe like a pair of middle-aged fishwives. Lord Hervey bragged when he received a letter from Algarotti, who had travelled to France, when Lady Mary did not. She begged Hervey to meet her to give her news of her love. Hervey cruelly ignored her, prompting her to write, 'what a stroke of Mercy a stroke of Lightening [sic] would be at this moment!' Hervey even wrote to Algarotti with news of Lady Mary's desperation, making fun of what he saw as her silly infatuation.[17] Truth be known, he might have benefited from some self-reflection in a similar regard. Algarotti, for his part, played both admirers admirably. Armed with his deep-hazel eyes, his high cheekbones, a coveted classical nose and his delicate lips, he denied them little but promised them nothing. He used them for their social clout, as any young man on the make might. After all, how others reacted to his beauty and charm was none of his business.

By May 1739, four years after his marriage to Elizabeth, Ste Fox was feeling the gap between Hervey and himself widen. He wrote to Hervey and chastised him for the increasingly humdrum nature of the letters he sent. Where was his once-effusive and reassuring affection, his barely concealed flirtations? It was enough to make Fox think that Hervey had lost his determined love for him altogether. Hervey replied, consoling Fox and reassuring him of his more than decade-long devotion. But Fox's intuition was correct. The light between them had finally started to flicker. More than that, Hervey's political brilliance was similarly beginning to dim.

In late 1737, Queen Caroline of Ansbach suffered an agonizing strangulated umbilical hernia. It quickly became clear that the queen would not survive. As she lay dying, the hernia perforated and 'spilled feculent succus entericus and fetid fluid onto the royal bed' and on to the floor beneath.[18] Surgeons rushed around the queen in her final weeks, making cuts and removing portions of her royal person in a futile attempt to save her life. Throughout her dismal deterioration Hervey occupied an important place by her bedside, an intimate proximity usually reserved for members of the royal family. Mercifully, the queen died on 20 November 1737 and Hervey wept sorrowfully with the king for her loss. Though it was not by any means his primary concern at the time, Hervey had just lost his greatest political ally and his own influence thereafter would be significantly tempered.

Meanwhile, despite his long tenure as prime minister, Hervey's other political ally, Sir Robert Walpole, had never succeeded in reuniting the divisions within the Whig Party. He had endured constant pressure and compromise in order to hold on to power for as long as he had. For example, his critics seized on a long-running trade dispute with Spain to goad the prime minister into declaring war in 1739. He was subsequently lambasted for his weak leadership during what was to be a prolonged conflict. There then followed an inevitably poor election result in 1741, which left Walpole weaker than ever before. Finally, on 11 February 1742, his position became untenable and, after over twenty years, Sir Robert Walpole resigned as Leader of the House of Commons, ending his tenure as de facto first Prime Minister of Great Britain. With the death of the queen and the fall of Walpole, Hervey's position in government was no longer secure. Therefore, five months after Walpole, Hervey resigned the Privy Seal on 12 July 1742 and retired from government. He spent the rest of that year attempting to convince his friends and former allies to curb the influence of the new Whig administration but he was no longer in favour. What he proposed mattered little.

It was at this point, and not immediately after his marriage, that Ste Fox, stepping more confidently into his own political potential, began to deliberately draw away from his former companion. For, in the void that had been created by Hervey's infatuation with Algarotti, Mr and Mrs Fox had discovered the potential joys of their own marriage. As she grew up, under the expert guidance of her mother, Mrs Fox had slowly but surely navigated her way to the very centre of her husband's emotional life, displacing the man who had once inspired so much joy, love, jealousy and excitement in her husband. Their union would eventually produce generations of one of the most formative dynasties in the British Empire. For now, though, Elizabeth's love and devotions inspired Fox to think and act for himself, in his own best interests. Those interests, it was clear, no longer included an intimacy with John, Lord Hervey.

Mrs Fox's early correspondence with her husband was naive and formulaic, understandable given her age. On 3 October 1736, for example, she lamented their separation, writing, 'My Dearest Ste ... to be kept separate from you Afflicts me more than you can possibly imagine.'[19] One can almost feel the pressure of Mrs Strangways-Horner's hand on her daughter's shoulder as she wrote. Mrs Fox's deliberate, studied handwriting, still maturing, acts as a tangible reminder of her youth.

But in an undated letter, thought to be from 1739 after Algarotti had appeared on the scene, things have noticeably progressed. The hand is less careful, less painstakingly precise and the sentiment more fluid:

> My Dearest Ste my only object of Delight & Joy . . . In me You may be always sure of the full profession of my Love . . . It will not be a vast while I hope before with Mama's consent we shall be every thing we wish to be to one another.

She finished her correspondence with a postscript, 'Let me know how your Chest do's.'[20] Mrs Fox proffers her epistolary care, providing a version of the comfort a Georgian wife was expected to furnish her husband with. This thoughtfulness, particularly in the absence of Hervey's usual attentions, was welcomed by Fox. Mrs Fox alludes to her other wifely duties too. She teases him with her wish that her mother might soon grant her consent to finally have sex with her husband. It is not she herself who keeps them apart, she assures him; her desire is palpable. We don't know precisely when Mrs Horner granted Fox conjugal access to her daughter, but by 1742, when she was twenty, Mrs Fox was pregnant with the couple's first child. In early January 1743 she and her household prepared for her lying-in. This period afforded elite mothers the opportunity to rest and recuperate in the run-up to, and for weeks after, the birth of their children.

Mrs Fox had chosen 31 Great Burlington Street as the site of her postnatal recovery. Its central location granted her access to physicians should they be required. In anticipation of her luxurious, frustrating confinement, Mrs Fox wrote confidently to her husband:

I went to our house in Burlington Street & saw the pictures Lord Hervey has got for us they look vastly well & I am quite happy to have my room furnished by the time I Lie-in because all the town will see it then[,] I enclose the list of them given me by Lord Hervey.[21]

The queer patterns of domestic life first nurtured by Hervey and Fox at this address had only been a temporary reprieve, now usurped by the more heteroregulatory sanctioned comings and goings of wives and childbirth. Hervey had overseen the decoration of the house more than a decade previously; now Mrs Fox set about reconfiguring the house to meet her own needs. Nonetheless, Hervey endured at 31 Great Burlington Street, through the pictures on the wall that Elizabeth had written about to her husband. They would oversee the birth of Lady Susannah Sarah Louisa Fox-Strangways (known as Susan) on 1 February 1743. There, in a once-queer domestic site, the Fox family would welcome the arrival of a new generation; a generation that Lord Hervey would never know.

In the spring of 1743, another episode of poor health took hold of Lord Hervey. He left London and returned to Ickworth, where Lady Hervey, his long-suffering wife, ever constant, was waiting for him. She doted on him, catering to his every whim. Though she would not have wished him sick, she relished his return. He was, once again, her own Jack. He had finally come home to stay. But he would not stay with her long.

John, Lord Hervey died on 5 August 1743. He was forty-six years old. In his final weeks, sensing the end, he redrafted his will, leaving most of his annuities to his children. His eldest son, George William Hervey, was appointed his sole heir, according to custom. Lady Hervey received no more than the very minimum promised to her in their initial marriage contract twenty-three years previously; an annual jointure of £300 (£60,000). Hervey could by now have afforded much more, so this would have raised eyebrows. In a further swipe, he also insinuated that his widow was not to be trusted following his death. She might, he implied, sell off certain of the Hervey properties that would impact his children's inheritance. And so he curtailed her ability to instruct on matters relating to property, as a widow usually would.

Given Lady Hervey's devotion and love across more than two decades, these callous curtailments baffled family members at the time and have confounded historians since. Some speculate that Hervey had lost his mind in the final months of his life, though there is nothing to suggest that this was the case. Frustratingly, we'll never know what was behind his desire to humiliate his widow from beyond the grave, but if I may, I'd like to offer an interpretation: the man was heartbroken and he lashed out. He had not wished to die in Lady Hervey's care at Ickworth, but to expire under the watchful eye of the love of his life, Ste Fox.

If Fox, now Lord Ilchester, grieved the loss of his former companion, the archives deny us a direct measure of his despair. In the absence of Ilchester's words, his actions help to shed light on his thoughts and feelings in the wake of Hervey's death. Lady Hervey, for example, acknowledged his tokens of affection during her time of grief: 'If Lord Ilchester has thought of me at all since he [sent me] excellent Pheasants, he must certainly think me a most unthankful wretch never to have said at least I thank you.'[22]

Later, in a letter dated 26 April 1755, more than ten years after Hervey's death, Lord Ilchester asked his wife, 'Have you seen Lord Bristol is he to be god father?'[23] In 1755 the earldom of Bristol was held by John's son George. Ilchester now sought his former companion's son and heir as godfather to his unborn daughter, Lady Frances Muriel Fox-Strangways. It was a touching tribute to the intensity of the time they shared together and solidified the long-term impact of the Hervey–Fox relationship within the traditional family unit. It formalized that relationship within the 'ties of affect as well as blood [which were] nurtured through the custom of godparenting . . . in order to cement close affiliation'.[24] The Hervey and Fox-Strangways families were therefore bonded once more, in formal terms, for the next generation.

Then there was the marble bust of John, Lord Hervey which Lord Ilchester had had commissioned in Italy in 1728 as the men travelled together at the very start of their relationship. Following Hervey's death, it remained at Ilchester's home in Redlynch. One imagines Hervey's likeness, proud and silent, rendered milky-white in the Somerset moonlight as the Fox-Strangways household turned in for the night. Who knows what confessions, lamentations, regrets and reminiscences Ilchester may have shared with his former companion's likeness in his remaining years.

Hervey's life with Fox is today best recounted in a printed collection of Hervey's correspondence. These were written to Fox by Hervey over more than a decade. They tell of love, lust, homemaking, jealousy, frustration and hurt. The full gamut of an intimate relationship. They were discovered in the Fox-Strangways archive, known as the Holland House Papers, where they remain. In 1950 these letters were edited and published by Giles Stephen Holland Fox-Strangways (1874–1959), the 6th Earl of Ilchester and the great-great-great-grandson of Ste Fox-Strangways. Ultimately, Hervey's words were preserved and presented for future generations by his companion's descendant. A delightfully queer heritage, I think. If Hogarth, with his depiction of the fruit basket lying in the dirt, had insinuated that the Hervey–Fox union would bear no fruit, these letters and the enduring legacy of their shared life have proved him wrong.

CHAPTER FIVE

Our Little Community

SOMETIMES SMALL DETAILS MATTER. The manner in which a door is closed might tell us whether the person exiting or entering through it was excited, exhausted or frustrated. That the door was closed is nothing singular, but the hand that closed it might change the world. So it is with the details that follow in this chapter. Reader, you will encounter cushions, candlesticks, bachelors, family names, friends and country houses. Nothing remarkable there, perhaps. But the order in which these incidental people, places and things deliberately (and sometimes secretly) arranged themselves centuries ago helps us to uncover an all too easily overlooked history that has helped to shape the present.

Despite his political woes and his inevitable fall from power in 1742, the first (and now former) prime minister, Sir Robert Walpole, had been a political animal through and through. His son, Horace (1717–97), on the other hand, was quite another sort of man. Horace was the youngest of six children and was not his father's heir. So although his future was technically less assured, he was also freer to make his own way in life. Though he served as

Whig MP for Callington in Cornwall from 1741 to 1754, the youngest Walpole's passions lay in collecting, literature, architecture and art. Today he is best known as the author of *The Castle of Otranto* (1764) and for his penchant for ostentatious Gothic architecture, an example of which can still be seen at his former home, Strawberry Hill House in Twickenham. The profound impact that Walpole's architectural and design taste had across Britain in the late eighteenth century helped to usher in a widespread devotion for all things Gothic in the nineteenth century. Gone were the restrained lines and simple symmetry of the Palladian style and in their place ornate, faux-medieval features began to appear including elaborate stained-glass windows and cathedralic pointed arches.

To assist him in these aesthetic pursuits Walpole assembled a set of influential fellow bachelors. These notable noblemen sat at the very heart of one another's social, emotional and creative lives. They played together, designed together, quarrelled together and regularly stayed in one another's houses. It was to other members of this group of tastemakers that each individual might turn when they were afraid, outraged, needed help with a housekeeper or if they had fallen in love.[1] In this way they were a community. And, as we shall see, their community was decidedly queer. Amongst their number were the likes of Thomas Gray (1716–71), a poet and scholar, and the diplomat Sir Horace Mann (1706–1786). George Montagu (1713–80; no relation to Lady Mary), the politician, moved in these circles too. Most important to Walpole was his esteemed friend John Chute (1701–76).

Chute was the youngest of no fewer than ten children: five boys and five girls. He was educated at Eton but, like Walpole, as a carefree youngest son he found himself at liberty to travel as he wished once his formal education was over. His European adventures went beyond the usual dictates of the Grand Tour, and Chute ended up spending many years in Italy as a young man.

Whilst there he developed a keen eye for art and architecture, sending many items of interest home to his family's country mansion, The Vyne in Hampshire. Fate, however, would eventually bring him back to England.

John's older brothers unexpectedly died one by one and his last surviving brother, Anthony, breathed his last in 1754. It was with Anthony's expiration that John now became an unlikely heir and, as master of The Vyne, was determined to modernize the old Tudor manor entrusted to his care. He allowed his imagination to wander as he planned his alterations, endlessly scribbling ideas on scraps of paper of how best to alter the house. In many cases, these scribbles soon transformed themselves into actual improvements. In 1770, for example, he designed a remarkable 'theatric' staircase, in the classical style, which directed his guests to the upper rooms. Walpole, given his own architectural talents, offered numerous suggestions as Chute scribbled and built, most of which Chute ignored. He was, nonetheless, grateful for Walpole's friendship and devotion. Despite their closeness, though, Walpole was not the primary focus of Chute's affections. That privilege was reserved for another man, Mr Francis Whithed (1719–51).

Whithed was Chute's distant cousin and the son of Alexander Thistlethwayte and his wife Mary Whithed. Upon learning that he had been named heir to a Whithed uncle's estate, Francis formally adopted his mother's family name in order to claim his inheritance. He was 'a fine young personage in a coat all over spangles'. He wore his brown hair pulled back and tied with a black silk ribbon. His eyes, a bluish-grey, were direct and knowing, whilst a playful smirk seemed to linger about his lips.[2]

Prior to 1747, Whithed had spent five years travelling across Europe with John Chute. During their time on the continent, Walpole had heard from their mutual friends that the two men had become inseparable. Chute himself, with uncharacteristic emotional candour, had even referred to Whithed as 'my other half'.[3] When Walpole had first met Whithed in Italy he thought him nice, if a little dim. Now that he was back in England and somewhat matured, Walpole found him 'infinitely improved'. A fitting companion for his closest friend.[4] Soon, though, the men in Chute and Whithed's orbit would come to understand their union as something more than friendship.

On 13 May 1747, Thomas Gray informed Horace Walpole of his intention to leave his mother's house and 'call at your Door, & that of the Chuteheds, if possible'.[5] On 26 June Walpole wrote to Horace Mann in Italy, gossiping about Lord Middlesex's loss of a lordship, stating, 'I intend to laugh over this *disgrazia* with the Chuteheds, when they return triumphant from Hampshire, where Whitehed [*sic*] has no enemy,' and in October of that same

Figure 8. Rosalba Carriera, 'Francis Whithed', 1741.

Figure 9. Johann Heinrich Müntz, 'John Chute', 1756.

year he wrote to Mann again, 'I am glad the Chuteheds are as idle as I am'.[6] Similarly, on 18 May 1748 George Montagu wrote to Horace Walpole from Chute's London house, 'Here I am with the poor Chutehed who has put on a shoe today for the first time. He sits at the receipt of custom [awaits visitors], and one passes most of the day here.'[7] These seemingly inconsequential passages from nearly 300 years ago can tell us a little about the visiting and relaxing habits of Chute's circle of friends. That in itself is useful. But there is another, altogether more precious detail from the past on display here too.

Just as Ste Fox and Elizabeth Horner-Strangways eventually became the Fox-Strangways after they married, so John Chute and Francis Whithed had become 'the Chuteheds' following their return from the continent. Walpole, Gray, Montagu and Mann deployed naming conventions normally seen in marriages between men and women to identify the Chuteheds as a single spousal unit. This takes on even more significance when we consider that the Chuteheds' union had also been legally reinforced when Chute adopted Whithed, making him his legal heir and beneficiary.

The idea of adult adoption as a tool with which homosexual men could legally cement their relationships came to light in America in the 1970s and 1980s. In 1982, for example, the Civil Rights pioneer Bayard Rustin adopted his younger partner, Walter Naegle. This move ensured that Naegle became Rustin's next of kin by default, benefiting from many of the allowances denied to same-sex couples, such as full visiting rights when Rustin was hospitalized towards the end of his life. Naegle was also the executor of Rustin's will. In the case of the Chuteheds, we find similar tactics being used two centuries earlier. This suggests that despite the lack of legal acknowledgement of same-sex spousal units in the eighteenth century, social customs might still reflect the importance of queer relationships. Tragically, however, the Chuteheds' plot to secure Francis Whithed as John Chute's beneficiary would never materialize.

On 1 April 1751 Horace Walpole imparted to Horace Mann some tragic news. 'How shall I begin a letter that will . . . give you as much pain as I feel myself?' He wrote, 'poor Mr. Whithed is dead!' Whithed had 'had a bad cough for two months', Walpole went on, but that did not stop his brother, a clergyman, dragging him 'out every morning to hunt, as eagerly as if it had been to hunt heretics. One day,' Walpole continued, Whithed and his brother 'overturned in a water,' following which 'the parson made [Francis] ride forty miles.' Whithed, who was only thirty-one at the time, thereafter 'arrived at the Vine [sic], Chute's home, half dead, and soon grew delirious'. Chute rushed to his companion's side and, upon seeing how ill he had become, 'sent back for two ... physicians' to attend Francis with haste. They attended him, but it was 'in vain; [Francis] expired on Friday night!' For Chute this loss was life-altering. Walpole wrote at the time that 'Mr. Chute is ... half distracted, and scarce to be known again'.[8]

Chute's sense of loss is palpable, and Walpole tells us that he was forever altered by Francis' death, no less than Prince Albert's death would alter the course of Queen Victoria's life in the following century. Despite the obvious depths of the Chutehed bond, many historians have ignored the clear importance of their blended name, presenting it as nothing more than camp frivolity. However, I would argue that the understanding and articulation of 'the Chuteheds' as one family, one household, amongst their wider social group is monumentally important, especially if we consider that these 'marital' manoeuvrings were part of an important queer tradition.

Take, for instance, those who had written about and condemned molly house culture in the opening decades of the eighteenth century. They took specific umbrage at the idea of molly 'marriages'. In 1709 the writer Ned Ward relayed details of how the mollies would 'Tattle about their Husbands', whom they had 'married' in secret ceremonies at the molly house.[9] Similarly, in Gabriel Lawrence's 1726 trial, the spy Samuel Stephens testified that the mollies went into private rooms together to 'marry' as we saw above.[10] We cannot be clear what these queer 'marriage' ceremonies involved exactly, but accounts confirm that the vernacular of 'marriage' was definitely used by and about queer men at this time. In the same way, English Professor Sharon Marcus has demonstrated the normalcy of female same-sex households in Victorian England, which functioned in plain sight because of the inherent associations between women's histories and the home.

Marcus showed how women who lived together might set about 'making marriage a plastic institution'.[11] The Chuteheds similarly moulded the institution to their own ends. However, that is not to say that marriage-like unions were the only model of intimacy within which gender non-conforming men and women in the past found emotional security. For many, their friendship groups dictated the tempo of their lives instead.

Many historians have described Georgian bachelorhood as a period of necessary tension and growth, a limbo, of sorts, between the spoils of childhood and the obligations of marriage.[12] It was a life stage to be transitioned out of with as little damage to one's reputation as possible.[13] Society's aversion to unmarried life was legislatively enforced, too. Parliamentary Acts such as the Marriage Duty Act (1695) levied unmarried men with a form of annual taxation if they remained unwed beyond the age of twenty-five, for instance. Though poor bachelors in receipt of alms were exempt, bachelors like Chute and his friends – those from the gentry and nobility – paid extra. An eighteenth-century bachelor, it was felt, had shirked his obligations as a potential husband and father in favour of a life given over to self-indulgence. What followed, contemporaries warned, was misery and ignominy.[14]

However, we have overlooked a significant element of this particular history, I think: that of the contented bachelor. More specific still, the contented bachelor who shared the significant intimate relationships of his life with other men. For within these often-queer coteries men forged lasting, loving and joyful bonds with one another in their determined avoidance of taking a wife. Once assembled, these gender non-conforming men gradually developed vital queer communities within which they sought comfort and constancy.

As far back as 1700 the writer William Seymar argued that 'a Celibate or Single life is the more perfect of the two [married or unmarried]'.[15] In his advocacy of an unmarried life Seymar insisted on a 'celibate' bachelor, thereby negating the sexual threat unmarried men posed to respectable Georgian women, and English society more generally, at this time. However, in the eighteenth century 'celibate' meant something ever so slightly different from what it does today. Dr Johnson defined it as 'Single Life. Where polygamy is forbidden, the males oblige themselves to [remain] *celibate*, and then multiplication is hindered.'[16] To be celibate, then, meant to be unmarried and to avoid procreation. Seymar's understanding of celibacy applied, therefore, only to sexual relationships between men and women, and indicated nothing regarding intimate relationships between men. The idea of the contented bachelor was not, however, solely confined to theoretical treatises on the matter. Whilst we have no indication that Chute, Walpole and their friends had read Seymar's work, we do know that they were well acquainted with another man who also wrote about the opportunities bachelorhood could offer 'literary' men, as he called them.

Dr Antonio Cocchi (1695–1758), whom we first met in Chapter Three, was a friend of John Chute's. It was through Horace Mann that Horace Walpole, John Chute, Francis Whithed, Thomas Gray and George Montagu came to be acquainted with Cocchi, and they welcomed him into their fold wholeheartedly. He was, after all, one of them. Cocchi was an Italian physician, writer and noted vegetarian. Having been Professor of Physic at the University of Pisa, Cocchi practised as a physician in Florence, becoming eminent amongst his peers. In 1736 he was admitted as a Fellow of the Royal Society and enjoyed a three-year stint in England before returning to practise once more in Italy. Incidentally, Cocchi was not only friends with Chute, but he had also attended to John, Lord Hervey when he travelled through Europe with Ste Fox. The men had remained friendly thereafter. As such, Cocchi's links to eminent queer Georgians was significant.

Cocchi was particularly close to Horace Mann, who acted as the British diplomatic representative to the Grand Dukes of Tuscany, eventually enjoying the rather florid appellation of Envoy Extraordinary and Plenipotentiary to the Grand Dukes' Court. Cocchi was a frequent presence amidst the many British and Italian bachelors that Mann entertained at his residence, Palazzo Manetti. On 29 November 1754, for example, Mr John Boyle, a visitor to the palazzo, wrote to his friend Mr Duncombe regarding the Cocchi–Mann intimacies in Italy. 'Mr Mann is fortunate in the friendship, skill, and care of his physician, Dr Cocchi,' Boyle observed, before going on to describe the idyllic, studious companionship between

Figure 10. Thomas Patch, 'British Gentlemen at Sir Horace Mann's Home in Florence', 1763–5.

the pair. He mused: 'could I live with these two gentlemen only, and converse with few or no others, I should scarce desire to return to England for many years'.[17] Despite Boyle's appreciation for the relationship between Cocchi and Mann, others back in England were far less willing to embrace this 'unconventional' lifestyle because, they suggested, of its sodomitical potential.

Cocchi's foundational *Del Matrimonio* was first published in 1762 in Italy, with an English translation, published in London, following in 1769. The treatise, which ran to several reprints, outlined the ways in which a man might have experienced a happy unmarried life, as Cocchi had.[18] Cocchi warned committed bachelors that 'they might bethink themselves seriously before they resolve on quitting the calm, serene, and placid shore of celibacy, to adventure on the rough, inconstant, and tempestuous ocean of matrimony'.[19] Like Seymar before him, Cocchi employs the framework of celibacy within which to advance the bachelor cause.[20] Cocchi assured those who recognized themselves in his work that they had no need of a conventional marriage with a woman in order to secure their well-being at home. Instead, his *Del Matrimonio* presented a manual for a new era in which men might more openly explore the contentment and complexities of their emotional lives with one another.[21]

However, the first translation of Cocchi's work for an English audience carried a telling caveat. There was something about Cocchi's proposal that made the English uneasy. 'Our readers, male and female, are once more desired to remember,' warned Paul Heffernan, Cocchi's translator, 'that the original author of this work was an Italian, and that it in no shape regards British husbands, wives, friends, or acquaintances.'[22] Heffernan reminded his readers that Italian bachelorhood was synonymous with Catholic bachelorhood which, in turn, was closely aligned with ideas of sodomitical intent in the minds of English Protestants. Heffernan and his publishers wanted to clarify that proper English gentlemen would never indulge in the types of intimacies that Cocchi wrote about. Heaven forfend! But Cocchi was no stranger to England or Englishmen. In truth, Cocchi's descriptions were just as reflective of the ways in which Chute and his friends lived as they were of any Italian bachelor. Indeed, his English friends, including Mann, Chute and Walpole, had most likely helped inform his theories. And just as John, Lord Hervey and Ste Fox had done a generation before, more and more of these aristocratic Englishmen decided that one of the safest and most fulfilling arenas in which to explore their same-sex contentment was in the privacy of their own homes.

John Chute's former home, The Vyne, sits comfortably in the Hampshire countryside. Its medieval origin means it lies lower in the landscape than a typical Georgian country house. Its homely red brick is nestled between lush trees which are, in turn, reflected in the grey surface of a pretty man-made lake. The house has been home to the Chute family ever since Chaloner Chute, John Chute's great-grandfather and Speaker of the House of Commons, purchased the estate in 1653. Speaker Chute had undertaken restorative building work to the house in his lifetime, for example adding a classical portico to the north face, but it was John who turned it into a home. It was here, particularly in the wake of Francis Whithed's death in 1751, that he would gather his closest friends about him for comfort.

Once he inherited The Vyne in 1754, the extent to which Chute set about domesticating it was remarkable. A rolling bill from Frederick Kandler, a goldsmith on Jermyn Street, London, to John Chute for 'plate, engravings and repairs' shows that Chute assigned £774:12:4 (£142,000) in 1756 alone for items which included elaborately decorated candlesticks, silver plates and dishes, sauce boats and a large chest for storage.[23] In 1757 Kandler added 'A new handle to a Coffee pot . . . taking Bruises out of 2 [others] . . . & mending a Tea spoon . . . D[itt]o [taking bruises] out of a Milkpot & cover & [adding] a new handle'.[24] From this seemingly humdrum inventory a lively picture of everyday life in the eighteenth century springs to mind; candlesticks placed on a mahogany dining table holding sets of flickering, dripping beeswax candles which illuminate fond faces. An oval terrine (tureen) synonymous with aristocratic culinary finesse was passed between guests, diners helping themselves *à la française*. Hands reaching across hands. Then came the tea set, still a luxurious commodity. The shining silver of Chute's repaired set catches the candlelight as the hot brew, flavoured by large, loose leaves of Bing tea, pours forth into genteel, anticipatory cups. The taste, as it was sipped, tickled the tongue. It was 'crisp in the Mouth, and the Smell of it very pleasant'. This particular tea was 'highly esteemed . . . in *China*', no less.[25] This, then, is not just a list of items; it is a catalogue of consumption, a history of long evenings spent with friends.

Most rooms at The Vyne were made significantly more homely during John Chute's tenure too. For example, when he inherited the property in 1754, the Gallery was a rather functional space and included 'A stove grate, a dust work fender, a fine Shovel . . . & poker . . . [mahogany] stools Covered with black Leather & brass nail[s], a [mahogany] table, 11 plaster heads & [the plaster] Head of a gentleman'.[26] However, by 1776 the room was a far more comfortable space. Chute had added decorative items to the room, including new glass to the windows and

> 2 Marble Tables on a carved & Gilt frame, 6 Maho[gany]-chairs & 2 Settees silk stuffed – backs and seats worked with silver, A Curious Ebony cabinet on a frame, Maho[gany] . . .

sofa [with] 3 cushions [and] 2 Bolsters – crimson check covers, 2 Blue & white-China Jars, [and] A curious inlaid writing Table.[27]

Chute's coterie of unmarried men helped shape the nature of his domestic comfort too. There was collaboration in interior decoration, for instance, as Thomas Gray demonstrated in a letter to Walpole. 'If you continue your intention of coming hither [to The Vyne],' Gray writes in September 1756, 'Mr Chute desires you would give yourself the trouble of looking among your prints (of Hollar or others) for an inside view of St George's Chapel at Windsor and be so good to bring it with you.'[28] Chute wished to incorporate a similar design at his own home. Privately this group of decorating bachelors called themselves 'the Strawberry Committee', after Walpole's Strawberry Hill. The committee, its members felt, ought to be suitably reflected in one another's homes as a result of their collaboration and so Chute renamed his Print Room the 'Strawberry Parlour' in acknowledgement of their efforts. The parlour was subsequently decorated with pictures of select members of the Strawberry Committee and trinkets reflecting their shared aesthetic bent.

It wasn't all happy, clappy, domestic creativity at The Vyne, however. There were times when the collaboration between the men caused tensions. For example, in 1755 Walpole put forward suggestions for the Oak Gallery and other rooms at Chute's home at a cost of £5,000 (£755,000). Chute, whose pockets were not as deep as his friend's, undertook his own (cheaper) alterations. Again, in 1757 Chute rejected a drawing Walpole submitted for a Gothic monument to John's ancestor, Speaker Chute. This second rejection prompted Walpole to lift his pen and vent to their mutual friend, Montagu, 'I am pretty sure I have [nothing worth seeing] to come at the Vyne, where I have done advising, as I see

Mr Chute will never execute anything.'[29] However, by the end of 1758 even Walpole was 'greatly pleased with the alterations' Chute had undertaken.[30]

Once gathered together inside its old walls, The Vyne offered Chute and his friends the opportunity to participate in important bonding rituals. The men held faux-religious ceremonies in the chapel there, for example, which included elaborate picnics, incense-burning and donning fancy dress. This helped contribute to what Walpole described as 'a most Catholic enjoyment of the chapel'. Walpole suggests that the men at The Vyne likely wore similar garb to the friar or monk costumes worn by the aristocratic men who attended other 'secretive' gatherings, such as the Hellfire Club. Members of the Hellfire Club met in not-so-secret locations throughout the eighteenth century so that they might indulge in excessive drinking, gambling and various sex acts. Yet Walpole's use of the word 'Catholic' as a descriptor for the bachelor meetings at The Vyne is all the more curious given the easy association between Catholicism and sodomy held by many English Protestants, as we have already noted.[31] What the exact 'Catholic enjoyments' at The Vyne entailed is hard to say, but lest there be any confusion, this was categorically *not* an opportunity to undertake devoted prayer. It was instead, I suggest, an elaborate form of queer bonding, solidifying a collective identity based on their shared gender non-conformity, deepening their sense of community. But whilst Chute, Walpole and the others might have been free to explore their identities behind closed doors, once they returned to the public sphere some of the very attributes that they celebrated collectively in private meant that the fear of violence was never far away. When these fears inevitably materialized, it was to other members of their community that they turned for understanding.

A letter from Thomas Gray to John Chute dated 7 September

1741 demonstrates his anxieties about the threat from those outside their clique. 'The Boys laugh at the depth of my Ruffles, the immensity of my Bag, & the length of my Sword,' he complained. 'If my pockets had anything in them, I should be afraid of everybody I met.' Intriguingly, Gray mentions that it was 'Boys' specifically that singled him out. 'Look in their face, they knock you down; speak to them, they bite off your Nose,' he went on. Then, he poignantly adds, 'I am no longer ashamed in public, but extremely afraid.'[32] What had Gray been ashamed of? And why was he only ashamed of it 'in public'?[33] Walpole wrote to Chute of similar fears on 4 August 1753: 'I felt strangely tempted to stay at Oxford and survey it at my leisure; but, as I was alone, I had not courage.'[34] The following year he wrote to their friend Richard Bentley on 9 July 1754 that he had not yet seen the tomb he had erected to his mother's memory in Westminster Abbey as 'none of my acquaintance were in town, and I literally had not courage to venture alone among the Westminster boys at the Abbey'.[35] Yet again, the lingering threat from a brute of unnamed 'boys' looms large. These 'boys', it appears, were determined to assert their ideas of what it was that constituted (or did not constitute) a 'real' man. Should one fall short in their view, as it appears Walpole and Gray had done, there would be consequences.

These fears and anxieties are communicated to Chute and Bentley in a manner that implies their innate understanding of this threat. Some of us understand them too, I think? When I first read these passages, it automatically called to mind being spat at, pushed, shoved and tripped by some of the other boys as I negotiated the corridors of my secondary school in the late 1990s. I was reminded too of having a small knife placed to my throat in the second (or was it third?)-year common area by another boy because (I think) all my friends were girls. Another memory returns of a once-forgotten punch to the chest that I received from a boy, no more than eighteen, as he passed in a larger group of lads whilst I was walking along Regent's Canal in Mile End in the early 2010s. I'd drawn his attention because I was holding my now-husband's hand. Now, more than a decade later, I still can't comfortably reach for his hand in public as a result. Once bitten and all that.

I share these personal experiences only because, I hope, they help to highlight something more immediate than mere archival analysis. Analysis is one thing; understanding is another. And when I first read these laments, it was an unspoken understanding that drew me in. The knowing that I too had experienced similar fears to the ones they expressed in the eighteenth century. As a historian I can analyse the contents of their letters, certainly, but as a queer man I understand their experience, or a version of their experience at the very least. But those shared, intergenerational queer wounds are not the focus here. They simply function to highlight an altogether more important history: that of persistence, resistance and insistence. Persistence in the face of violent opposition to the depth of one's ruffles, the radical resistance of a marginalized community even in the face of systematic heteroregulation, and the determined insistence that one should be able to hold one's partner's hand in public without being punched in the chest for doing so.

So often when we examine the history of same-sex desire, we are confronted with two concepts which go hand in hand: first, that some people in the past conducted the most important intimacies of their lives with other people of the same sex and, second, that they were gravely worried and ultimately punished for doing so. There is truth in both assertions, but that is only part of the story. Read between the lines and an altogether more radical history emerges, a hidden past wherein the pursuit of joy emerges as a tangible facet of our queer inheritance. Men like Chute, Whithed, Mann, Walpole, Gray, Montagu and others knew this and sought their joys together, both in marriage-like unions and as part of a wider proto-queer community. They were not alone. Nor were they miserable, despite their fears. Their homes became safe spaces in which they could spend time, explore and contest the boundaries of their gender non-conforming identities.

It would be naive of us to imagine that the spaces Chute, Walpole and the others cultivated were not protected by their race and their social status. These country houses were a far cry from the more brutal experiences of the working men at Mother Clap's molly house, for instance. But this queer community is no less noteworthy for that. The care, devilment, campery, love, secrecy, fun, comradery, fear, passion, sex, bitching, infighting and empowerment that they fostered was powerfully felt within its fold. We feel it too, when we read their letters or encounter it in the very fabric of their homes. In that way, if you were to visit The Vyne, Chute's home, today, your visit ought to be much more than a Sunday afternoon enjoying fruit scones (jam before cream incidentally). It is instead an invitation to step across a previously unexplored queer threshold, to visit and participate in the vitality of the eighteenth-century queer country house, to reclaim its hidden past, and the queer community it served, for ourselves.

CHAPTER SIX

The Speculation

THE SUN HAD NOT yet risen on 21 October 1777, but the sense of anticipation ran high. The Chevalier d'Éon, the troublesome captain of the French dragoons, spy and diplomat, awaited his fate in a sixteenth-century Parisian town house located on the rue d'Anjou. Rue d'Anjou was one of the older bustling tributaries that webbed about the newly built Palais de L'Élysée. The Chevalier's lodgings sat, tightly tucked, between two other wooden-framed buildings. This house had once belonged to Diane de Poitiers (1500–66), the powerful mistress of King Henri II (1519–59). Over time, the structure had withstood the fall of the royal House of Valois-Angoulême and witnessed the glorious rise of the House of Bourbon, whose illustrious son Louis XVI now occupied the French throne.

From the outside the house induced a feeling of jaunty disequilibrium, the happy burden of its age. It was spread across four floors, with the first and second *étages* boasting balconies. Atop the structure, a tented roof differentiated the house from the other hodgepodge schemes up and down the street. Beneath its rafters a small window overlooked the comings and goings below. The

Chevalier's rooms were, most likely, on the second floor. Though aged, they will have had a rustic charm that might have suited him quite well had the circumstances of his stay been different.

At seven that morning a curt knock came at the Chevalier's door. He attended to it. Before him stood the officious Mademoiselle Bertin, dressmaker to Queen Marie-Antoinette. She was accompanied by two female aides-de-camp sporting shallow-crown straw hats adorned with rose-red ribbons. Recently returned to France, the Chevalier had (in the main) been a great supporter of the king's late grandfather, Louis XV, and had come home to offer his fealty to the new king.[1] Quite bizarrely, however, before he would receive the Chevalier, Louis XVI had a very specific demand and, according to the Chevalier's memoir, Bertin had been assigned to ensure that demand was met: the Chevalier d'Éon must appear at court as a woman.

'My honourable Captain and wise Demoiselle d'Eon,' the dressmaker began, addressing the Chevalier using both male and female appellations, 'your fate is no longer a mystery . . . It is now only a matter of adorning your virtue with the decorum required by law.' Indicating her artillery of silks, Bertin went on, 'Here is the trousseau that the King commanded, that the Queen has designated for you, and that I made for you . . . If you leave the building in men's clothing, you will be arrested and taken to a convent. Please then, do voluntarily what will be done to you forcibly.' But d'Éon had no desire to assume female dress.

'Just leave me as I am,' he pleaded, 'I have lived for forty-eight years this way.'

Bertin would not yield.

'Today, by order of [the] King and the law,' she declared, 'the bad boy must become a good girl.'

Quickly realizing that his opposition to the formidable dressmaker was futile, 'a peace agreement between the warring parties of the nether regions' was negotiated. Thus the Chevalier reluctantly removed his male attire and succumbed to the torture of a 'steaming hot cleansing bath' which softened his rough, sun-damaged soldier's skin into something more ladylike. D'Éon's first *toilette* took four hours and ten minutes in all. His hair was coiffed and powdered, his *maquillage* meticulously applied, and his jewellery fashionably chosen. Bertin had expertly strategized each pluck and preen. D'Éon finally stood in front of a mirror and looked at his new, female self. In that moment, she felt nothing but despair. 'This is my torment,' she managed. 'Whether it be good or evil, I cannot change it.'[2]

The potential reasons for this royal decree have long since stumped journalists, historians and gossipmongers alike. Some at the time claimed that the Chevalier had, in fact, been born female and that Louis XVI wished her to readopt her womanhood before he would permit her attendance at Versailles. Others since have claimed that the king simply wished to formally acknowledge the Chevalier's inherent gender non-conformity by accepting her in France as the woman she longed to be. Following this line of thinking, modern commentators such as the BBC have felt confident enough to refer to d'Éon as 'the world's first transgender spy'.[3] In the midst of such modern sureties, when I first approached the research for this chapter I believed that I would encounter documentation that bolstered this version of the Chevalier's history. Much to my surprise, however, that is not at all what I uncovered.

Charles d'Éon de Beaumont was born into modest privilege at his ancestral home in Tonnerre, Burgundy on 5 October 1728. His father, Louis, was a man of the law, a local noble and a one-time mayor of Tonnerre. We do not know much about his mother, Françoise. Even her maiden name is disputed – de Chavanson or de Charenton, depending on your source. Charles was the couple's third child and followed their daughter, Marguerite-Françoise, and a boy, Théodore-André, who had died in infancy the previous year.

After some time with a doting wet-nurse, Charles was educated at Collège Mazarin, before studying law at the Collège des Quatre Nations, Paris. A precocious student, by the age of nineteen he was already making a name for himself as a gifted lawyer. So much so that by 1756 d'Éon had come to the attention of the Prince de Conti, a cousin of Louis XV. He subsequently brought the then twenty-eight-year-old Charles into the king's secret service, the infamous and elusive *Secret du Roi*.

Clandestinely recruited, members of the *Secret* worked alongside (and sometimes against) official French ministers and diplomats in France and overseas. They alone were privy to the king's true wishes and whims. Louis XV, for example, often issued simultaneous but contradictory orders to his diplomatic corps and his secret agents on the same day, 'his left hand countermanding the instructions of his right'.[4] This unexpected recruitment meant that Charles d'Éon de Beaumont found himself, if not quite at the very heart of French political life, certainly in one of the vital arteries that helped the muscle beat.

Having entered royal service, d'Éon was soon appointed secretary to the French ambassador in Russia. His secret task, however, was to establish a confidential line of communication between the French king and the Russian empress, Elizabeth, which he achieved. Whilst in Russia, d'Éon also carefully negotiated the diplomatic fallout of the ongoing Seven Years' War (1756–63), a global conflict which saw superpowers France, Britain and their respective allies clash over the borders of their foreign territories. D'Éon soon became frustrated with the slow pace of his diplomatic efforts, however, and, with no prospect of a peace in sight by 1760, left his diplomatic role to take up arms in the war instead.

The Speculation

In battle, as in diplomacy, d'Éon excelled. He was appointed captain of the dragoons and his mounted infantry fought bravely against the Prussians and Royal Scots in 1761. But war is an expensive business and, after seven years, public opinion in both France and Britain had turned against the conflict. D'Éon was thus sent to London as a member of the French negotiating team, led by the Duc de Nivernais, the ambassador there, to agree terms for a desperately necessary peace. Simply put, the French could no longer afford to be at war. And the British knew it. Once terms had been agreed and formally drafted, it was d'Éon who was chosen to hand-deliver the Treaty of Paris, as it became known, to Louis XV, a great honour indeed.

Though the sought-after peace had been achieved in London, in Paris the terms of the treaty were seen as an embarrassing defeat. The French had now lost the vast majority of their land in North America and had been annexed from their lucrative trading routes in India. Given their perceived loss, d'Éon was once again deployed on diplomatic business to London. Officially he would act as secretary to the Duc de Nivernais, but in truth his task was to be Louis's eyes and ears at the heart of British imperial power. The plan was that Louis, and the *Secret*, would use information gathered by d'Éon to co-ordinate a surprise invasion of Britain. This invasion, it was hoped, might recoup some of their lost honour. D'Éon was to 'conform' to Louis's will and, importantly, 'never mention anything of it to any living person, not even my [Louis's] ministers'.[5] In London, Nivernais was only too pleased to see d'Éon return to his side. 'I cannot sufficiently extol his zeal, vigilance, amiability of disposition, and activity,' he enthused upon his arrival.[6]

As a sign of his admiration, on 30 March 1762 Nivernais invested d'Éon with the insignia of the Royal and Military Order of St Louis. Henceforth d'Éon was to be addressed as the Chevalier d'Éon and was granted a windfall of 60,000 livres (£500,000) as befitted his new title. On 20 July 1762 *The Bath Chronicle and Weekly Gazette* recorded that 'The Chevalier d'Eon Minister Plenipotentiary from France, had a Private Audience of His Majesty to deliver his Credentials,' thus officially securing his role. On the surface of it, all was going well for the new Chevalier in London. His true intentions went undetected and he played his part to perfection.

Back in France, however, government ministers, unaware of Louis's intriguing, slowly began to consider d'Éon's political manoeuvrings rather suspicious. Even more so after Nivernais was recalled to France and d'Éon temporarily undertook ambassadorial duties in his absence. D'Éon, as the ministers saw it, was now operating well beyond his station. Further, d'Éon's profligate spending had peeved the cash-strapped government officials at home. But these tensions had only just begun.

Relations between d'Éon and the French government deteriorated even more significantly when the Chevalier received news that the Comte de Guerchy would be appointed as the new French ambassador in London. Upon Guerchy's arrival, d'Éon was expected to step back from his unofficial ambassadorial role and resume his secretarial duties once more. D'Éon was none too pleased. He considered Guerchy unqualified for the position and predicted that his own undercover duties would be compromised by the arrival of the new ambassador. D'Éon sent hot-headed letter after hot-headed letter to France pleading his case which in turn only served to anger Louis XV's ministers all the more. How dare d'Éon question their authority?

To settle this impasse between his ministers and his spy, the king was required to act fast; he must either recall d'Éon or back him in his bid for the ambassadorship. D'Éon was confident of the king's support, he was a member of the *Secret* after all, and the *Secret* was more closely bound to the king than his ministers. Yet when word eventually arrived from Louis XV, it was not in d'Éon's favour. Louis had bowed to the wishes of his ministers and recalled his spy to France. Outraged and feeling utterly betrayed, the Chevalier rejected the orders of the king to whom he had always remained so loyal. He would not return to France under such circumstances.

Politically isolated and smarting, the Chevalier now approached a select group of British ministers with a proposed deal. He promised the British a valuable cache of letters regarding various facets of French diplomatic strategy, on the condition that they offer him protection from any attempts made by the French to recall him to France. Though the letters he handed over were embarrassing for the French, certainly, at this point he decided to withhold details relating to any planned French invasion. They might be required later, if things got even worse. As it happened, the British were very satisfied with the Chevalier's offerings and agreed to his proposal. So when French diplomats eventually approached the British to extradite the Chevalier, the British refused their request.

Across London the Chevalier was toasted as 'a person of approved bravery . . . as a man, a person of probity and honour' for having sided with the British and provided them with secret documentation from the French.[7] Even so, he thought it prudent to leave the confines of the royal court given his now unofficial status in London and retreated to 38 Brewer Street, Soho, where fewer official eyes were watching. If, however, the Chevalier had hoped to continue his life at Brewer Street as a private citizen, he was to be sorely disappointed.

In February 1764, as a result of his obstinate treachery, the French officially stopped the Chevalier's annual pension of 12,000 livres. This was devastating news for the Chevalier, who had already racked up considerable debts on wine imports, fine clothing and books that the French government had been expected to pay for. Now word spread across the English capital that the Chevalier was no longer in favour with the French, and that no royal livres would be forthcoming to settle his debts. As a result, he was beset with demands from his English creditors. Quite suddenly, then, far from his days of glory and acclaim, the Chevalier d'Éon found himself on the slippery road to ruin.

By March 1764, the Chevalier was in such dire financial straits that he felt he was left with no choice but to publish a portion of his correspondence with the French government in order to make money. Once again, the letters for publication were carefully chosen. They would not reveal the French invasion plan, would not implicate Louis XV in any of the French incompetencies to be detailed and dared not expose the *Secret du Roi*. This likely indicates that the Chevalier hoped for some form of reconciliation with his monarch and his family of spies, despite the current tensions. The letters would, however, shed light on the quarrelsome nature of Louis's ministers, including Claude Louis François Régnier, Comte de Guerchy, the new minister-plenipotentiary at the British Court.

The *Lettres, mémoires et négociations particulières du Chevalier d'Éon, ministre plénipotentiaire auprès du roi de Grande-Bretagne* (1764), as the publication became known, enjoyed significant circulation when it was printed. The confusion and infighting the Chevalier's publication documented made the French look absurd, an insult they could scarce afford in the wake of their recent international losses. The Chevalier was, single-handedly, chipping away at France's reputation on the international stage when his initial secret task had been to bolster it. Naturally, Louis XV and his ministers were concerned about what the Chevalier might do next.

Attempting to capitalize on this new-found influence, the Chevalier wrote to the French informing them that the British

The Speculation

government had offered him £40,000 (£6.2 million) to hand over the rest of his correspondence. Though this sum seems unlikely, the Chevalier confidently stated that he expected the same or more from the French to surrender the remainder of his letters and save the administration any further international embarrassment. Outraged by the publication of his letters and the Chevalier's demands, the Comte de Guerchy retaliated and sued him for libel in the English courts. Given the standing of those involved, the hearing was held quickly at the Court of the King's Bench on 3 July 1764. D'Éon did not appear but was found guilty nonetheless, thus denting the Chevalier's negotiating position with the French. Yet de Guerchy sought further revenge, and dramatic rumours began to circulate that the count had gone so far as to engage a hitman to kill the Chevalier for betraying his king and country. It had all turned into a rather torrid diplomatic misstep, both for the Chevalier and the French government. This embarrassing infighting would have to stop.

An irate Louis XV recalled de Guerchy to Versailles in order to curb the diplomatic discontent in London. Without the French ambassador prodding and poking the Chevalier, perhaps he would take stock and remember where his true loyalty ought to lie. Back in Versailles, Charles de Broglie, a senior agent of the *Secret*, had simultaneously convinced Louis to offer the Chevalier an olive branch. De Broglie advised the king to reinstate the Chevalier as a spy in London, realizing that it was better to use and placate him rather than risk further retribution. They also knew that the Chevalier was in no real position to refuse the reinstated annual payment he would receive as a result. Resolved to follow de Broglie's guidance, and in an attempt to quieten his wayward spy, Louis XV duly offered to reinstate the Chevalier's annual pension, on the condition that he return all incriminating letters in his possession.

But the Chevalier was suspicious of his king now. Had he not been let down by him and the *Secret* before, when he hoped they would support him above de Guerchy in the matter of the British ambassadorship? Nonetheless, he took his chances and agreed to relinquish some of the letters in his possession but refused to return the rest until he had received a one-off payment of £116,341 (£17.8 million), which he claimed would serve to clear his debts. By any standard these reported debts are substantial and it is possible that the Chevalier inflated the seriousness of his circumstances in order to extract more money from the French than he needed. This is lent support by the fact that even though no such settlement was agreed upon, a tentative truce was concluded. The Chevalier would resume his surveillance of the British political class and report back to Louis XV as before.

Tellingly, it was at about this time, in 1769 or thereabouts, that rumours regarding the Chevalier d'Éon's sex began to snake their way through the corridors of power. Some historians have claimed that he had displayed hints of gender non-conformity prior to this – that he had begun to wear female clothing as far back as his days in Russia, for instance. But there is no contemporaneous evidence of that in the primary-source material, only later conjecture not backed up by evidence. Instead, I would like to proffer my own interpretive possibility as to why these rumours began when they did. My theory is supported in three ways. First, in what we have discovered in the timeline outlined above. Second, and crucially, a key letter that has been overlooked in accounts of the Chevalier's gender non-conformity. And finally, witness testimony which was provided at a later trial regarding the Chevalier's sex.

To my first point: the Chevalier d'Éon had ruffled the perfectly preened feathers of several French ministers and the King

The Speculation

of France. He had been tried and found guilty of libel against the French minister-plenipotentiary to the British court. Though Louis and his *Secret* had agreed terms with the Chevalier for the return of any further scandalous letters in his possession, the Chevalier had only partially complied with their demands. As a result, he still posed a threat to France's international reputation. It is my hypothesis, therefore, that the rumours regarding the Chevalier's sex emerged at this specific time because the king, following advice from de Broglie and the *Secret*, wished to discredit the Chevalier in anticipation of any future leaks. And so, aware of the impact that rumours regarding the Chevalier's gender (and by implication his sexuality) would have to his political cachet in Britain, the *Secret* fabricated a scandal that chipped away at the privilege automatically placed on him by his manhood by insinuating that he was not a man at all. The story went that d'Éon had been born female and, in cahoots with her family, had assumed male attire in order to inherit land and titles. But now that she had been discovered she must return, King Louis XVI insisted, to her female attire and her true self.

In the eighteenth century, the idea of a woman assuming male clothing to assert power and autonomy was by no means unheard of. The French and British alike would have been aware of the unnamed soldier often referred to as 'The Rider', for instance, who had joined the Swedish Army in the first decades of the century whilst presenting as male. Later, in 1769, the very same year that the rumours regarding the Chevalier began to spread across Europe, Anna Sophia Spiesen was discovered to have assumed male attire to serve in the Dutch Army under the assumed name of Claas Paulusse. These things happened, but that didn't mean they were accepted. A woman daring to enter the public or political sphere at this time, in whatever guise, was seen as an utterly foolish creature. This sentiment was summarized by Joseph

Figure 11. Anon., 'The Trial of M.D'Eon By A Jury of Matrons', Town and Country Magazine, 1771.

Addison when he condemned 'Ladies of Fire and Politicks' in *The Freeholder* on Monday, 30 April 1716, for instance. He observed: 'A States-woman is as ridiculous a Creature as a Cott-Quean. Each of the Sexes should keep within its particular Bounds, and content themselves to excel within their respective Districts.'[8]

By May 1771, word of the Chevalier's supposed gender-deception had spread like wildfire, much to the embarrassment of the Chevalier, who refuted the slander. That month the *London Evening Post* reported that wagers regarding the Chevalier's 'true sex' amounting to £60,000 (£8.5 million) had been placed on the London Stock Exchange. The following month the satirical print 'The Trial of M. D'Eon By A Jury of Matrons' appeared in *Town and Country Magazine*, poking fun at the nature of the gossip and ridiculing the Chevalier (Figure 11). In the print, the Chevalier wears a military hat and the medal of the Order of

The Speculation

St Louis dangles from his neck. These were the sartorial markers of his distinguished manhood on display for all to see. He stands, however, bare-arsed before a jury of older women, assembled in their wisdom to determine the sex of the person before them. This print stripped the Chevalier almost naked before the nation and reflected the level of interest the debates over his sex had sparked amongst the British public.[9] People believed he was a woman, or at the very least doubted that he was a man. This brings me to my second piece of evidence in support of my theory that it was the *Secret* who deliberately spread the misinformation regarding the Chevalier's sex: a key letter, written by the Chevalier in 1771 to Charles de Broglie.

In this letter the Chevalier claimed that he knew the reasons behind the erroneous claims that he was a woman. His revelations came in two deceptively simple sentences. First, he admitted to de Broglie that, although in his forties, he was mortified to 'still [be] as Nature made me'. Simply put, the Chevalier had never had sex. For late-eighteenth-century men, virginity or chastity in the right context was a virtue, but this context was specific and limited. Chaste adult men who devoted their lives to religious orders, for instance, might be tolerated. Beyond that it was seen as odd, threatening even, and aroused suspicions of same-sex desire. Virginity was, however, far more comfortably associated with idealized forms of unmarried womanhood.

The Chevalier continued that since he had never felt the least temptation to 'sensual indulgence, this has given my friends in France, as well as in Russia and England, grounds for imagining in their *innocence* that I was of the *female* sex'.[10] Essentially, the Chevalier disclosed that he was sexually uninclined and that this disinclination, coupled with the knowledge of his virginity and chasteness, had inspired his 'friends' (of whom de Broglie was one) to infer that he was a woman. These details may seem incidental, but they are important because they shine a light on how the Chevalier became so utterly linked to womanhood in his own time. Additionally, his words are significant because they also counter popular histories of what we now call 'asexuality'. These histories have suggested that the origins of asexual identity emerged in the late nineteenth century, but the Chevalier's testimony establishes that it existed as early as the mid- to late eighteenth century instead.

These important and often overlooked contextual details contained in the Chevalier's letter to de Broglie demonstrate that the *Secret* certainly had enough private information regarding the Chevalier's sexuality and sexual history at their disposal to use it to bring him to heel when he threatened them. The Chevalier himself tells us that these rumours were put about by his 'friends', after all.

In later life, d'Éon would offer a more heroic account of how she came to be known as a woman. As she told it, her discovery had come on a rainy day in either 1770 or 1771 when she was riding over Westminster Bridge on her trusty steed, Bucephalus (meaning ox-headed). The Chevalier's horse shared his name with that of Alexander the Great's horse, the most famous in classical antiquity. And so, just as the fall of Bucephalus marked the fall of Alexander, so too did the fall of the Chevalier's horse spell an end, of sorts, for him.

D'Éon claimed that whilst driving the horse too fast in the rain, he slipped and was thrown unceremoniously across the cobblestones of Westminster Bridge. Coming to, d'Éon noticed blood oozing from his groin and trickling in streams across the cobbles. Passers-by saw this too, apparently, and came rushing to d'Éon's aid. In a desperate attempt to save him, they cut away his male clothing to stop the bleeding and found that the Chevalier (male) was, in fact, the Chevalière (female).

The Speculation

This is all well and good, except that it did not happen. This retelling was part of the fictional material assembled by d'Éon that would inform much of her 'memoirs'. Had an event this dramatic actually occurred on the busy cobbles of Westminster Bridge in the early 1770s it would have been recounted in newspapers, pamphlets, ballads and poems, plays and private correspondence within days. Instead, there is nothing at all. What's more, the Chevalier continued to dress in male clothing in the early 1770s, which would have been impossible had she been discovered as he claimed. Nonetheless, 'discovered' she was.

In 1771 the appearance of a new print, 'The Discovery', spread across London (Figure 12). In it the Chevalier d'Éon is presented as a fashionable woman. Her hair is worn high atop her head,

Figure 12. S. Hooper, 'The Discovery or Female Free-Mason', 1771.

whilst the voluminous ruffles of her sleeves frame her arms. In her hands she holds the symbols of a gentleman and a soldier, the staff and the sword. Scattered on the table to the left lies a copy of *Lettres du Chr D'Eon* and *L'Hist. du Chr D'Eon*, identifying the subject of the print quite clearly.

Over her head we see another sword. A military hat hovers, waiting to be worn. In the right of the image, a man's suit jacket has been discarded in favour of the elaborate frock she has on. The implication here is that the Chevalier's sex is to be determined by her costume. She may adopt the robes of either sex at any time and, as a result, she is not to be trusted. Further elaborating on this, two telling pictures flank 'The Discovery's' effeminate subject.

To the left of the picture Mary Toft, the notorious 'rabbit breeder' of Godalming in Surrey, delivers forth her rabbit babies. In 1726 Toft began 'giving birth' to all manner of animal parts, including the heads of rabbits, cat's legs, and in one particularly prolific day, nine dead rabbits. This afforded Toft significant celebrity status in her time, even catching the attention of George I, who dispatched a surgeon to get to the bottom of what was going on. It wasn't long before it was discovered that Toft and her female relatives had been sneaking rabbits and animal parts into Mary Toft's room and inserting them into her before she 'delivered' them. It was all an elaborate hoax.[11]

In the top right of the picture another celebrated hoax is referenced, the Bottle-Imp of 1749. This was an idea concocted by the Duke of Montagu and another noble friend, who joked that if they could find a conjurer that could somehow, magically, jump into a quart bottle, all of London would flock to see it. And so, sans conjurer, they placed an advertisement in a London newspaper calling on Londoners to witness their non-existent conjurer present 'you with a common wine-bottle'. This bottle could then be examined by any member of the audience, they reassured them, and once they were satisfied, the bottle would be placed in the middle of a table. Then, before their very eyes, their conjurer 'without any equivocation goes into it'. But that was not the end of it; once inside the bottle, the conjurer would proceed to 'sing all the popular songs of the day'. The crowd, including royalty, paid their entry fee and gathered to witness this supposed true marvel, only for it to become very clear very quickly that they would be treated to no such bottle singing that day. Needless to say, 'a general row ensued' and the aristocratic hoaxers were unmasked.[12]

All that is to say that, in 1771, many English readers supposed the story of the Chevalier to be best understood alongside these two prominent hoaxes. Perhaps they felt that the debate regarding his sex had been concocted for financial gain and mischief, as it had been in the Bottle-Imp case? Or maybe that it was an attempt on the Chevalier's part to gain some form of celebrity status. Though neither accurately summed up the Chevalier's case, as 'The Discovery' demonstrates, there was significant contemporary doubt as to the veracity of the claims that the Chevalier d'Éon had been born a girl and then lived her life as a man. But if a fall from a horse or strategically planned French rumour did not herald d'Éon's move from Charles to Charlotte, a royal death would soon set the course for this extraordinary history to unfold.

At 3.15 p.m. on 10 May 1774 Louis XV died. He had endured weeks of bloodletting and various treatments for persistent, excruciating headaches, but when the hour finally arrived the sixty-four-year-old king passed peacefully in the splendour of his private apartments at Versailles. Thus ended the second-longest reign in French history. But despite his longevity and his moniker 'Louis the Beloved', many in France were pleased to see the back of him. He had, after all, depleted the French coffers through his warmongering and his expensive tastes. Further, as we have already noted, France's position on the international stage had been significantly undermined by his secretive, underhand machinations. It was, the people agreed, time for a change.

The new king, his grandson, Louis XVI, would have to make some modifications in order to stabilize the monarchy. He began by disbanding the *Secret du Roi*, preferring to conduct his diplomatic activities by more conventional means. Following its demise, and sensing an opportunity to finally bring the wayward Chevalier to heel, the new king's ministers once again attempted to have him return his letters once and for all. But without adequate repayment the Chevalier would not budge. Not coincidentally, then, the rumours regarding the Chevalier's sex intensified once more.

On 13 November 1775, the Chevalier placed a letter in the *Morning Post* asking readers 'not to renew any policies [bets] respecting my sex'. He asked for all previous bets to be annulled and warned that, should his wishes not be respected, 'I should be obliged to quit a place which I regard as my second country.'[13] But the gossip and intrigue did not abate. On 18 November 1777 it was reported that one Domenico Angelo, a friend of the Chevalier's who lived on King's Square (Soho Square) in London, offered the now poverty-stricken Chevalier £10,000 (£900,000) 'upon condition that the said Chevalier D'Eon should suffer himself to be examined by two surgeons and two midwives, in order to ascertain his sex'. The Chevalier replied, 'My dear Angelo, I know your friendship for me, and ten thousand pounds are a considerable sum; however, the persons that propose it must wait till I am dead, and then if they please they shall be welcome to make their examination, and to kiss my backside.'[14] Despite this spicy retort, the press attention he commanded and the resulting society gossip made it increasingly difficult for the Chevalier to remain in London.

The Speculation

Eventually, a significant financial agreement was reached between the Chevalier and the French court. The agreement must have come as a relief to the Chevalier. The sums agreed would rid him of the majority of his debts, plus his pension of 12,000 livres would be reinstated, as the late king had promised. In return, the Chevalier would finally relinquish his secret papers and could safely return to France. There was one unusual final condition, however. Louis XVI was aware of the strength of the rumours that circulated concerning d'Éon. And so he decreed that, following a medical examination to confirm he had been born female, the Chevalier must wear only female attire thereafter. If he did not adhere to this order he would be imprisoned. However, Louis stipulated that the Chevalier would retain the cross of the Order of St Louis. The Chevalier agreed to these terms, naively believing that 'because of my obedience and my former titles, on my return to France I would be allowed to wear men's clothing' as before.[15]

Before the Chevalier left for France, however, England had one more slight to inflict. Wagers on his 'true sex' were still outstanding – they had accrued over some six years by this stage – and those invested in the outcome finally demanded answers, and money. It was decided that a trial would be held to determine, once and for all, the biological sex of the Chevalier d'Éon, and by so doing all bets could finally be settled.

On Friday, 4 July 1777 a headline in *The Derby Mercury* declared: 'The SEX of D'EON *Determined*'. The article revealed that on the previous Tuesday in the Court of the King's Bench at Guildhall, a judge, Lord Mansfield, and a 'Special Jury' met to determine whether the Chevalier was male or female. As the Chevalier himself was not on trial, he was not present to hear discussions about his intimate private life and anatomy. The outcome of the trial, it was noted at the time, 'is of the utmost Importance to every Person concerned in the Policies opened on the Sex of the Chevalier D'Eon'.[16] Mr Hayes, a surgeon from Leicester Fields, had brought the action against M. Jacques, a French broker and underwriter who had initially taken bets on the Chevalier's sex. Hayes believed he was due a significant return if it transpired that the Chevalier was indeed a woman.

The atmosphere in the courthouse was jovial as Monsieur Le Goux, a surgeon, was called to testify. Le Goux claimed that he had been acquainted with the Chevalier since Nivernais, the former 'Ambassador from the court of France', had lived in England. As a medical man, Le Goux's testimony was eagerly anticipated. When his revelations came they were determinedly clear. The Chevalier d'Éon was 'to his certain Knowledge . . . a Woman'.

Lord Mansfield pressed the Frenchman further; how did he know this? What was his proof? Le Goux testified that he had attended the Chevalier five years previously, in 1772; 'unfortunately for herself, as well as her Sex, [she] laboured at that Time under a Disorder which rendered an Examination of the afflicted Part absolutely necessary . . . This Examination led, of Course, to that Discovery of the Sex.'[17] As eighteenth-century legal testimony went, this was near-conclusive evidence. A professional medical man could surely be trusted with the truth.

Next, another Frenchman known to the Chevalier, Monsieur de Morande, was called to the stand. De Morande testified that on 3 July 1774 the Chevalier had told him that he was truly a woman. When de Morande proclaimed his doubt, the Chevalier 'had even proceeded so far as to display her Bosom on the Occasion'. The Chevalier had also, according to de Morande, 'exhibited the Contents of her Female Wardrobe'. Having been thus aroused by the Chevalier's bosom and 'Sacques, Petticoats, and other Habilliments', de Morande could no longer contain himself. He 'accosted her in a Stile of Gallantry respecting her Sex'. Encouraged by the

The Speculation

Chevalier, de Morande soon established 'manual Proof of her being in Truth a very Woman'.[18] With this, *The Caledonian Mercury* reported that 'the whole Court, which was very full', erupted in 'one universal fit of hearty laughter'.[19]

After further legal parries, Lord Mansfield then instructed the jury. If it were up to him, he stated, neither party would emerge victorious. In his eyes this was nothing more than a petty gambling debt. 'D'Eon dressed as a Man', he concluded, but, 'She would have fought Duels. She was Captain of Dragoons. Resided here as Ambassador.' She was, in effect, a 'Woman in Masquerade'. As a fascinating point of order, Mansfield reminded the jury that 'It was not the Power of any Person to compel D'Eon to disclose her Sex', but the witnesses had spoken, and he was convinced. The jury ought to be too. *The Derby Mercury* reported that they 'without Hesitation, gave a verdict for the Plaintiff [that d'Éon was female] ... The Sex of Mademoiselle D'Eon being legally substantiated in a Court of Judicature.'[20]

It is, I think, noteworthy that both men called to provide 'proof' of the gender of the Chevalier were French. And indeed, that the person accepting bets in the first place, M. Jacques, was also French. This, then, brings me to my third and final reason for determining that the *Secret* and then the French government were involved in deliberately disseminating the false rumours that the Chevalier was a woman. The Frenchmen involved in this trial all had noted links to either Nivernais, the wider French diplomatic corps or the now abandoned *Secret du Roi*. We cannot know for certain that they originated the rumours, but we certainly know that they deliberately delivered false testimony during this trial in order to humiliate and discredit the Chevalier. In turn, so tarnished was his reputation in England that he was now left with few alternatives but to return to France. Thus in August 1777, the month after the trial, the Chevalier announced that he was to 'quit with grief my dear England, to retire to my native country, near an august master, whose protection and kindness further assure my quiet than all the Magna Charta [sic] of this Isle'.[21] Finally, the French had him where they wanted him.

On Thursday, 14 August 1777 it was reported that 'the Chevalier D'Eon or Mademoiselle De Beaumont, after fifteen whole Years Residence in this Isle of Liberty, amidst imminent Perils and Dangers, Troubles and Trials, set out . . . on her Return to her Native Country'. The Chevalier was now being referred to as a woman in the British press. The trial, as far as the press were concerned, had settled the matter conclusively. D'Éon was a woman, though she had not yet donned the garb. *The Derby Mercury* noted that she had set off for Versailles with a small retinue in a plain post-chaise, with four uniformed officers in attendance. 'It is said,' they reported, 'that after she has waited upon her Sovereign [in France], she will dress in the Habit of her Sex.'[22]

Once the Chevalier returned to France, he becomes a little more difficult to track. We know that he remained there for eight years before returning to England in 1785, and that when she did she was a very different person to the one who had left in 1777. Upon his arrival in France, despite the wishes of his king, the Chevalier initially presented himself in male clothing, in full military uniform. He requested that he be permitted to continue to dress as he had, and that he might once again resume active service in the army. But the French did subject d'Éon to their threatened medical examination, which concluded that he was biologically female, so his request to remain dressed as a dragoon was denied and he was instructed to 'resume' wearing female dress. The former spy who had sold state secrets to the British, humiliated the French on the world stage and effectively held the secrets of Versailles to ransom could not simply

The Speculation

return to France as though nothing had happened; Louis XVI had to make an example of him. 'The bad boy must become a good girl.'[23]

It was at this point, according to d'Éon's heavily fictionalized memoir, that Mademoiselle Bertin presented herself to the Chevalier in Paris and clad him in the female attire assigned by Louis XVI and Marie Antoinette. 'I preferred being a woman', d'Éon wrote in one passage, however truthfully, 'to rebelling against the voice of my master', the king.[24] Once again, though, the Chevalier's account of his womanhood does not ring true. For in 1779 he was arrested and remanded by the French authorities at Château de Dijon for over two weeks because he had reverted to wearing his military uniform. As punishment for her transgression, d'Éon was subsequently confined to her family estates at Tonnerre, before relenting and returning to Versailles as a gentlewoman once more. Charles de Beaumont would now be known as Charlotte de Beaumont. During this time, d'Éon had concluded that the degradation she had been subjected to in England was preferable to the humiliation and imprisonment she experienced in France. Thus she made several requests to be allowed to return to England, all of which were initially denied. However, eventually the royal court relented and a request in November 1785 saw permission granted.

Back in England, familiar headlines were soon in circulation once more. Mademoiselle the Chevalier d'Éon, as they called her now, had taken up with a man, some claimed. Others said that she had 'lain' with a lady. Another report stated that she finally paid arrears to a wet-nurse who had spent all this time caring for a child that d'Éon had secretly given birth to when she was still passing as a man.[25] Even English playwrights immortalized the transformation of the Chevalier from dragoon to damsel:

> Did not a lady knight, late Chevalier
> A brave smart soldier in your eyes appear?
> Hey! Presto! Pass! His sword becomes a fan,
> A comely woman rising from a man.[26]

Mademoiselle d'Éon returned to her old lodgings on 38 Brewer Street. On 5 March 1786 James Boswell, the Scottish lawyer and diarist, encountered d'Éon in her female form and crudely concluded, 'She appeared to me a man in woman's clothes, like Hecate on the stage.'[27] Despite these remarks, d'Éon was warmly received as a French oddity in London and, in this age of spectacle, that afforded her some advantageous social connections. She was received by the Duke of Dorset at his country seat in Knole, for example, and was entertained by Lord Chancellor Loughborough, with whom she had been friendly prior to her transformation. Despite continuing to live on the pension granted to her by the late King of France, old habits die hard, and it was not long before she found herself in debt once more due to her extravagant taste and social life. To help meet the familiar financial burden of this new debt, however, Mademoiselle d'Éon would take her fencing sword in hand, gather her pride and make such a captivating display of skill and charm that it would secure her place in history.

On 9 April 1787 a specially selected group of men and women gathered together at Carlton House at the behest of the then twenty-four-year-old Prince of Wales, the future George IV. In the blue Ante Room of that great house the prince had had a makeshift fencing ring erected. Blue and gold drapery was added to match the decor of the room and, around that, a row of blue and gold seats were positioned. A larger chair was reserved at the head of the ring, between the south-facing windows, for the prince himself. He had already gained a reputation for being 'rather too

The Speculation

fond of women and wine', so events such as these were hotly anticipated by his fashionable set.[28] By this time the prince had already fallen for, and secretly married, his Catholic consort, Maria Fitzherbert.

As the guests took their seats the soft sound of silk, lifted to sit, hissed through the room. Fans fluttered as ladies exchanged calumnies behind them, eyes darted around the room. A group of well-dressed gentlemen assembled beside the prince's seat. Proximity to the prince was key, especially given the tensions between him and his parents, George III and Queen Charlotte. The Prince of Wales was the future, and if the quiet rumblings at court proved to be true, that future may be upon them sooner than some anticipated.

George and Maria were a dashing pair. He was dressed in a royal-blue overcoat embellished with the bejewelled insignia of the Order of the Garter. A black felt riding hat perched atop his powdered hair. She, the very breath of spring in a salmon-coloured riding outfit, sported a black felt hat to complement her husband's. Once they had taken their seats the entertainment could begin.

Entering from an open door on the other side of the room, two figures made their way towards the ring. The first, dressed in crimson and sporting a tidy wig, was the notable French celebrity the Chevalier de Saint-Georges, Joseph Bologne. A Guadeloupean, he was the son of Georges Bologne de Saint-Georges, a white plantation owner, and an enslaved Creole woman. In addition to being an accomplished fencer, the Chevalier de Saint-Georges was a virtuoso violinist and composer whose musical skill was said to have rivalled that of Mozart.

Saint-Georges had been sent to England by the Duc d'Orléans, Louis-Philippe, to court favour with the Prince of Wales as political unrest and popular uprisings broke out in many regions across France. The French working poor questioned the disparity between their own relative poverty and the excesses of the French elite, and the duke, with these tensions in mind, hoped to secure the prince's support should he become 'regent' amidst this tumult. French abolitionists also felt that Saint-Georges would be an ideal candidate to advance the movement in London and so, with no small weight on his shoulders, the thirty-one-year-old had set off. His presence alone would have been enough to make the ladies swoon, but it was his opponent who caused a real stir that particular Monday afternoon.

Dressed all in black, except for her white chemise, large white cap, and the blazing-red ribbon attached to her medal of the Order of St Louis, d'Éon's appearance was met with both shock and delight. As the *Ipswich Journal* later reported, 'The novelty of a lady in petticoats engaging [in] the most experienced and able matters of the noble science of defence, excited universal pleasantry.'[29] Once royal formalities had been observed, the famous fencers undertook the required saluting ceremony. First they saluted one another, then the referee, before a final acknowledgement towards the gathered crowd. Then Mademoiselle the Chevalier hiked up her skirts, exposing a glimpse of her white cotton underskirts, and launched her initial attack. D'Éon would, ultimately, emerge triumphant, much to the delight of those gathered.

Back in France, a dismal harvest in 1788 meant that already scarce food supplies had now run desperately low, resulting in still deeper civil unrest. Then, on 14 July 1789, the Parisian populace stormed the Bastille, a fortress which was seen as a symbol of either royal power or tyranny, depending on how much bread was in your cupboards. In the regions beyond Paris peasants took up arms against their feudal lords too. As a result, in fear for their lives, on 4 August 1789 the French National Assembly declared the abolition of the French feudal and tithe system. Then, on 26 August, it published the *Déclaration des droits de l'homme et du citoyen* (*The*

The Speculation

Figure 13. Alexandre-Auguste Robineau, 'The Fencing-Match between the Chevalier de Saint-Georges and the Chevalier d'Éon', c.1787.

Declaration of the Rights of Man and of the Citizen), which proclaimed liberty, equality and the right of all citizens, regardless of their rank, to resist oppression. Louis XVI, however, refused to sign any such declarations, realizing that they essentially spelled the end of the monarchy. As a result a significant proportion of the population in Paris once again rose in revolt, marching, this time, on Versailles on 5 October. The outcome was that the royal family were unceremoniously removed from their palatial hideaway and held in Paris under armed guard. France would never be the same again.

Having devoured details of these revolutionary events in the English press, d'Éon felt compelled to act. Had she not, after all, served her country diligently before? She wrote to the National

Assembly in Paris asking to 'resume her helmet, her sabre, and her horse' for France. 'I wish to finish my career by dying for my country,' she proclaimed.[30] When the letter was read aloud to the Assembly on 12 June 1792 it was received as a joke, a rare moment of levity amidst the terrors of revolution. As the *ancien régime* in France collapsed, so too did many of the ongoing financial settlements that had rested with the monarch. D'Éon's pension quickly fell into arrears before disappearing altogether, and this presented yet another significant financial crisis for the Chevalier, who was now forced to use every ounce of resourcefulness, charm and ingenuity at her disposal to survive.

First she sold her library of books, one by one. Next, when books could no longer provide, she sold her jewellery, some of which had been given to her by the King and Queen of France. As a result of the crisis unfolding in Paris, these particular items became all the more valuable on the English market. Sadly, there was no family she could turn to in her despair, her elite relatives having lost their heads in Paris and her mother and sister having passed away. Following their deaths, d'Éon's French lands and properties had all been confiscated by the state, so all paths to prosperity seemed blocked. This unrelenting sequence of penury and isolation would grind Mademoiselle d'Éon's indomitable spirit to the very depths of despair. 'Given that nothing can change my destiny,' she lamented, 'I spare myself the useless pain of asking for it . . . What remains in this life is a matter of indifference to me.'[31] Despite this, however, her will to survive knew no limits and she soon rallied once again.

By 1793, her pension gone, her books, jewels and best dresses (but not her male military attire) now sold, d'Éon was left with no choice but to sell her notoriety to get by. Fencing sword in hand once more, she partnered with Mrs Bateman, an actress and female fencer, to showcase her talents once more, this time for the crowds at the popular Ranelagh Gardens and the Haymarket Theatre,

The Speculation

London. Though she was now sixty-five years old, Mademoiselle d'Éon was said to have parried 'as though in the vigour of youth'.[32] She thrilled her audiences once more. Such was the reception and demand, d'Éon soon found herself touring Britain and Ireland as a celebrity. She was, after all, the gender non-conforming, headline-generating, fencing French dragoon. Along with her reputation, she brought spectacle and intrigue with her wherever she went.

On 20 June 1795 *The Staffordshire Advertiser* alerted its readers to her recent visit. 'MADEMOISELLE D'EON', the newspaper declared, made a 'GRAND ASSAULT D'ARMES' in the Free Grammar School. By now she was touring with 'an Englishman, a Professor in the Art of Fencing'. D'Éon's ability in combat, the *Advertiser* remarked, 'is yet unrivalled in history'.[33] According to the *Advertiser*, she also showed 'her astonishing agility . . . in a public room at Liverpool'.[34] She had entertained in Birmingham and in Ireland.[35] In Gloucester, we are told, d'Éon would be received by the 'Right Worshipful' Mayor on 31 August 1795 at the Grand Jury room, at the Booth Hall. Doors were set to open 'at Six, with Fencing to begin precisely at Seven – Admittance, Ladies and Gentlemen, three shillings'.[36] Advertisements like these littered regional newspapers, ensuring healthy ticket sales and a respectable return. And, some 230 years later, it was one of those very advertisements that served to highlight yet another vital but forgotten part of d'Éon's history.

When I first read *The Gloucester Journal* of Monday, 31 August 1795 I brushed past it. It was just another d'Éon advertisement, much like all the others. I had extracted the details I needed from them. Or so I thought. It was only in the course of reviewing my notes for this chapter that I realized how important the information contained there really was. *The Gloucester* ad reads: 'The Chevaliere will appear in the same Uniform which she wore at the time when she served as

Captain of Dragoons, and Aid-de-Camp.'[37] D'Éon was identified as a woman, yes, but, crucially, she was dressed as a man. Previous histories of Mademoiselle the Chevalier d'Éon have maintained that despite the fall of the *ancien régime* – and with it the demand for her to wear women's clothing – d'Éon had never again assumed male garb, indicating a new-found comfort in her female identity. Because of this, and because of the enduring nature of the image painted for the Prince of Wales by Alexandre-Auguste Robineau (Figure 13), it has always been assumed that d'Éon toured and fenced dressed as a woman. However, the detail contained in these tour advertisements calls into question whether d'Éon even appeared or fenced in female attire at all after her performance at Carlton House, particularly as the advertisement for her Gloucester appearance is not unique. On Saturday, 9 January 1796 her show in Bath was also to be conducted 'in the same Uniform which she wore at the Time when she served as *Captain of Dragoons*, and Aid-de-Camp to Mareschal Duc *de Broglie*, in Germany'.[38] This overlooked evidence demonstrates that previous assumptions that d'Éon dressed exclusively as a woman after she returned to England are incorrect. Following numerous refused appeals to two successive Kings of France to be allowed to stay in or reassume her male uniform, d'Éon could now dress as she wished. This, we now know, meant she dressed in both male and female clothing depending on her desire and need. D'Éon deliberately used the long-standing confusion and gossip regarding her sex to bamboozle her audience. The tensions she had previously attempted to avoid regarding her gender performance now became part of her 'brand'. However, despite the ingenuity with which d'Éon monetized the public obsession with her sex and gender, disaster loomed at the tip of a fencing sword.

It was 26 August 1796, and d'Éon had taken to the ring in Southampton to display her fencing skill, as she had at various locations on many occasions over the past several years. Her 'opponent' on this occasion was a Frenchman, Monsieur de Launay. Amidst the usual lunge and riposte, the flèche and parry, de Launay's light, flexible fencing foil shattered and accidently pierced d'Éon's flesh on the right side, badly wounding her. 'An unfortunate accident lately happened to the well-known Chevalier D'Eon,' *The Reading Mercury* recounted a few days later. The short article went on to detail that the foil had 'entered [her] 4 inches above the right breast'. Luckily, 'medical assistance was at hand', and though her life was never in peril her livelihood was, as she would never fence again.[39]

Without money or occupation, d'Éon now faced ruin once more. Back in London, she was forced to quit her lodgings at Brewer Street and moved into smaller premises at 26 New Milman Street with Mrs Mary Cole, a naval widow. Cole and d'Éon, having both fallen from more fortunate circumstances, pooled their limited resources in order to survive. In March 1798 *The Caledonian Mercury* described d'Éon as 'one of the most intrepid, intelligent, and extraordinary characters, which the world ever produced'. It lamented, however, that she was now reduced to 'living in great distress, and nearly without the common necessaries of life'.[40]

Her dire financial predicament, however, elicited charity from several friends and acquaintances. Queen Charlotte assigned d'Éon an allowance of £50 (£4,750) per year for the rest of her life, for example. Whilst this only went so far, the royal seal of charitable approval had wider value. It also appears that William Douglas, the 4th Duke of Queensberry, better known in his lifetime as 'Old Q', covered some of her expenses too. He even granted her £1,000 (£95,000) in his will, though as she predeceased him she never benefited from this charity.

'When I have money,' d'Éon tells us herself, 'I eat and drink as any other would. When I have no money, I stay in bed and work [write] from morning to night. I survive on bread, cheese, lettuce, vegetables, and fruit.'[41] To the modern reader this intake may seem somewhat well rounded, but in comparison to the excesses that d'Éon had previously enjoyed it marked a significant reduction in her situation. In 1804 d'Éon's debts finally caught up with her and she was unceremoniously confined to a debtors' gaol for about five months until her housemate, the devoted Mrs Cole, was able to gather together the funds to secure her release.

Desperate, d'Éon now signed a contract with Messrs Richardson of London to finally publish her memoirs and reveal 'the truth' about her life and her sex. Having turned down many previous offers, d'Éon was reluctant to tell her sensational story now, but poverty had no rules. D'Éon's memoirs were never completed, but she did begin to bring together the material that would go some way towards informing them, a significant portion of which survives today. It is widely accepted that much of what she wrote was pure fiction, playing into the dramatic lies that had surrounded her life in order to encourage sales and generate income.

Sadly, though, if money had been the reason why d'Éon finally agreed to write her memoirs, that money did not come quickly enough. Towards the end of 1809 she was finally forced to sell her prized possession, her cross of the Order of St Louis. A combination of speculation and revolution had cost Mademoiselle d'Éon everything: her career, her clothing, her jewellery, her books, her medals and, most important of all, her very identity.

On 21 March 1810, at the respectable age of eighty-two, the Chevalier d'Éon died peacefully at New Milman Street, London. Within days, it was arranged that her body was attended to by an array of gentlemen, 'perhaps 10 or 12 in all, including a professor of anatomy, two surgeons, a lawyer, and a journalist', to carry out the long-awaited autopsy which would determine her sex conclusively.[42] Those assembled included the British courtier

The Speculation

and politician Francis Seymour-Conway, Rear Admiral Sir Sidney Smith, Mr Wilson, a professor of anatomy, Mr Thomas Copeland, an army surgeon, and Marie-Vincent Talochon, or 'Le Père Elysée' as he was also known, former surgeon to the now-headless Louis XVI, who had attended d'Éon in her final years. The results of that autopsy, and the multiple prints and column inches that they inspired, show that even in death the question of d'Eon's sex would deny her a peaceful, dignified rest.

An anatomical drawing held in the vaults at the British Museum details the findings of that autopsy. It was produced in 1810 by (or after) Charles Turner, the noted English mezzotint engraver. An inscription below the drawing in question states: 'Drawn from the Body of the Chevalier D'Eon, May 24. 1810'. Rendered in exacting fleshy tones above this description is 'the penis and emaciated thighs of . . . the Chevalier D'Eon'. In the image, the white drapery that covers the lower portion of her body has been raised and rested atop her stomach to unceremoniously expose and record her genitalia. It is an intrusive image, even now, and one I don't feel comfortable sharing in this book. It is, however, authentic.

'I hereby certify that I have inspected & dissected the Body of the Chevalier D'Eon,' wrote Thomas Copeland, the army surgeon, beneath the drawing. He goes on to confirm that the autopsy has been carried out 'in the presence of Mr. Adair, Mr. Wilson, & Le Pere Elysee, & have found the Male Organs in every respect, perfectly formed'. The document is dated 23 May 1810 and is written from Golden Square, Soho, London. It is signed by Copeland and other witnesses.[43]

On 24 May 1810, the day after the autopsy, *The Sun* ran the story that the 'questionable gender' of the Chevalier d'Éon had finally been determined. She was, they concluded, 'a perfect male!'.[44] *The Pilot* published details from Copeland's certificate, again stating that d'Éon was *'male . . . at the time of his or her decease'*.[45] The

General Evening Post found itself confounded by d'Éon's seemingly ever-changing sex, stating glibly that she was 'Sometimes *the one*, sometimes *the other*'.[46] This confusion persisted well into the twentieth century too.

The author John V. Grombach wrote to the famous sexologist Albert Kinsey on 20 May 1953, asking if Kinsey thought d'Éon might be a 'hermaphrodite' who somehow managed to change his genitalia over the course of her life? Grombach refers to this as the '$64 question [*sic*]'.[47] Kinsey, having ignored several letters from Grombach, eventually impatiently replied. 'We are scientific observers and recorders,' he stated matter-of-factly, 'and have rather strictly abstained from guessing what history might be when we do not know enough of the facts to put the matter together.'[48] Feeling a little more generous, Kinsey went on to inform Grombach that there was no known case of a 'hermaphrodite' having naturally changed their genitalia.

Robert Baldick, the British scholar of French literature, once referred to the Chevalier d'Éon as 'that pathetic human being'.[49] J. M. J. Rogister, in his entry for the Chevalier in the *Oxford Dictionary of National Biography*, refers to her as 'indisputably male'.[50] Others have referred to d'Éon as a 'cross-dresser', as having 'come out as trans' and as gender-fluid.[51] None of this is entirely correct, however. The Chevalier was far from pathetic. Indeed, Edmund Burke referred to her as 'the most extraordinary person of the age . . . we have seen no one who has united so many military, political, and literary talents'.[52] Neither was she 'indisputably male'. That idea was very much disputed in her lifetime, as we have seen.

In her memoir, the Chevalier tells us that she 'became a girl against my wishes'.[53] Indeed, her enforced womanhood is described as the 'origins of my misfortunes'.[54] Her gowns and jewellery, hand-picked by Marie-Antoinette, became the 'golden chains of my new slavery'.[55] Despite modern assertions that the Chevalier d'Éon was a proto-trans hero(ine), hers is not the language of a woman finally revelling in her true identity; rather it is the sentiment of a detainee. And that, I propose, is what we have previously failed to fully grasp about this history: that the Chevalier's womanhood was not born of liberation but of punishment and incarceration. It was symptomatic of a patriarchal and misogynistic system of French governmental control that valued manhood above all else and denied the Chevalier his in order to control him. In truth, we can never really know how the Chevalier d'Éon understood his gender identity, but the burdensome nature of his enforced womanhood is plain for all to see.

Piecing together a true and complete history of Charles de Beaumont, the Chevalier d'Éon, is like attempting to catch individual raindrops in a downpour. Yet here we are even so, more than 200 years later, just like the Georgians, still trying to identify, still trying to classify, still trying to settle a bet. This particular dispute, though, is not ours to settle. The Chevalier d'Éon has crafted a history that is his own, and underneath the delicate embroidery of that creation her stitches are too finely sewn for us to properly unpick. If the Chevalier's sex and gender identity fascinated the Georgians and intrigues us now, it offered no such curiosity to her, and after all that is written here that is all we need to know. 'I am what I am,' she tells us, 'I declare that the intention of the Lord Creator in creating this multiplicity and this diversity of men and women on this earth has been to render them all equal in the eyes of God and His law.'[56]

CHAPTER SEVEN
That Feverish Dream Called Youth

WHEN, IN 1822, THE Yorkshire landowner Anne Lister (1791–1840) visited the famous Ladies of Llangollen at Plas Newydd in Wales, she was utterly charmed. For Lister, like many queer people since, the ladies demonstrated an all-too-rare glimpse of gender non-conforming joy and domestic possibility. However, despite her revelatory experience, the *real* story, Lister felt, lay beyond Llangollen. Having left Wales, Lister later mused in her diary, 'Much, or all, depends upon the story of their former lives, the period passed before they lived together, that feverish dream called youth.' What follows here, then, is the history that Anne Lister never knew. In order to unravel it we take our leave of Wales at Holyhead and board a vessel travelling west upon the oft-ill-tempered Irish Sea bound for Ireland (*Éire*). Then, disembarking at Waterford (*Port Láirge*), we travel by coach some thirty-five miles north to the amiable city of Kilkenny (*Cill Chainnigh*). It is here, in 'the Marble City', that this lesser-known history unfolds.

At the time of the Restoration of King Charles II in 1660, Kilkenny is loosely recorded as having been home to a civilian population

Figure 14. Kilkenny Castle today.

of approximately 3,802. But, as Georgian Ireland gave way to the reign of Queen Victoria, the number of people living in the small city had grown nearly sixfold to about 25,000 people. Throughout this period, more than 75 per cent of Kilkenny's inhabitants are recorded as having attended the Catholic Mass.

Just beyond the high street which cut through the city centre, a fortress-like castle loomed on the banks of the River Nore. Originally constructed in the twelfth century, this grey-stone monolith, all turrets and buttresses without, tapestries and fine local limestone within, had been the seat of the Butlers of Ormonde for over four centuries. The Butler family, despite their Anglo-Norman origins, had been so long in Ireland that it was said they had become 'more Irish than the Irish themselves' by the late eighteenth century.[1] Whilst this is an oversimplification, to be sure, it does reflect the fact that the Butlers were Roman Catholic and keen Jacobites. Further, like the vast majority of the Irish population at the time, they had also endured significant legal, civil and religious impediments under the Penal Laws.

The Irish Penal Laws were introduced by the Protestant English minority from 1695 to subjugate the Irish Catholic majority and, in some cases, Presbyterian factions, so that the Irish could not effectively organize to overthrow colonial rule. These laws meant that Catholics were barred from holding public office; practising, teaching or administering their religion freely; obtaining a commission in the army; or entering professions such as medicine or the law. Catholics were not permitted to possess arms nor read or speak Irish, which, for many, was their native tongue. Infamously, as every primary-school child in Ireland can tell you, they were also denied ownership of any horse worth more than £5 (£750), at a time when a decent saddle horse cost about £15 (£3,000). Most impactful of all, though, the Popery Act of 1703 ensured that Catholics could not inherit estates in full. The English convention of primogeniture ensured that, where possible, landed estates were inherited intact by the first-born son. However, for Catholics it was decreed that lands should be divided equally amongst all legitimate sons, thus subdividing their landholdings and diluting their power and influence.

Given these restrictions, many Irish Catholic gentry families took up temporary residence in Catholic strongholds like France. As a result, Miss Eleanor Charlotte Butler was born on 11 May 1739 at Cambrai, not far from the Belgian border. Her parents were Walter Butler, the *de jure* 16th Earl of Ormonde (1703–83), later described by a contemporary as an 'ignorant & ill-bred man', and his wife, the mighty Eleanor de Montmorency Morres (1711–93), known as Madam Butler. She, according to the same adversary, was 'a bigoted Roman Catholic'.[2] By all accounts, though, their daughter, Miss Eleanor, thrived during her early life at Cambrai, demonstrating an aptitude for all manner of subjects and ideas.

Across the Channel and back in Ireland, Sarah Ponsonby was less fortunate. Her early life had been continuously interrupted by a series of tragedies which would take her to the very brink of destitution.

Sally Ponsonby (1755–1831), as she was affectionately known in her youth, was born to the illustriously named Chambré Brabazon Ponsonby (1720–62) and his second wife Louisa Lyons (1730–58) in 1755. Little Sally was just three years old when her mother died. Soon afterwards her father took his third wife, Mary Barker, but 'shortly after died himself, making no provision for his daughter Sarah, imagining that she would have her share of his property'.[3] However, following her husband's death, the Widow Ponsonby gave birth to 'a posthumous child' (Chambré Brabazon Ponsonby-Barker) who became sole heir of his father's estate. The Widow Ponsonby then married Sir Robert Staples but died just a few years later. And so, at the age of thirteen, alone in the world, Sally was taken in by Lady Betty Fownes, her father's cousin, at Woodstock, in the southern part of County Kilkenny.

Woodstock was the seat of a supposedly enlightened 'Protestant Ascendancy' family. This term, which appeared towards the close of the eighteenth century, described a certain type of Protestant Irish landowner who forcefully settled Irish-owned land during the Cromwellian invasion in 1649. The Fownes family were originally one such set of settlers. By the late eighteenth century, these families were said to have 'ascended' to civic and political dominance due, in no small part, to the effectiveness of the Penal Laws.

Lady Betty Fownes cared deeply for her cousin's daughter and chose Miss Parke's boarding school in the city centre as an appropriately polite institution for her to continue her education in 1769. Like other similar schools in Ireland at the time, Miss Parke likely educated a small number of boarders and day scholars in her own private house, where the Fowneses could have expected Sally to become proficient in languages, music, drawing and needlework. Miss Parke's young ladies would also have emerged as confident dancers; knowing just the right allemande spins to entice, and the appropriate hold in the cotillion to preserve one's dignity whilst capturing a roving bachelor's heart.

At about this time, Eleanor returned from France to Kilkenny Castle on the occasion of her brother John's wedding. John had converted to Protestantism in 1764 and so had managed to secure himself a wealthy Protestant heiress. When it came to his sister, Eleanor, however, the question of marriage had passed her by, despite her 'good complexion & . . . fine set of teeth'.[4] Now aged twenty-nine, it was thought that she was too 'satirical' and too 'masculine' to interest the opposite sex. Very soon Eleanor found herself bored and frustrated with life at the castle, so her mother suggested that she offer her services as a tutor at Miss Parke's school. Miss Parke was grateful to have her, such was Eleanor's learning, and she assigned her to a 'very nice slight looking little girl' named Sarah or 'Sally' Ponsonby, who was fourteen at the time.[5] Sarah was, it turned out, a diligent pupil. 'She learnt all she could from her teachers, she wrote fluently, spelled correctly & read whatever books fell her way.'[6] As the years progressed, both the Butler and Fownes families could not help but note the intensity of the relationship that was developing between Eleanor and Sarah, despite their age difference. This intensity was fostered by an extensive (now missing, likely destroyed) secret correspondence between the pair which lasted well beyond Miss Ponsonby's time at Miss Parke's.

Following her schooling, Miss Ponsonby was welcomed at Lady Betty's home, Woodstock, where she lived in relative comfort, though not without worry, for 'Sir William Fownes was not a kind husband to his excellent wife', according to his granddaughter, Caroline.[7] Family lore had it that Sir William was far from satisfied that Lady Betty had not provided him with a male heir, '& believing Lady Betty was in a declining state of health, he fancied that the time was approaching which would leave him at liberty to marry a young wife'.[8] Conveniently for Sir William, a candidate for the not as yet vacant position had recently taken up residence right under his own roof. Sir William inflicted all manner of unwanted attention on Miss Ponsonby. Eventually, his harassment became so unbearable that it instigated a wonderfully stern riposte from her.

'I desire to be informed in writing & only in writing,' Miss Ponsonby demanded of her would-be suitor, 'whether your motives for behaving to me, as you do, is a desire that I should quit your home.'[9] She made it clear that whatever feelings Sir William thought he had for her were not reciprocated. She was filled with nothing more than a 'disgust & detestation' of Lady Betty's spouse and 'adopted a reserved mode of behaviour' when in his presence. If he persisted in his unwanted attentions, she declared, then she would take it as an indication that Sir William wished 'me to inform them [his wife and family] what you have already honoured me with'.

It is doubtful, in truth, that Miss Ponsonby would have uttered a word against him. In a letter to her friend Mrs Lucy Goddard, a Dublin socialite, she made clear that her main cause of concern in this matter was that she might offend Lady Betty, to whom she was utterly devoted. 'I would rather die,' she confided, 'than wound Lady Betty's heart.'[10] Sir William, however, did not need to know that, and her spirited responses seem to have kept the old codger in his place for the time being.

Miss Ponsonby also confided to her friend that she and Miss

Butler of the castle continued to conduct a clandestine, intimate correspondence. What she failed to share with Mrs Goddard, however, was that within the sheets of the queer devotionals that flew between Woodstock and the castle, a secret plan had been set in motion. This plan would free Ponsonby from the lecherous attentions of Sir William and liberate Miss Butler from the dreary routine of castle life, which threatened to stifle her vitality. What followed was an Irish adventure story the likes of which would not have been out of place in the works of Jonathan Swift and would have put Jane Austen's domestic heroines to shame.

On 'Tuesday Nigh [sic]', 31 March 1778, such a commotion had taken Woodstock by the neck that Lady Betty sent urgently for the sensible, cosmopolitan Mrs Goddard to ease their anxiety. 'I can't paint our distress,' Lady Betty wrote, before proceeding to paint a picture of their distress. 'My Dear Sally leapt out of a Window last Night and is gone off. We learn Miss Butler of the Castle is with her. I can say no more,' she continued, before summoning the gumption to do so. 'Help me if you can. We are in the utmost distress and I am sure you pity us. God Bless you.'[11] Lady Betty might well be distraught. The reputation of young women in Georgian Ireland was no laughing matter, particularly a young woman in Sarah's precarious position, with neither parents nor fortune. Had she ruined herself with this escapade? How could she hope to find an all-important husband now?

The night prior to her flight, Miss Ponsonby had come to Lady Betty, knelt beside her and wept bitterly. At the time, Lady Betty was watching over her sickly daughter and assumed Sarah's tears fell from worry. Little did she know that as far as Miss Ponsonby was concerned, this was her final goodbye. After the Fowneses had settled into an oblivious slumber, Miss Ponsonby changed into men's clothing in order to conceal her identity. Then, accompanied by her faithful dog, Frisk, she crept stealthily from her room, made her way across the landing, down the stairs and into the parlour of the grand house. From there she simply opened a window and, with Frisk in her arms, leapt to the ground below. She then secured a pistol under her arm and accompanied a 'confidential Labourer', whom she had paid handsomely for his discretion, to a barn beyond Woodstock. No doubt, as the barn doors opened she felt a rush of relief wash over her. For there, in front of her, beaming in anticipation, stood her secret correspondent, Miss Butler. Reunited, they quickly left the barn to set off on the next part of their journey together. This would take them to the port at Waterford, from where they planned to abandon Ireland for good. Their adventures had begun.

Early the next morning, 31 March, the small Kilkenny village of Inistioge was a hubbub of action and intrigue. Butler, Eleanor's father, having ascertained that his daughter was missing, made haste in riding the sixteen miles to Woodstock 'to enquire for his daughter', assuming that Miss Ponsonby might be able to tell them something of the man he assumed his daughter had eloped with. When he arrived, Mr Butler was informed that a search was already under way there, as Miss Ponsonby had also disappeared. Clearly, the two had escaped together. With this new information Sir William bounded into action, sending servants scattering from Woodstock in every direction in pursuit of the missing Misses.

Sir William's servants scoured the routes in and out of Inistioge. This eventually led them to the barn where the fugitives had met before heading onwards together. Following a sweep of the grounds, one vital clue was found, 'a ruffle' from Miss Butler's clothing. Having thus conclusively established that Butler and Ponsonby had been in this particular barn and passed this specific way, it was deduced that the only logical route they could then have pursued was south, to Waterford. Confident that they were now in hot pursuit, Fownes and Butler condensed their search party into a smaller group of men headed by Butler himself and Captain Wymms of the Kilkenny Volunteers. Behind them, a cavalry set out in search of the two missing women.[12]

There are several competing accounts of what happened next, one involving another barn hideout near Waterford. Most likely, though, the ladies made their way to the docks and realized that they had missed the last sailing to Wales. Stranded, they would have to take lodgings in Waterford overnight and continue their escape across the sea the following day. The next morning, 1 April, the Butler search party arrived in the port city and set about questioning the locals as to the whereabouts of Miss Butler and Miss Ponsonby. We cannot be sure what information they managed to gather, but we know that they were eventually alerted to the location of the two escapees because Ponsonby's dog, Frisk, had been so unsettled by the downgrade in his circumstances that he had not stopped barking all night.

Soon, the search party had formed a blockade around their accommodation. Within, aware of the hopeless nature of their situation but defiant in their elopement, Miss Butler reportedly drew a pistol and aimed it squarely at the door, waiting to greet their unwelcome guests. They had come this far and they would not turn back without a fight. But by the time her father's men burst through the door (think of poor Frisk!), Miss Butler and Miss Ponsonby knew their escape had been foiled and surrendered willingly. Word was instantly sent to Kilkenny Castle and Woodstock that Butler and Ponsonby had been safely recovered in Waterford and that they would soon be transported back to Kilkenny. Upon receiving this news, an impatient Lady Betty demanded a coach be brought round to transport her to the port so she could assess the situation for herself. Simultaneously, on receiving their update, a Butler delegation set out on the same journey from the castle.

Lady Betty arrived at the docks first. She quicky concluded that both women were well, though Miss Ponsonby seemed to have caught a cold and couldn't stop sneezing. Lady Betty bundled the two runaways into her coach and hurriedly set off, back to Woodstock. However, within just a few turns of the Woodstock coach wheels, their path was blocked by the Butler party, who demanded Eleanor be handed over to them. She was to be placed under 'house arrest' in a relative's grand house in Borris, Co. Carlow, they informed Lady Betty, until the Butlers could decide what might become of her. On hearing this, Miss Butler fell to her knees and 'begged and intreated' that she be allowed to stay with Miss Ponsonby at Woodstock. However, the Butler contingent was insistent and unceremoniously 'helped' Miss Butler, 'half-fainting', into their carriage, which departed at speed for Carlow.[13] Soon after their arrival, it would be determined that Miss Butler could not be trusted to stay in Ireland at all. The Butlers had grown angry with their daughter, who, they felt, would 'feel the bad management of this rash & unaccountable action . . . during the rest of her life'.[14] The only option available to them was to deposit Miss Butler in a convent in France. There she would be hidden, forgotten and, frankly, no longer a thorn in their side.

Once they were alone in her coach, Lady Betty could not conceal her dread from Miss Ponsonby. What, or, worse still, who, had enticed Miss Ponsonby and Miss Butler from Kilkenny? Miss Ponsonby informed her guardian that their escape had not been undertaken on a whim but that it had been thoroughly planned for some time. 'Their plan', Lady Betty informed Mrs Goddard in Dublin, 'was to go to England, take a house and live together'. Though shocked at the clandestine and co-ordinated nature of their escape, Lady Betty was immensely relieved that 'there was no man concerned with either of them'.[15] Despite their unseemly departure, and the gossip that would undoubtedly ensue, if there had been no men involved reputations might yet be salvaged! With a fretful Lady Betty placated, home she and Miss Ponsonby coached to Woodstock.

Under the watchful eye of Lady Betty, a heartbroken Miss Ponsonby took to her bed, laid low by the cold brought on by her escapade. In the days following her rescue her condition worsened, and the physician was sent for. After a brief examination the physician delivered the weighty news to Lady Betty and Sir William that he had 'a great fear for her life'.[16] But even during her fevered, 'delirious' incoherence, Miss Ponsonby made it known that 'her heart was still bent upon going . . . with Miss Butler'.[17] A frightened Lady Betty wrote, once again, to Mrs Goddard in a desperate appeal for her advice. 'Oh what I would give that you were here to advise this dear girl. I fear that I shall lose her after all my care & pains.' She concluded her missive with an appreciation for the strength of the bond between her ward and Miss Butler: 'I think her still in very great danger.'[18]

As Miss Ponsonby's health showed gradual signs of improvement, letters from an incarcerated Miss Butler in Carlow arrived day after day to Woodstock. Upon receiving her companion's letters, Lady Betty tells us, Miss Ponsonby would become greatly distressed. And so Lady Betty now wrote in no uncertain terms that Miss Butler should curtail the 'volumes' of letters that continued to arrive at her house for, she implied, they were impeding the recovery of Miss Ponsonby. For whilst Miss Ponsonby suffered, Miss Butler was, by all accounts, 'very well, dines with the family, & seems cheerful'.[19] News that the Butlers planned to send their daughter to a convent in France eventually reached Lady Betty and she too thought it the best course of action given the circumstances. In fact, she lamented, 'I wish she [Miss Butler] had been safe in one long ago, which would have made us all happy. She has cost me many an unhappy hour & I fear will cost Sally many years of unhappiness.'[20]

Meanwhile, unbeknownst to Lady Betty, Sir William Fownes had approached Miss Ponsonby and 'said that he was sorry for his past folly' towards her. She had, he implied, misunderstood his intentions and if she could see fit to forgive him and remain at Woodstock then he was willing to double her allowance. But if Miss Ponsonby felt obliged to placate Lady Betty, she felt no such obligations towards Sir William. Regaining some strength, she told him that were 'the whole world . . . kneeling at her feet, it should not make her forsake her purpose – she would live & die with Miss Butler'.[21] Sir William was not her master, she retorted confidently. And if he or anybody else tried to retain her at Woodstock against her will, 'she knew her own temper so well, that she would do what would give her friends more trouble than anything she had hitherto done'.[22]

By mid-April, Miss Butler had ceased to communicate with her family and had grown tired of her confinement in Carlow. Given what was understood to be the hopeless nature of her case, she appeared to relent and eventually agreed to enter a French convent, as her mother and father desired. She would do so, however, on one condition. They must allow her a final meeting with Miss Ponsonby, a final goodbye. Miss Butler wrote in desperate terms to the kindly Lady Betty asking that she intercede on her behalf with the Butlers, that they might accept her terms before she set sail for France. Lady Betty couldn't believe that the stubborn Mr and Madam Butler would ever allow such a meeting to take place and so sent the letter of intercession, confident that the request would be denied. To her surprise, it was not. The Butlers agreed that their daughter and Miss Ponsonby should be allowed one final half-hour together. Miss Ponsonby quickly readied herself and took a coach to Borris so that she could see her companion. Once reunited, we might imagine many tears, kisses and embraces exchanged between the two women, but we do not know for certain what they discussed. However, we do know that it was during this meeting that the ladies hatched one final plan. It was agreed that on Sunday, 17 April 1779, under the cover of darkness, Miss Butler would make her escape from the house in Carlow. She would, once free, then travel to Miss Ponsonby at Woodstock, where Miss Ponsonby would oversee the secret preparations to receive her.

Mary Carryl had long been Lady Betty's housemaid and, as one of the 'lower order' of staff, would have occupied a mostly unseen

Figure 15. William Crane, 'Mrs. Mary Carol [sic]', c.1840.

role in the extended 'household family' at Woodstock. We do not know when Mary was born, only that when she was, she was born into a poor family in Ross, County Wexford. Her tombstone tells us that she died in 1809, so she was likely somewhere between twenty and forty in 1779, when these adventures unfold. Her duties at the big house would have been varied and taxing. A typical day for Mary included making beds of a morning, opening windows to air the rooms, serving tea to Lady Betty, Miss Ponsonby and the others in the afternoon, polishing stairs, fireplaces and items of furniture when the family were not about, and mending items of clothing as the nights drew in. We don't know why Miss Ponsonby chose Mary, but it would turn out to be one of the most fortunate events that could have befallen the housemaid.

That Sunday night, or very early on the Monday morning, as the rest of Woodstock slept, Mary went into the parlour and slid open the window through which a waiting Miss Butler quietly bundled herself. Then Mary, accustomed to slipping through the house unseen, guided the visitor upstairs to Miss Ponsonby's bedroom. There Miss Butler would remain for the next several days, hiding in a cupboard when necessary and subsisting on food that Mary Carryl smuggled to her.

News of Miss Butler's latest escape instantly reached Woodstock. Her family assumed that Miss Ponsonby had taken flight again too. To Lady Betty's great relief, she was able to send word to the castle that her Sally was safely accounted for in her rooms. So imagine Lady Betty's surprise when, some days later, an unknown man who worked for the Butler family presented himself at her house saying 'that he could discover where she [Miss Butler] was' hiding. Sir William asked, 'Where?' To which the man dutifully replied, 'In your Honour's house. She was let in through the . . . window on Sunday night.' At that, Lady Betty sprang to her feet, dashed upstairs and burst into Miss Ponsonby's room, where she found the fugitive and her ward, crying together in a desperate embrace.[23]

For the next fortnight, Woodstock became the focus of local gossip. The unnamed man who had revealed Miss Butler's hiding place had swiftly departed again, leaving Miss Butler at Woodstock with Miss Ponsonby and the bewildered Fowneses. As the peculiarity of their predicament revealed itself to them, Miss Butler moved amongst them like a jolly spectre, sometimes at table, sometimes hidden. It was clear, however, that Miss Ponsonby, now twenty-five, and Miss Butler, nearing forty, continued to plan their lives together away from Kilkenny.

Sir William, desperate to rid himself of Miss Butler, wrote again and again to her father pleading with him to come and take his daughter home, or at least remove her from his home so that she would stop trying to persuade Miss Ponsonby to leave. Butler, however, had had enough. He wanted nothing more to do with his troublesome daughter. She was Sir William's problem now and he ought to deal with her as he saw fit. That was until Tuesday, 28 April 1779, when Mr Butler had a change of heart and decided to resolve the matter himself.

Mr Park, the Butler family solicitor, called at Woodstock to relay the happy news that Butler would concede defeat and agree to his daughter and Miss Ponsonby living together, on the sole condition that they leave Ireland for good. Mr Park had been instructed to remain at Woodstock to discuss all necessary financial arrangements with Sir William and Lady Betty. As negotiations proceeded, Mrs Goddard, who had finally arrived at Woodstock, took it upon herself to warn Miss Ponsonby that Miss Butler had 'a debauched mind' and that 'they never would agree living together'.[24] Miss Ponsonby let her speak, then ignored her cautions entirely.

On or before Sunday, 3 May the matter of the financial settlements for Miss Butler and Miss Ponsonby was finally agreed upon and their departure set for the very next day. A cloud of anguish descended over Woodstock that afternoon. Sir William's prayers offered no comfort and even a round of Game of the Goose brought little distraction. The object of the game was to throw dice in order to progress around a board to the sixty-third spot. Each spot was decorated with goose eggs, some of which contained an obstacle, the costliest being Death. If a player landed on the death spot they had to return to the very beginning. The board game was meant to symbolize the hazards one encounters throughout one's life so, in hindsight, it was probably not the best-chosen activity for that particular day. As they played, only Miss Butler and Miss Ponsonby remained upbeat, knowing that the coach had already arrived to take them away.[25]

The following morning, even the unseasonably cold and wet spring weather could not dampen the ladies' spirits. Nobody from the castle turned up to wish Miss Butler goodbye. She would not, in fact, be mentioned in family circles for some time to come. We are left to imagine the tender farewell between Lady Betty and her dear, sweet Sally. Lady Betty will have known that she would, most likely, never see her charge again. Miss Ponsonby sought out Mrs Goddard too, to wish her well, but Mrs Goddard would not see her friend.

And just like that, Eleanor and Sarah were on the road to Waterford. Like so many Irish people before them, and significantly more thereafter, these two Kilkenny women left behind the land they had once, sometimes reluctantly, called home. From the busy port of Waterford they took to the skittish Irish Sea in a 'sail boat' and made the crossing to Milford Haven in Wales. After travelling the region for a short time, it was eventually Llangollen, the

Figure 16. James Henry Lynch, 'The Ladies of Llangollen'.

'pretty Village, on the River Dee', that persuaded them to settle there.

Once settled at their 'little cottage' that would one day charm the world, they sent to Ireland for their faithful accomplice, Mary Carryl. The summons came at just the right time for Mary, who had been dismissed from Woodstock for 'throwing a candlestick at a fellow servant & wounding her severely',[26] earning her the moniker 'Moll the Bruiser'.[27] Mary would remain in the ladies' employ at Llangollen for almost thirty years thereafter. She eventually quit their service in 1809 when death claimed her, prompting the ladies to erect a memorial to 'Our Matchless Mary' in St Collen's cemetery, Llangollen. Beside her, when her time came, Lady

Eleanor Butler was laid to rest in 1829 followed, not too long afterwards, by Miss Sarah Ponsonby in 1831. All three remain in death, as they had been in life, side by side in Llangollen.

Today Woodstock is marketed as 'Kilkenny's Natural Escape'. Drive beyond Inistioge and you'll eventually enter a world of monkey-puzzle avenues and formal gardens. Once you've parked, passing the obligatory coffee truck and having dodged your way through an assault course of maniacal children on scooters, the Palladian house Miss Butler and Miss Ponsonby once knew comes into view, though to them it would be virtually unrecognizable. It was destroyed in the first week of the Irish Civil War, July 1922, by the IRA, who wished to scupper any plans 'Free State' forces might have harboured to use it as a garrison. So, for some, the ruins of this once-grand house have come to represent the toppling of an old colonial order and the reclamation of the Irish land for Irish people. But for me, what's left of Woodstock will always be something more personal than that. For this is the site of a uniquely queer revolt. The IRA may have knocked down its walls in the twentieth century, but the remaining ruin and rubble speak to a series of moments in the late eighteenth century when Miss Eleanor Butler and Miss Sarah Ponsonby took a polite but determined stand. Here they planned a life together that others around them could not yet dare to imagine. Here it was they bent and moulded familial and societal expectations to meet their own ends. As a Kilkenny man myself, their history grounds me in a place where I once thought I could never truly belong because of my queerness. I am of that land, as were they, despite our respective subsequent scatterings. Our queerness is timeless. It runs through the ancient limestone underfoot and hangs in droplets from the sturdy bows of the evergreen. These are our roots; feel how mighty they are.

CHAPTER EIGHT
Inflammable Materials

As you may have noticed, the idea of houses, homes and their importance to queer people in the eighteenth century is a vital component of this history. Women like Lady Eleanor Butler and Sarah Ponsonby, despite their many obstacles, eventually used their womanhood and its associations with domesticity to bring together a celebrated shared home in Llangollen, for instance. Men like John, Lord Hervey and John Chute, acting within the long-established cotquean tradition, also managed to quietly carve out queer homes for themselves and their respective companions. However, some men (and women, doubtless) had no desire to replicate heteroregulated domestic traditions in their same-sex relationships. Others were deliberately denied them. What follows is an example of two such interlinked histories. But before we begin, we must correct some historical misconceptions.

Powderham Castle sits on the banks of the River Exe in Devon and was originally built in 1391 by Sir Philip Courtenay as a family home. Though it has undergone significant remodelling since the fourteenth century, the castle remains in the private ownership of the Courtenay

Queer Georgians

family and is currently overseen by the 19th Earl of Devon, Charlie Courtenay. Within the walls of this great fortress one encounters histories of French knights, the Wars of the Roses, the English Civil War and the Second World War, such is its historic legacy. In recent years, however, as a result of the 19th Earl's commitment to remembering some of the queerer elements of Powderham's past, more and more attention has been turned to one of his Georgian ancestors, the intriguing but archivally elusive William 'Kitty' Courtenay, the 9th Earl of Devon (1768–1835).[1] Kitty was involved in a number of sodomitical scandals that made headlines across Georgian England. The most famous of these took place, so we are told, in the supposed 'privacy' of Powderham Castle. In fact, so closely linked with the Courtenay homestead is this famous scandal that it has since become known simply as the 'Powderham Scandal'.

Powderham. November 1784. It was early morning, and the household had not yet risen. Mr William Beckford (1760–1844) had spent some weeks at the castle with his wife, Lady Margaret Gordon

Figure 17. Samuel Buck, 'The East View of Powderham Castle in the County of Devon', 1734

(1762–86). Both were guests of Lord Courtenay (Kitty's father), then occupier of Powderham. Beckford was, they said, England's richest commoner. His father, Alderman Beckford, had amassed his substantial wealth as a direct result of the violent subjugation of enslaved African people across thirteen sugar plantations in Jamaica. Following the Alderman's death in 1770, his son's inherited wealth stood at £1,000,000 (£135,750,000), not to mention his late father's assets and stocks.

Once he came of age, Beckford sought to connect his 'new money' with an ancient, aristocratic lineage and so approached the 4th Earl of Aboyne regarding a possible match with one of his daughters. Accordingly, on 5 May 1783, William Beckford married Aboyne's daughter, Lady Margaret, thus securing her family's financial position and taking Beckford one step closer to the peerage he so desperately desired. But that November morning, as Powderham Castle began to stir, Lady Margaret lay alone in her bed, for her husband occupied another's.

Elsewhere in the house, one Mr Moore, tutor to the then sixteen-year-old Kitty, 'heard a creaking & bustle [in the corridors] which raised his curiosity'. The unusual noises came, he thought, from his charge's rooms. Concerned, Moore made his way along the corridor in the direction of the noises. Soon he came to Kitty's bedroom door, stopped and listened awhile before lowering his eye to the keyhole, in perfect gothic fashion. Through the keyhole Moore was confronted with what he deemed to be an utterly indecent and altogether shocking 'operation'.[2]

We are left with two different versions of what Moore might have seen that night. One possibility is that he happened upon a heated argument between Kitty and Beckford regarding an incriminating letter in the teenager's possession which was said to have exposed an ongoing intimate relationship between the two. In this version of events, Beckford was so enraged that the letter had not been destroyed that he was horsewhipping the teenage boy in his chambers. Other retellings go further and state that Moore actually discovered Kitty and Beckford together in bed, *in flagrante delicto*. One way or another, armed with this intimate knowledge, the tutor supposedly quickly set about informing his pupil's father, Lord Courtenay, of what he had seen.

If we believe this version of the story, another man also played an important role in what was to come. That man was Lord Courtenay's brother-in-law and a distinguished peer, Alexander Wedderburn, better known at the time as Lord Loughborough. Loughborough was a member of the House of Lords, one-time Attorney General for England and Wales, and a future Lord High Chancellor of Great Britain. It is said that in the aftermath of Moore's discovery, Loughborough somehow seized a bunch of explicit letters that had been sent between the pair and had taken them to the press. The motive? His hatred of William Beckford. Such was his animosity that Loughborough was willing to risk the reputation of his own family to expose his enemy. As a result of Loughborough's actions, Powderham would soon become known as a den of iniquity. Lord Courtenay would be ruined and his son, Kitty, forced into exile, or worse, potentially put to death. But this received version of events has never really made much sense to me. Why on earth would Loughborough risk so much solely to get at Beckford? Doubtful, I returned to the newspaper reports regarding the scandal as they appeared in 1784 in the hope of ironing out some of these narrative inconsistencies. To my great surprise, these articles contained some small but significant clues that had been previously overlooked, ignored or forgotten. These details, I believe, not only exonerate the long-maligned Loughborough but also demonstrate that we have diligently clung to incorrect information about this scandal for nearly 250 years. What follows is an attempt to correct those misconceptions.

*

Here's what we know based on numerous sources from the time. A tutor, most likely Moore, definitely saw something one night in November 1784 that involved William Beckford and Kitty Courtenay. By 27 November, wisps of gossip relating to what he had discovered appeared in the *Morning Herald*: 'The rumour concerning a *Grammatical mistake of Mr. B*—— and the *Hon. Mr. C*——, in regard to the genders, we hope for the honour of Nature originates in *Calumny* [slander or libel]!'[3] The *Herald* reported rumours they hoped were untrue. They had no proof nor was there any mention, it is worth noting, of revelatory letters from Loughborough.

Two weeks later, the *Morning Herald* printed an update. It reads: 'If anything could heighten the detestable scene lately acted in *Wiltshire*, by a pair of fashionable *male lovers*, the ocular demonstration of their infamy, to the young, and beautiful wife of one of the monsters, must certainly have effected it.' Beckford and Kitty were both exposed and disgraced, they became 'infamous' in a matter of weeks and their story had moved from the realms of tittle-tattle to fact. But note here that the scandal in question is reported to have occurred in Wiltshire, some eighty miles away from Powderham Castle in Devon. How can we account for that discrepancy? Shoddy journalism? It seems not, for a Christmas Day letter from Charles Greville to Sir William Hamilton, which gave a less formal account of the scandal, also points to Wiltshire as the site of these queer misdeeds.[4] There is good reason for this too because Fonthill Splendens, Beckford's magnificent country seat, just so happened to be in Wiltshire.

All things considered, Beckford probably wasn't at Powderham Castle in November 1784 anyway. He had written from Fonthill to his friend Samuel Henley on 13 October telling him that 'we have been in Devonshire and passed a month at Powderham Castle'.[5] It is unlikely, therefore, that he had returned to Powderham again in November. Incidentally, during his September/October stay at Powderham, Beckford had indeed been bothered by Loughborough ('I have been wonderfully vexed and griped with L[*oughborough*]'), but the Beckford–Courtenay relationship had not been exposed during that stay.[6] We have, I think, got the details of this scandal all wrong. Here, based on multiple contemporary sources, is a more likely version of events.

Following Beckford's visit to Powderham Castle in October, he and his wife had returned Lord Courtenay's hospitality by hosting his son William at Fonthill Splendens the following month. Given the boy's age, he was accompanied by his tutor. That is why Moore was within earshot of Courtenay's rooms and why he discovered the scene between the 'fashionable *male lovers*'. And whilst Lord Loughborough did pursue 'corporal or legal Punishment for Mr Beckford's Violation of young Courtenay', he did so once their affair had been exposed and the rumour mill went into overdrive.[7] Loughborough claimed that Beckford, as the older party, had taken advantage of his teenage nephew. In this context, Loughborough's actions were a noble attempt to protect his family's honour rather than an attempt to tear it to shreds, as previously thought. If he was in possession of any letters between the pair, it is far more likely that he held on to them to mount a case against Beckford in the courts, but we have no archival proof that he ever had them.

Further, not even Beckford and his wife initially suspected that Loughborough had leaked details of the scandal to the press, much as they felt harassed by his threats of legal action. There was another man, more closely linked to Beckford, of whom they were far more suspicious. We know this because in the immediate aftermath of the scandal, on 22 November 1784, Lady Margaret Gordon, Beckford's wife, wrote to her aunt, Lady Gower. In her letter she laments Loughborough's legalistic and violent 'behaviour', naturally, but points the finger for the leak at her brother. She writes, 'I . . . think I should convince you how much to blame my brother has been.'[8]

It is almost certain that she was referring to George Gordon, 9th Marquess of Huntly (1761–1853), as her half-brother Lord Douglas Gordon was only seven at the time. Perhaps Gordon wished to free his sister from the disreputable clutches of a rumoured sodomite, despite his wealth? Or maybe, given the parlance of the day, Lady Margaret referred to one of her *brothers-in-law*. Beckford's father had sired six illegitimate sons and two illegitimate daughters, after all. There is a chance that one of these illegitimate heirs wished to disgrace their younger half-brother and claim some of their father's substantial inheritance in the process.

Figure 18. Joshua Reynolds, 'William (Thomas) Beckford', c.1782.

Whatever the leaker's motives, given the evidence presented here it would, henceforth, be more accurate to refer to the scandal in question as the Fonthill Scandal rather than the Powderham Scandal. This incidental detail matters, as it more accurately encapsulates the imbalanced power dynamic between Beckford and the youth, Courtenay, in 1784. This discovery also serves to set the scene for what came next, and the disruptive ways in which their individual queer histories would unfold.

Details of the Fonthill Scandal quickly infiltrated London drawing rooms and contaminated country piles like mould. William Beckford was wholly ruined. Friends abandoned him, he was not received in society and his hopes of a peerage were utterly dashed. On top of all that, his wife was distraught. Now faced with the threat of legal action, imprisonment and possible death, Beckford thought it prudent to remove himself and his wife from England. So on 30 December 1784 the *Morning Herald* reported that 'The Fonthill Fool is . . . in Italy.' Beckford would spend most of the following decade exiled on the continent.

Within two years, though, Lady Margaret had sadly died. She passed away just twelve days after the birth of her second daughter, Susan Euphemia (1786–1859), on 26 May 1786 at Château-d'Oex in Switzerland. Her tragic fate elicited much sympathy back in England and blame for her passing was placed squarely at Beckford's feet. 'I was stabbed to the heart by the loss of Ly. Margaret,' Beckford wrote in the wake of her death. 'And what was the balm poured into my wounds? A set of parag[raphs] accusing me of having occasioned her death by ill usage.'[9] Beckford never remarried, not out of any lingering devotional obligation to his wife, though he had loved her, but because his amorous attentions thereafter were exclusively geared towards men. Foremost amongst these was a handsome Portuguese musician named Gregório Franchi.

*

Inflammable Materials

For over 200 years, Gregório Franchi has been confined to the peripheries of the past. He has languished in Beckford's shadow, not forgotten but tantalizingly out of view. He has by turns been referred to as Beckford's agent, which is somewhat accurate, his devoted 'best friend', which seems likely, and his live-in pimp, which is perhaps a little fanciful.[10] But none of these categorizations adequately describe the complexities of their relationship. Franchi was all of these things and so much more. For the purposes of this chapter, then, I use the term 'companion' in the hope of more appropriately reflecting the nuances of their shared business interests, sex lives, and the deep love and affection they held for one another.

Gregório Felipe Francisco Franchi was born on 25 May 1770 in the Salvador district of Lisbon, the second son of Loreto Franchi (c. 1730–c.1811), an Italian singer employed at the Portuguese court, and Maria Prassede Girardi (c.1730–89), originally from Pescia, Tuscany. Gregório was primed to follow in his father's footsteps and was an accomplished musician-in-training. He attended the Patriarchal Seminary or College of Music, which had been founded in 1713 by King João V. Instruction at the conservatory college was focused initially on singing, but gradually came to include keyboard skills across harpsichord and organ, whilst demanding proficiency in grammar, writing and Catholic doctrine. It was in a private rehearsal room at the College of Music that Beckford, then twenty-six, first encountered the talented seventeen-year-old Franchi on 28 May 1787. Beckford sat and listened to Franchi's music, allowing the young man's Haydn, played on harpsicord, to quiet his busy brain.

They met again just over a month later, on 1 July, and this time Beckford recorded his impressions following their meeting. 'I think his eyes are grown larger than ever,' Beckford blushed, 'and fix themselves so inveterately upon me that I cannot help colouring ... These Portuguese youths are composed of more inflammable materials than other mortals.'[11] Beckford was smitten and wrote that he desperately wished to see Franchi again the very next day. According to Beckford's private journal, 'caresses [and] kissing' soon followed.[12]

A year after their initial meeting, in May 1788, Franchi was sent for from Lisbon to join Beckford in Madrid. This arrangement marked a near-permanent union that would last well into the following century. Franchi, on his arrival, carried with him a letter from his father Loreto which, in effect, handed over his son to the protection of the Englishman:

> With tears in my eyes I commit my son Gregory to Your Excellency, and recommend him to you, believing and hoping that your protection may be the true beginning of his fortune ... I hope to obtain from Your Excellency the kindness of persuading my son that he forget not to help his mother ... I only desire that he may show himself worthy of your incomparable protection.[13]

In many ways, this letter operates within accepted master/protégé expectations. But considering the intimate favour, considerable time and sexual attention Beckford had already heaped on his young companion, the document can also be read as a sort of queer 'marriage settlement' between Loreto and the infamous Englishman. Franchi senior agreed to transfer the responsibility for his son to Beckford. And, just as other eighteenth-century marriages were often arranged with family fortunes in mind, Loreto hints that this union will protect Franchi family interests despite Beckford's reputation.

Gregório Franchi also opted for a traditional, legal union with

Inflammable Materials

a woman in 1795 when he married Bárbara Maria de Castelo de Lage at the Shrine of Our Lady of Joy, Portugal. Bárbara was the daughter of Francisco de Lage, a Knight in the Order of Christ and a Gentleman of the Royal Household. Beckford was instrumental in putting together their marriage articles, just as Hervey had overseen Ste Fox's marriage, and granted them both an annuity. Following his marriage, Franchi was admitted into the Order of Christ alongside Bárbara's father, conferring on him the title of the Chevalier Franchi. Bárbara herself was granted a position as *Fidalga de Cota de Armas*, a noblewoman of the coat of arms. There was no love lost between Franchi and his wife, however, and he often complained to Beckford that she was stupid: '*Bete, bete, bete, à faire trembler*; I do not like betes.'[14]

Very soon after the Franchi nuptials in 1795, Beckford, hoping some other scandal had displaced his own, made the decision to return to his country estate in Wiltshire. It is likely that his return was in no small way prompted by his intimacies with Franchi, with whom he now wanted to cultivate a domestic space. Together, as the promise of the nineteenth century loomed, the two men would design, build and establish the most notoriously queer household that England had ever known. A household unlike any other.

Whilst Beckford and Franchi navigated the twists and turns of their return to England, William Courtenay, 3rd Viscount Courtenay, as he was now styled following the death of his father in 1788, had never really left. Naturally, Kitty had undertaken the customary trips to Europe as befitted a young man of his station. But, despite his role in the scandal, Powderham Castle remained his home throughout the 1780s and 1790s. He was no recluse either, jovially joining the *beau monde*. Lord Courtenay was on intimate terms with the delightfully unserious young men and women who moved in the same circles as the Prince of Wales. For him, unlike Beckford, it was as if no scandal had occurred at all. In that way, Loughborough's attempts to highlight his age and Beckford's 'violations' had worked. It should come as no surprise, then, that Courtenay marked his twenty-first birthday, his official 'coming of age', with a lavish three-day private party at Powderham from 30 July to 2 August 1790 which was attended by his fashionable friends. The festivities began with an outrageous masquerade ball which was, sartorially at least, something akin to the Met Gala today. Courtenay himself dressed in a rather camp interpretation of 'Van Dyck style', resembling the court garb of a

Figure 19. Richard Cosway, William 3rd Viscount Courtenay in his coming-of-age masquerade attire, 1790.

seventeenth-century aristocrat, as it was so often depicted by the Flemish artist. Further, he, unlike his guests, attended this opening event unmasked. He was, after all, the host. Lord Courtenay needed to be seen.

To accommodate his guests in the most extravagant style, Courtenay had altered the landscape around Powderham with several 'temporary structures, and exquisite decorations and illuminations' to heighten the otherworldly atmosphere of the castle grounds.[15] The *Public Advertiser* reported that Courtenay's lavish display of wealth and frivolity was, truly, something to behold. Artificial flowers wound round each temporary pillar and post, whilst 'upwards of ten thousand lamps' ornamented the trees. Courtenay's tables were decorated in expensive linens and featured elaborate centrepieces, with 'Friars, Nuns, Harlequins, allegoric Forms, Music, the Family Coronet, Arms, Motto, &c. – all very striking and pretty'.[16] It has been estimated that this series of events cost somewhere in the region of £9,000 (£1.1 million), an eye-watering sum even for an aristocrat. Those in attendance, like 'Bridget Purling-Stream', were all suitably gobsmacked by the fruits of said expenditure; 'Lord bless us what a fine humbledy jumbledy it was,' Bridget recalled a week later.[17] We know that Beckford had taken note of Courtenay's coming-of-age party too as a newspaper clipping detailing the celebrations was found amongst Beckford's belongings after his death.[18] In another world he would have attended. In another still, he would have hung on Kitty's arm.

That is not to say, however, that Courtenay was left entirely untarnished by the Fonthill Scandal. One contemporary anecdote had it that he was once spotted heading to court in the most marvellously extravagant carriage. Captivated by his splendour, an old woman reportedly asked a passer-by if he knew who the fine carriage belonged to. She was informed that it might be one of 'the sheriffs come to present an address from the city of Gomorrah'.[19] Still, Courtenay felt no need or desire to hide himself away. Beckford, on the other hand, wished for nothing more.

Once back in Wiltshire, William Beckford immediately set about erecting a high wall round Fonthill Splendens. If the intention was to keep prying eyes out, ironically the wall only served to attract further attention. What did the once-exiled Beckford and his new Portuguese companion have to hide? Tongues wagged once again when, in 1796, Beckford engaged the architect James Wyatt, known for his skilful commitment to the Gothic architectural style, to construct a brand-new country house on the Fonthill estate. Fonthill Splendens had only been completed in 1770, less than thirty years before, but Beckford's new mansion would replace the Palladian structure with something altogether more dramatic. Many, including the art historian Whitney Davis, have drawn a line of queer architectural inheritance between Walpole's Strawberry Hill and Beckford's new house, Fonthill Abbey. By so doing they insist on the inherent queernesses of the Gothic style.[20] The Abbey represented a chance, Beckford thought, to start again. 'Farewell to fantasies, suspicions, and threats!' he promised Franchi. 'Let us leave the past and turn to the future.'[21]

Despite this fresh start, things soon turned sour between Beckford and his architect. Wyatt failed to attend crucial on-site meetings and ignored Beckford's instructions, so the project quickly fell behind. Beckford was adamant that lost time had to be regained, so Wyatt proposed that a set of night builders be employed, at substantial extra cost, to hasten progress. So, each evening after dark, a set of nocturnal builders scaled the wooden scaffolding round the growing structure, torches in hand, and set to work. 'Beckford builds a Babel by torchlight,' it was commented, 'to gain an immortal, though infamous celebrity.'[22] In all,

Figure 20. James Wyatt, 'Design for Fonthill Abbey', 1798.

500 people worked day and night to deliver the build. As it began to take shape it resembled a striking ruined convent, said to emulate the Portuguese abbey of Batalha, a nod to Franchi's homeland. It wasn't until 1807, however, that Beckford and Franchi made the unfinished abbey their permanent home and demolished Fonthill Splendens.

Amidst all this building, tension and anticipation, it has all too easily been forgotten that Fonthill Abbey was not just Beckford's home, it was Franchi's too. Franchi travelled Europe to secure the finest pieces of art that would hang on their walls. And it was Franchi who often procured, designed and adapted items that would furnish their home. These ideas, items and inspirations are littered throughout his letters to Beckford. That is not to say that Franchi had any legal ownership of the Abbey, but the fact that this was their joint home was communicated in monetary terms. In 1808, for example, Beckford referred to the financial commitment of Fonthill as 'ours' and regretted the waste of money 'we' had previously undertaken. This expenditure was therefore viewed as fundamental to the Beckford–Franchi household, not just a collaborative interior design project.[23] Further, once gathered together inside, the interweaving tempos of their shared living arrangements demonstrate the many ways in which the Abbey fulfilled many of its desired domestic functions for both men.

The rain kept metronomic time on the windowpanes and obscured the Wiltshire countryside beyond the ever-rising Gothic Abbey, in which Franchi stood, wrapped against the cold, letter in hand. He understood by now what was expected of him and was punctual with his missives. The 'vexatious Turk', a member of the all-male household staff employed by Beckford and Franchi, suddenly appeared behind him in the room. His real name was Alidru and he was Albanian, not Turkish, but geography would not stand in the way of Beckford's fancy. Ali-dru deposited a delivery for Beckford on a table and promptly left without acknowledging Franchi. Tension between the two was not unusual. Meanwhile 'Mme Bion', another member of staff, coaxed heat from the fire, the flames glowing on the lad's handsome face.

Soon Beckford would return from his ride, miserable from having been caught in the unexpected downpour, and the air in their 'cathedralic' home became taut with the inevitability of his gloom. Franchi placed a letter for Beckford containing various quotidian updates on the harpsichord, where Beckford would reach for and consume it whilst he dried off. A longcase clock dropped seconds upon seconds into the room. The fire rumbled and crackled. True contentment, however, would prove elusive until Franchi returned to the harpsichord later that evening and took his place at the keys. Then, slowly, something like peace would emerge from Franchi's melody and the house would finally relax.[24]

Despite the domestic functions that Fonthill inevitably fulfilled, it is clear that Beckford was unable to cultivate the same type of queer domesticity that Chute and Hervey, say, had sought. The new Fonthill, with all its incomplete beginnings and endings, was more than a house but never really a home. It was a radical, sexual site. In a letter dated 8 September 1807, Beckford asked Franchi to keep an eye out for a particularly attractive young man whilst the latter visited Bath. He wrote: 'If it is at all possible, go to see an angel called Saunders who is a tight-rope walker at the Circus Royal and the certain captivator of every b[ugge]r's soul.'[25] The frankness of Beckford's correspondence, though originally written in Italian, hints at the acknowledgement of a wider network of 'buggers' who were known to one another throughout England at this time. Also worth noting here is that, between them, Beckford and Franchi (and presumably others) had started to reclaim words that were used against them. Where 'bugger' was once only seen as a slur, it was used by Beckford to denote a wider community of same-sex-attracted men to which he and Franchi belonged. Rather fascinating too is that other members of this 'buggering community' came to Fonthill Abbey specifically in search of sex.

Franchi's largely unexplored archive, kept in the Bodleian Library at the University of Oxford and part of which I had translated for the first time during my PhD research, proves particularly interesting in this regard. Writing from Fonthill to Beckford in September 1822, Franchi stated:

Neither Bestorum nor Estorum have arrived yet. Father Phillippo and the rich subdeacon have arrived. Filipus the painter,

Dibdin, [and] the bookseller Payne arrived today. This week is going to be tremendous . . . they all will bugger.[26]

Franchi wrote to Beckford in a deliberately confusing mix of Latin, Italian and Portuguese, encoding his message. This passage offers a rare explicit example of the pleasures of sex shared between men in the early nineteenth century. Franchi's words point towards the private possibilities that were available to aristocratic and gentry men. They also demonstrate the queer potential of Fonthill Abbey to blur (even if temporarily) conventional class divisions. The mixture of men accounted for in Franchi's letters ranges from handsome working-class servants to middle-class booksellers, as well as others drawn from Beckford's own rank. They were accommodated intimately at the Abbey, both emotionally and, we can now confidently reveal, sexually.

Once assembled, these men would be served (and possibly serviced) by some of Fonthill's coterie of all-male staff. This intriguing, ever-changing rotation of players was identified, just as those in Margaret Clap's had been, by female monikers. They included Marion, Silence, the Infamous Poupee, Mme Bion, Miss Long, Miss Butterfly and the ominously named 'noblewoman' Countess Pox. Beckford noted that 'it's cruel to hear of fair boys and dark Jade vases and not to buy them'.[27] And so collect them he did. Beckford wrote to Franchi again in 1811, enquiring as to which of the household staff he should sample next: 'Who will be my Eve?' he enquires of his absent companion, demonstrating that whatever understanding they had between them was not a monogamous one.[28] Beckford was not short on options for, as he himself tells us, there were many local families who had handsome young sons that they wished to add to the Beckford and Franchi collection. On 18 November 1808 Beckford wrote to Franchi regarding a possible new member of staff who had been suggested by the boy's mother: 'I have no great opinion of youths recommended with such ardour by their mothers, sisters and friends,' he told him. 'This one will be some ragamuffin – and we have enough ragamuffins here. Take no steps until we have talked it over together.'[29] When he was intrigued by a potential new boy, however, Beckford understood that wooing the lad's mother was key. 'A boy jack-ass,' he enthused in 1811, 'would it not be possible to inspire his divine mother to bring this fair treasure here? In that case I should be all sugar and the most paternal of all fathers.'[30]

It is worth considering the ages of the boys in question here, I think, as Beckford's determined pursuit can make for uncomfortable reading, particularly in our own time. Often the exact ages of the young men he writes about are not provided in his correspondence, but we know that Saunders was seventeen, for example. It is also worth noting that the term 'boy' might still be applied to working men in their early twenties, though there are certainly times when it is inferred that the boys Beckford references are fifteen or so. Considering their age and the blatant imbalance of power at play here, it is very easy to read these interactions as exploitative and abusive. In the context of the time, though, such considerations were non-existent. Until 1875, for example, the age of consent for girls in the United Kingdom was twelve (fourteen for boys); it was subsequently raised to thirteen before being raised again to sixteen in 1885. In the United States, until 1880 the ages of consent in the majority of states had been set at ten or twelve, though Delaware was an outlier in setting its legal age at seven. Such legalities are impossible for us to fathom, but it is crucial to highlight them in order to explain that the age and power dynamics we encounter at Fonthill were in no way exclusive to queer households. As such, these occurrences existed within the social and legal expectations of the day and operated within broader aristocratic conventions of power and sex – apart from the fact that Beckford and the objects of his desire were exclusively male.

Interestingly, the idea that working-class mothers in Wiltshire wished to place their sons in Beckford's household despite his reputation suggests that there was some form of recognition regarding the queer nature of the Beckford–Franchi household beyond the walls of Fonthill Abbey. It was, nonetheless, still an elite household and could offer the handsome sons of working-class mothers a chance at a different life. That said, rumours that linked Beckford to sodomy were no trifling matter. And had one of the young men from his household accused him of sodomy it could have been ruinous, as Lord Courtenay at Powderham was about to find out.

Sometime towards the end of December 1810, Lord Courtenay suddenly boarded a yacht 'and set sail . . . for America'.[31] His flight came approximately six months after the Bow Street Runners, London's prototype police department, had raided the White Swan, a molly house in London. When, owing to a lack of evidence, some of those taken up were released from Bow Street the following day they were attacked by a group of working-class women who had gathered to further disgrace the men. So rough was the women's treatment that many of them barely escaped with their lives.

Ultimately, six men were convicted of sodomy. Two others, Thomas White, a sixteen-year-old drummer of the Guards and John Newbolt Hepburn, a forty-two-year-old low-ranking commissioned officer in a West India regiment, were hanged at Newgate Prison. Beckford felt for their plight: 'Poor sods – what a fine ordeal . . . What a pity not to have . . . a magic wand to transform into triumph the sorry sequence of events.'[32] It is worth noting that according to the *Oxford English Dictionary*, at or about this time 'sod' was used as a derogatory or offensive abbreviation for 'sodomite'.[33] But Beckford once again demonstrates that this abusive term had been reclaimed within the proto-queer community in the same way 'bugger' had. Courtenay, like Beckford, will have been only too aware of the headlines and the hangings regarding the White Swan too. Within this heightened climate of targeted hate, it was not long before suspicious eyes in Devon turned towards the chief resident at Powderham Castle.

The landscape artist Joseph Farington, for instance, tells us that he spoke to a Chudleigh apothecary by the name of Mr Yard following the raid in London and that they talked about the rumours regarding Lord Courtenay's involvement with a male member of his household staff. The stories emerging from the castle were 'daily becoming more particular'.[34] Many of Devon's increasingly influential middle class now called for Courtenay to address these troubling reports, 'before the Magistrate'.[35]

Courtenay was in trouble, and he knew it. In the face of such speculation he had no choice but to flee the country, just as Beckford had done nearly two decades before. Though Beckford and Courtenay never communicated again after the Fonthill Scandal, Beckford watched these events unfold with curiosity. He did not write on the matter, but amongst Beckford's collection of clippings researchers have located the following passage:

> It is understood that Lord Viscount C. whose precipitate retreat from this country has been the subject of such general conversation, took shipping at Liverpool, with the intention of visiting, as it is said, the Brazils. As Lord C. has declined appearing to answer the charges laid before the Magistrate, a bill of indictment will, it is said, be preferred against him at the ensuing Assizes for the county of Devon.[36]

Courtenay, it was said, had 'wept like a child' before he was forced from his home.[37] Leaving England on the *Jane*, he set sail for New York accompanied, we believe, by his cousin Edward-Robert Clack, George Woods, his 'faithful servant', and another man named William Howe. Initially he travelled under a 'feigned name', but soon tired of the charade. Courtenay told his companions that he wished to resume his original identity, 'but was told it would be dangerous on acc[oun]t of the Sailors whose prejudice . . . might have bad effects'.[38] They were right to be cautious; Courtenay had escaped his homeland, but just in the nick of time.

Not long after his departure, a formal indictment was issued in England outlining Lord Courtenay's crimes, and in April 1811 a document signed by Magistrate Follett formally accused him of sodomy. The 'assault', committed 'feloniously wickedly Diabolically and against the Order of nature', had occurred on 12 December 1810, and involved the willing participation of one William Fryer, a labourer from Courtenay's estate who also stood accused. The source of the information was a member of Lord Courtenay's household staff. The lovers had been 'moved and seduced by the instigation of the Devil' in order to undertake their 'venereal affair'. Though the crime they had committed ought 'not to be named among Christians', Follett had no choice but to style it in legal terms. Lord Courtenay and Mr Fryer stood accused of 'Buggery'. It wasn't long before the charges against Courtenay became part of wider public discourse and, on 9 September 1811 the Irish magistrate Mr Robert Day recorded that Lord Courtenay was a 'disgusting Sodomite'.[39] Courtenay's reputation lay in tatters.

The details that follow regarding Courtenay's movements in America have been pieced together from numerous British and Irish press reports. Given the newspapers' distance from New York, and accounting for the time it would have taken news of his comings and goings to reach them there, numerous, often conflicting versions of Courtenay's life in America have emerged. For example, the *Exeter Flying Post* appears to give the incorrect location for the estate where Courtenay lived and an Irish newspaper, *The Freeman's Journal*, of 1 October 1813 falsely stated that Kitty had 'married a young Lady of that country [America] . . . by whom, he has already a son and heir'.[40] Nonetheless, we can piece together enough detail to track his movements in and around New York at this time.

By 6 April 1811 Lord Courtenay and his entourage had taken up residence in a modern villa in Bloomingdale, a district on what is now the West Side of Manhattan, some ten miles from the city. If, however, he had expected to be welcomed in America with open arms, a rather frostier reception awaited him. Where once Lord Courtenay had been received by royalty, he was now 'shunned by all classes of people'.[41] His reputation preceded him.

Claremont, Courtenay's villa, was 'singularly elegant [and] . . . of superior taste'.[42] Its interior was 'judiciously' arranged, 'blending comfort with . . . tasteful embellishments'. It sat in twelve 'enchanting' rolling acres described by contemporaries as 'healthy and beautiful'. The garden at Claremont was noted, and the estate's peach yield abundant. 'Young forest trees' provided Courtenay with ample shaded walks, especially during the warm summers. Despite its bucolic setting, Claremont was situated only four and a half miles by road from the centre of New York City.[43] The estate must have seemed a rather ideal place to exile oneself if one could not enjoy the comforts of one's real home. However, the outbreak of war between the United States and Britian in June 1812 meant that the potential of Lord Courtenay's American idyll was to be denied. By July the State Department decreed that the ongoing conflict necessitated all British subjects to register in their respective districts so they could be monitored. Courtenay did so, but by 9 July he had been removed from Claremont to Poughkeepsie.[44]

Once moved and further monitored, Courtenay must have felt that New York was no longer the home from home he had hoped for. And so, on 19 March 1814, he appealed for permission from the State Department to allow 'myself and family to leave this Country by the first Vessel that parts as a Cartel from any Port . . . especially from Boston or Newhaven'.[45] Though it took some months, his appeal was eventually granted, and at approximately two o'clock on 26 October 1814 William Courtenay, along with his American household staff, set sail from New York on the *Gustav Adolph*, bound for continental Europe.[46] Maybe he could settle there and finally stop running.

Despite being safely ensconced at Fonthill Abbey, Beckford had begun to feel similarly unmoored. Franchi, acting on his behalf in various business interests, was often away from the house. In these instances, Fonthill Abbey took on an altogether doleful aspect. For Beckford, the longer the build at Fonthill continued, and in the absence of his companion, the more the Abbey became 'the most shameful cesspool known to the annals of architecture'.[47] Fonthill Abbey, Beckford now knew, had ultimately failed to eradicate the trauma of his scandal and exile. Despite his attempt, he had failed to make a home. He wrote to Franchi on Monday, 17 April 1812, 'some people drink to forget their unhappiness. I do not drink, I build. And it ruins me.'[48] The house, and his past, haunted Beckford. The building swayed and groaned in the Wiltshire wind: 'All last night, I fancied I heard the ghosts,' he complained, 'sobs and groans and dying lamentations . . . Truly I can't live in this way – it isn't living at all.'[49] Again, in February 1815 Beckford observed: 'This place makes your flesh creep as soon as night falls. Yesterday I thought that everything was coming down.'[50]

By now Beckford faced financial ruin too. Amidst all this talk of palatial country houses and lavish interior design, we must remember that as an enslaver Beckford relied heavily on an income that was generated on the backs of the forced labour of up to 3,000 enslaved Black African people across his plantations in Jamaica. This ill-gotten income helped to finance his architectural whims in Wiltshire. In 1807, however, Parliament enacted the Slave Trade Act, which prevented the sale of enslaved people across the British Empire (without actually eradicating the institution itself). In light of this Act, and with the recurrence of several poor sugar-producing seasons in Jamaica, the yield from the Beckford plantations became less and less profitable. Beckford referred to this series of events as his 'sugar disasters', and ultimately they meant that he could no longer afford to finish Fonthill Abbey. 'I am planning all reforms imaginable,' he wrote to Franchi when his cash flow had finally dried up, 'I am stopping all building little by little.'[51] Begun in 1796, by 1822 Fonthill Abbey was still not entirely complete. In his dogged pursuit of the finest house in England Beckford had left himself near-penniless and wholly miserable.

It is no surprise, then, that Beckford and Franchi decided to sell Fonthill Abbey in 1822. Beckford would vacate the property and recuperate in Bath, whilst Franchi readied the house for sale. Franchi engaged the services of Christie's to sell it and its contents and, after fifteen years of keeping the public out, the gates of Fonthill were now unceremoniously flung open in order to facilitate the sale. 'Fonthill soon attracted the swarm,' one contemporary account noted, 'and was filled to overflow, by the buzzing tribe.'[52]

Amidst this considerable interest, an auction was scheduled to begin on 17 September 1822 and catalogues with admission tickets had been sold across Amsterdam, Brussels, England and Paris. However, in a dramatic turn, the auction was cancelled at the last minute when a gunpowder magnate, John Farquhar, agreed to buy the entire estate for £300,000 (£32 million). Beckford was free at last. 'Fonthill is sold very advantageously,' he rejoiced. 'For twenty years I have not found myself so rich, so independent or so tranquil.'[53] Franchi was equally delighted at first. He saw an opportunity for them both now that they were free of Fonthill's financial drain. Perhaps they could begin to cultivate a quiet, more sedate life together?

Ultimately, however, their companionship slowly began to disintegrate once they fled Fonthill. It was as if the monstrous Abbey had bound them together over the course of the last twenty-five years. Now that it was no longer their concern, Beckford took comfort in his money, buying an impressive new property in Bath and constructing follies in the vicinity of his new home. Over time he deliberately isolated Franchi; the pair now lived apart, leading Franchi, who had relied on Beckford for so long, to financial and emotional destitution. Beckford, meanwhile, comfortable with his lot once more, refused to see his former companion or even write to him. Whilst Beckford continued to count his coins, Franchi, now abandoned to a bedsit on Baker Street in London, was left penniless and bewildered by a 'distorted mind'.

Gregório Franchi died on 5 or 6 August 1828, divorced from his intimacies with Beckford and embittered as a result. He was buried in the cemetery of St Marylebone on 9 August 1828. In an act of queer kinship, Beckford's daughter, the Duchess of Hamilton, paid for his funeral costs and erected a headstone to his memory. There he remains amongst artists, actors, politicians and other notable individuals; but whilst history has granted some of Franchi's graveyard companions a legacy that draws an intermittent trickle of people to their gravesides, they do not look for Franchi. He has been cruelly obscured by the very man to whom he provided constancy and love for the majority of his adult life.

Sadly, William Courtenay died away from his home too, in Paris on 26 May 1835. He was sixty-six years old. Before he died, however, in 1831, despite his now scandalous reputation, he succeeded in re-establishing the Courtenay family earldom and assumed the title of 9th Earl. Kitty's bequest to the Courtenay family, therefore, was profound. However, despite this legacy and the current earl's determined remembrances of his queer ancestor, it was not always thus at Powderham. In 2008, for example, Devon County Council was forced to revoke the 18th Earl's licence to host civil marriage ceremonies at the castle following his refusal to allow 'gay weddings' at the property.[54] That licence, under the 19th Earl, has now been restored.

It appears there may have been some historical alterations to the 9th Earl's archive at Powderham too. Ask any researcher who has spent time leafing through the chaotic assortment of documents there and they will agree that there is remarkably little personal documentation remaining which belonged to him. No diaries, no extensive personal correspondence, not much at all. During my own visit I heard tales of possible archival tampering by staff members long gone who had been instructed to 'clean up' the 9th Earl's legacy. If that is true, then important documents regarding Kitty may have been hidden or destroyed, similar to the alleged ways in which Ste Fox's intimate letters to Hervey were disappeared by the generations of Fox-Strangways that came after him. Despite the archival gaps, though, we must continue to tell these histories as best we can, even when the telling becomes uncomfortable.

Kitty's history is easy to embrace, in many ways; an ostentatious aristocrat, sadly maligned by a legal system determined to root out and punish same-sex desire. Kitty was loved by his family and, despite his privilege, he felt an enduring responsibility to his tenants and his community, even when he decided to leave Britain. All that, plus his once-carefree flamboyance, endears him to us even now.

William Beckford, on the other hand, is a different matter. To spend any significant time with the Beckford papers is to encounter a difficult man, an abusive man, an enslaver. The leaves of his archive are an unpleasant place to dwell. Whilst working through his words, I found myself taking inadvertent steps closer to the gloom; dark clouds began to gather as a result of his never-ending moaning and his exploitative nature. It has been suggested that Beckford ought to have a new biography and that I might be well placed to write such a book, given my broader historical expertise. But I could think of nothing worse than spending any more time than I already have 'with' him. Nonetheless, Beckford's history acts as an important reminder that the queer past cannot solely focus on heroic pursuits and the determined opposition to regulated expectations. Ben Miller and Huw Lemmey's work has shown this again and again.[55] In some instances, particularly those that involve wealthy aristocratic men, though their queerness marked them out as 'other' they also used their privilege to exploit household staff or subjugate Black enslaved peoples. It is important to recount these unpleasant parts of the queer past too, even when that unpleasantness is perpetrated by an icon of our community, as we shall see in the next chapter.

CHAPTER NINE

Geranium Sylvaticum

ON THE NORTH-WESTERN SIDE of Goodramgate in York, England lies Holy Trinity Church. This, archaeologists have discovered, has been a religious site since the twelfth century, but the majority of the quaint sandstone building that awaits you today dates from the fifteenth. As you walk through the eighteenth-century red-brick archway at No. 70 Goodramgate, the bustle of a busy shopping street gives way to birdsong and a remarkable sense of peace. The grounds are littered here and there with sinking headstones, whilst a short stone path leads you to an inconspicuous entrance and, in turn, on to wonderfully uneven flagstones. Once inside, if you're lucky you'll find flickering candles in wrought-iron stands attached to the most exquisite boxed pews, a post-Reformation addition, inviting you to sit and reflect. The honey-coloured interior vibrates with a chorus of forgotten pleas, offered up to the rafters across the centuries. But beyond its undeniable beauty, Holy Trinity Church is also an unlikely queer landmark. For it was here, we are told, that Miss Anne Lister and Miss Ann Walker (1803–54) 'exchanged vows' on 10 February 1834.

According to some historians, journalists and Lister enthusiasts, the Lister–Walker union was 'a historic lesbian church wedding'.[1] In *Gentleman Jack* (2019), the hugely successful TV series based on Lister's life, Sally Wainwright depicts this historic union; Lister (Suranne Jones) and Walker (Sophie Rundle) approach the church in a carriage. Bells peal as the women exchange rings, kissing one another in blissful anticipation. They then leap from their carriage and Lister looks at us directly, smiling broadly in acknowledgement of the momentous occasion.

Inside, under the warm glow of candlelight, both women are seated together in a pew. They look to one another in agreement, smile and prepare to take the sacrament. Then they kneel, side by side, take the body and the blood, exchange a knowing glance and progress back down the aisle, intimately intertwining their little fingers as they go. Seated again on their pew, Lister and Walker swap another loving look. It is done. They are wed. It makes for a wonderful piece of drama.

In 2019 the York Civic Trust erected a blue plaque, trimmed in the rainbow colours, on the wall outside Holy Trinity Church which has become a 'must-see' on queer tours of England.[2] It reads:

> Anne Lister
> 1791–1840 of Shibden Hall, Halifax
> Lesbian and Diarist;
> took sacrament here to seal her
> union with Ann Walker
> Easter 1834

A fitting reminder of a groundbreaking and previously hidden history. Except, I am sorry to say, the plaque does not quite reflect the true nature of the Lister–Walker union, particularly as it relates to that specific site. That, as we shall soon discover, was a far more

Geranium Sylvaticum

complex affair and more nuanced than a single well-intentioned memorial can communicate.

Anne Lister was born in Yorkshire to Rebecca Battle (1770–1817), wife of the downwardly mobile Captain Jeremy Lister (1753–1836), on 3 April 1791, a day assigned to the memory of St Richard of Chichester, patron saint of all coachmen.[3] Captain Lister, as the youngest son of the Shibden Hall Listers, had no claim to the family estate and so embarked upon a military career in order to make a living. He and Mrs Lister subsequently went on to have a family, though they endured the sad loss of three sons and a daughter. John Lister (1789–89) died whilst in the care of his wet-nurse, Jeremy Lister (1801–2) died in similar circumstances and an unnamed, stillborn daughter was born and died in 1806. Later, the only surviving Lister son, Samuel Lister (1793–1813), a junior-rank officer in the 84th (York and Lancaster) Regiment, died by drowning whilst stationed in Fermoy, Ireland. Thus the Lister legacy was left in the hands of Anne and her younger sister Marian (1798–1882).

Anne was bright and educated privately, first at Ripon and then at the Manor School in York. Whilst at York, Lister lodged with Miss Eliza Raine (1791–1860), the orphaned heiress of an English East India Company doctor and an Indian mother. At fourteen, the girls found comfort and constancy together in a room in the eaves of the Manor, which they affectionately referred to as 'the slope'. There Lister and Raine cultivated an intense teenage romance which would, eventually, sour and result in Miss Raine's confinement to psychiatric care. Though she is often skipped over in retellings of Lister's history, the tragedy of Eliza Raine has been the inspiration behind many literary imaginings. Some critics have claimed that it was, in fact, the story of Miss Raine that inspired Charlotte Brontë to summon Bertha Rochester in *Jane Eyre* (1847).

Figure 21. Shibden Hall.

The Irish author Emma Donoghue has also provided a thrillingly astute and heartbreaking imagining of the Lister–Raine affair in her 2023 novel *Learned By Heart*. But by 1815, done with school and Miss Raine, a now twenty-four-year-old Anne Lister abandoned the monotony of her home life at Market Weighton and went to live with her unmarried uncle, James Lister, and his unmarried sister (also named Anne) at Shibden Hall in Halifax.

Shibden Hall's roots run deep into the West Yorkshire landscape. At times it can appear as though it has sprung up from the earth by itself, rather than having been placed upon it. Today it is a coherent blend of architectural trends, reflecting its long and varied history, though arguably its most iconic feature is the half-timbered face of the house in the Tudor style. In 1815 Shibden Hall lay at the centre of the waning Lister 'empire', which had been established in the early seventeenth century and was built on the once-buoyant enterprise of the Lister textile mills. It was within the context of this relative privilege that Anne Lister realized that she might yet shape her place in the world on her own terms.

On Wednesday, 25 December 1816, an impatient Anne Lister confided to her diary that she 'Wished I could persuade my friends to let me try & do something for myself.' She was sure that she could 'make two or three hundred pounds if I might . . . do as I liked'.[4] Lister continued defiantly that 'I should not scruple to throw off my petticoats' in order to achieve her ends.[5] In April 1820 Lister wrote that she possessed 'the civility of a well-bred gentleman'. Later, in May 1821, she recorded that she had imagined herself 'in men's clothes & having a penis'.[6] If manliness (particularly in its elite form) was the standard by which further privilege might be obtained in late-Georgian society, it is clear that Anne Lister aspired to meet that standard and harness its privilege.[7]

Lister's masculine fluency was also widely acknowledged by her contemporaries.[8] For example, on Sunday, 28 June 1818, as Lister strode along Cunnery Lane within the Shibden parkland, she noticed three working men standing idly by a gate. As she neared, she caught a whiff of their trite bravado from afar as they jostled one another in preparation for her passing. She knew what was coming next. She'd heard variations on the same theme many times since she had returned to Halifax from York. As she passed, one of the men observed, 'That's a man,' to the great amusement of his pals. Lister walked on, unfazed. Then, from within the abusive chortling emerged an enquiry: 'Does your cock stand?'[9] By now Lister had left the laughing men behind, but the encounter made enough of an impression for her to record it in her diary that night. This was, clearly, an act of verbal aggression, but within it was a tacit recognition that Lister could participate in certain public codes that inferred masculinity.

However, Lister's masculinity also meant that in some polite circles she was treated as an outcast. On 15 September 1823, for instance, whilst staying at Scarborough, the Misses Morritt and Goodric thought it beneath them to 'pay me [Anne] some civility'. They would not receive Lister in private at all and barely acknowledged her in public. The source of this snub, Lister later deduced, was a Miss Fountaine of Bath, who had in 1814 'told [the Misses Morritt and Goodric] . . . that I was masculine & said what they have never forgotten'.[10]

Throughout her life, Lister would enact this commitment to her masculinity in four interconnected ways. Principally, in her determination for taking a wife who ought to occupy a traditional role in her household, but also in her interactions with the law of the land, in her political beliefs and in her devotion to her faith. We shall explore Anne Lister's desire to take a wife in depth below, but it is worth pointing out here that, despite her sex, as heir to the Shibden estates she stood to benefit from a legal strategy that ultimately reinforced male control over the vast majority of women. In that sense she might be read not as a radical disrupter but as the exception that reinforced the rule. This idea is further bolstered by Lister's role as a committed Tory and Anglican, through which she worked to preserve the rights and privileges of the landowning aristocracy. In these ways Anne Lister was a patriarch.

Beyond her widely acknowledged masculinity, Lister also conducted the significant intimate relationships in her life with other women. As is well documented, she enjoyed a string of sexual affairs throughout her life which are recorded in great detail in her diary. She fell madly in love with some of these women too. Mariana Belcombe (1790–1868) was, arguably, the love of Anne Lister's life. Belcombe was the spirited daughter of a York physician under whose care Eliza Raine had been placed following the disintegration of her Manor School relationship with Lister.

Geranium Sylvaticum

Miss Lister and Miss Belcombe first met at Langton Hall, home of the Norcliffe family, in 1812. By 1814 they had formed a sexual and emotional intimacy so strong that they promised they would spend the rest of their lives together. By 1816, however, despite these promises, Miss Belcombe had become Mrs Lawton, the mistress of Lawton Hall, following her marriage to Charles Lawton, a wealthy Cheshire landowner. Inevitably the Lawton marriage prompted Lister to question if 'M[ariana] and I will ever get together' openly and on their own terms, as they had promised one another.[11] Lister correctly predicted that this marriage would keep the new Mrs Lawton from her bed, driving a wedge between them.

By July 1821, Lister had not seen Lawton for a year and a half. In that time Lister had flirted with the idea of taking other women in her place. A local girl from Halifax, Emma, had proved a jolly plaything, for example, but no more than a harmless distraction. Come the summer of 1821, though, Lister and Lawton had finally arranged to meet in Newcastle once again. Lister was nervous at the prospect of seeing her love after so long. Would she feel differently about her now? Had the time and distance between them altered their affections? Faced with the imminent prospect of their reunion, in the late afternoon of 22 July 1821 Lister downed 'two glasses of wine after dinner' to steady her nerves.[12]

She need not have worried. Secreted away in the privacy of their Newcastle lodgings, the embers of their old intimacies sparked and reignited with ease. Lister was soon 'thoroughly convinced of M[ariana]'s attachment & devotion to me'.[13] They had persisted, despite Lawton's marriage, and Lister, ecstatic at finding their love as strong as ever, now wished to formalize their union.

That Sunday night, 22 July, Lister and Lawton pledged their faith to one another, privately exchanging rings to mark their union. They then 'agreed to solemnize our promise of mutual faith by taking the sacrament together' when they were both next at Shibden.[14] They would live at Shibden Hall when Lister inherited, with Aunt Anne and Marian, Lister's younger sister, if the latter did not marry. It would be a brilliantly belligerent female enclave, with very little need for men. A jubilant Lister wrote, 'I love & trust her & shall henceforth only hope that we shall one day be happy together.' They would find a way. They must, Lister surmised, seeing how distraught Mrs Lawton was when they parted ways once more on 29 July. Lister, however, was hopeful that their time apart might not be so extended as before. Had not Mr Lawton 'been unwell & in a bad humour all the week' after all? If they could not contrive their lives together whilst Mariana remained married, perhaps her imminent widowhood would see to it for them? No such luck. Charles Lawton soon rallied and would stick around for some time to come, as inconvenient husbands tend to do.

What Mrs Lawton needed, Lister decided, was an example to follow, then she could muster up the courage to abandon Lawton Hall and join Lister in West Yorkshire. As luck would have it, Lister had read an intriguing article in *La Belle Assemblée* about two ladies so devoted to one another that they had conspired to leave their native Ireland and set up a shared home in Wales. Come the summer of 1822, then, taking Mrs Lawton and her Aunt Anne with her, Lister set out to pay a visit to Plas Newydd in the Vale of Llangollen.

July 13 1822. Anne Lister was not, at first, enamoured of north-eastern Wales. The undulating hills seemed naked and alien to her, whilst the limestone quarries sank great unsightly giants' footprints into the landscape. Upon arriving in the little town of Llangollen itself, however, more of the romantic rural idyll she had pictured emerged in the settling dusk.

Geranium Sylvaticum

The Listers had started their journey from Shibden Hall on Thursday, 11 July, meeting Mrs Lawton at Northwich, Chester, the following evening. On Saturday the 13th the trio then undertook the four-and-a-half-hour journey to Llangollen by carriage and, when they arrived, were relieved to find comfortable repose at the King's Head New Hotel. The inn was located close to the bridge that led in and out of the little town and Lister could hear the waters of the River Dee burbling nearby.

Since settling at Plas Newydd more than forty years earlier, Lady Butler and Miss Ponsonby had become unlikely celebrities. It was not so much that 'the Ladies', as they were known locally, were two women living together – that, in itself, was not unusual – but the depths of their shared love and devotion had caused a stir. Once they found Plas Newydd, it was said that Butler and Ponsonby 'never slept out of it a single time' again.[15] By 1822, the ladies had transformed their Welsh stone cottage into a Gothic fantasy, in keeping with the tastes of the day. They added intricately carved oak panelling that had been reclaimed from much older churches to the walls and dramatic stained glass throughout. The gardens had been artistically remodelled too. Small Gothic follies, such as an imitation ancient ruin, littered the grounds, whilst a collection of exotic fruit thrived in their greenhouse. Around the garden, pinned to carefully chosen trees, poetry extracts fluttered in the Welsh winds.

The home Butler and Ponsonby had created at Plas Newydd was thought to be so singular and so idyllic that it was featured in numerous fashionable magazines like the one Lister had read. Once word got out, the ladies were inundated with requests to visit them in Llangollen; some people even wished to stay a while in the cottage. Illustrious guests included Sir Walter Scott, Percy Shelley, Lord Byron and William Wordsworth.

Wordsworth was so impressed by his visit that he wrote a sonnet addressed 'To Lady Eleanor Butler and the Honourable Miss Ponsonby, Composed in the grounds of Plas-Newydd, Llangollen'. It reads:

> A stream to mingle with your favourite Dee
> Along the Vale of Meditation flows;
> So styled by those fierce Britons, pleased to see
> In Nature's face the expression of repose,
> Or, haply there some pious Hermit chose
> To live and die—the peace of Heaven his aim,
> To whom the wild sequestered region owes
> At this late day, its sanctifying name.
> Glyn Cafaillgaroch, in the Cambrian tongue,
> In ours the Vale of Friendship, let this spot
> Be nam'd, where faithful to a low roof'd Cot
> On Deva's banks, ye have abode so long,
> Sisters in love, a love allowed to climb
> Ev'n on this earth, above the reach of time.

And, whilst she never visited, Queen Charlotte (already patron to the Chevalier d'Éon) convinced her husband, George III, to grant Butler and Ponsonby a royal pension too.

It is also clear, in keeping with queer traditions already examined in the case of the Chuteheds, for instance, that the Butler–Ponsonby union was read as a marriage by contemporaries too. Princess Caroline, for instance, concluded: 'Lady Eleanor Butler and Mlle. Ponsonby . . . must be mad, I should think, to choose to leave the world, and set up in a hermitage in Wales,—*mais chacun a son goût*,—it would not be mine . . . I do dread being married to a lady friend. Men are tyrants, *mais* the women—heaven help us! They are *vrais Neros* over those they rule.'[16] Anne Lister had no

Figure 22. W. L Walton, 'Plas Newydd', 1840.

poetry to write there; instead it was this idea of being 'married to a lady friend' that drew her to Wales.

Upon her arrival in Llangollen, Lister had 'strolled thro' the town to Lady Eleanor Butler's & Miss Ponsonby's place', but having not yet declared herself, she dared not contravene the rules of Georgian visiting customs which dictated that as she was unknown to them she ought to write ahead. She therefore refrained from presenting herself that evening. Instead she made her way back to the hotel, where Lister tells us that she, Aunt Anne and Mrs Lawton ate heartily of 'excellent roast leg of mutton, & trout, & very fine port wine, with every possible attention'.

Back in their rooms and sated, Lister took pen in hand and set her intentions to paper. 'To the Right Honourable Lady Eleanor Butler & Miss Ponsonby, Plâs Newyd [sic],' she began,

> Mrs & Miss Lister take the liberty of presenting their compliments to Lady Eleanor Butler & Miss Ponsonby, & of asking permission to see their grounds at Plâs Newyd in the course of tomorrow morning. Miss Lister . . . had intended herself the honour of calling on her ladyship & Miss Ponsonby . . .[17]

The response came that Lady Butler was, sadly, too ill to receive guests but that they might be permitted to see the grounds at 12 p.m. the following day.

On Sunday, only Lister and her aunt walked to Plas Newydd, where they were greeted by the gardener, 'a good sort of intelligent man, much attached to his mistresses after having lived with them 30 years'. Lister, no stranger to landholding and land management, chatted to him about the ladies' cows, their milk and the superior cream which they cultivated from it. 'My expectations were more than realized,' she wrote that evening, 'I could have mused for hours, dreamt dreams of happiness, conjured up many a vision of . . . hope.'[18] The life she had imagined for herself and Mrs Lawton was indeed possible. A version of it existed in Llangollen. She had experienced it, smelt the summer grass, flirted with its carefully cultivated bloom. Still, she had not seen the ladies themselves and wondered, given local stories of Lady Butler's continued ill-health and Miss Ponsonby's associated grief, if she ever would. 'I am interested about these 2 ladies very much,' she pined in her diary. 'There is something in their story & in all I have heard about them here that, added to other circumstances, makes a deep impression.'

Finally, on Tuesday afternoon, 23 July, ten days after the party had arrived, Anne Lister received word from Miss Ponsonby. She would 'be glad to see me this evening'. Lady Butler would be resting but to chat with Miss Ponsonby would in itself be a thrill. Lister wondered 'what will she think of me' as she washed and cut her toenails in anxious preparation for her visit. She dressed in smart, clean clothes before setting off.

Anne Lister arrived at Plas Newydd at 7 p.m. that evening and was led to the breakfast room, where she waited for her host. After a tense minute or so, a toothless Miss Ponsonby, now somewhat frail in her sixty-seventh year, 'waddled' into the room. Ponsonby sported a

> blue, shortish-waisted cloth [riding] habit, the jacket unbuttoned shewing a plain plaited frilled habit shirt – a thick white cravat, rather loosely put on – hair powdered, parted ... down the middle in front, cut to a moderate length all round & hanging straight, tolerably thick.[19]

Altogether, Lister concluded, Miss Ponsonby cut 'a very odd figure'. Odd was something Lister could relate to. Despite Ponsonby's gumminess and her waddle, Lister was immediately taken in by her delicate manners and intelligent conversation. Lister found that although Ponsonby was not a manly woman (like herself), she had a certain *'je-ne-sais-quoi'* about her nonetheless.[20]

Together, these two women filled the breakfast room at Plas Newydd with polite chit-chat concerning literature and Lady Eleanor. Miss Ponsonby then asked Lister to join her for a walk through the garden. There they chatted further about Lister's own home, Shibden Hall. As they talked, Miss Ponsonby reached down and picked a sprig of geranium for Lister's absent aunt and a rose for Lister herself. There, amongst the brilliant pink of the gynodioecious cranesbill, a plant which might bear only female flowers, Lister silently and unknowingly inherited a queer legacy. A legacy that had been carefully cultivated by Butler and Ponsonby before her. A legacy that she might, one day, pass to another.

★

Although we do not know how Miss Ponsonby felt about Lister's visit that day, it made a lasting impression on Lister. Later that night, whilst writing in her diary, she made plans to 'dry & keep the rose' Ponsonby had given her, a keepsake from her visit and a reminder of the idyll she might shape for herself. However, despite being buoyed by their earlier conversation, Lister now 'felt low'. She had hoped to excite Mrs Lawton with the realities and possibilities of Llangollen. Instead, with the scents of Plas Newydd still swirling about her, it was becoming ever more obvious to Lister that her version of what Butler and Ponsonby had achieved could no longer include Mariana Lawton.

Mrs Lawton had been feeling 'some delicacy' about the tensions between her devotion to her lover and her duty to her husband. She may not have loved the man, 'yet the kindness & obligation' he had towards her made her uneasy to be ever 'calculating the time or thinking' of his demise. Even whilst they remained at Llangollen, Lister began to feel Mariana Lawton slip away from her. 'Seeing M[ariana] has been no comfort to me,' she lamented on 17 July 1822. 'When I asked her how long she thought it might be before we got together . . . she seemed to fight off answering.'[21]

That night in Wales Lister lay with Mrs Lawton once more, but 'was almost convulsed with smothering my sobs'. A near-decade-long love affair fought for its final breaths, rattling remembrances of earlier electrifying sparks. What did Lister have if she lost Mrs Lawton? Whom could she call her own? If Lawton felt the weight of Lister's sobs through the mattress that night 'she took no notice' and let her companion's tears fall.[22]

Lister's relationship with Mrs Lawton had been important to her for two reasons. In the first instance, she loved Mariana dearly. More important still, Lister believed that a marriage-type union with Mrs Lawton could grant her (Lister) further respectability and autonomy, much in the same way that marriage did for single

Geranium Sylvaticum

men. Lister held fast to a traditional ideal of the Yorkshire squire: the Hall, the land, the mills, the rents and the wife. The Ladies of Llangollen had certainly secured widespread respectability and autonomy because of their union; it was not unreasonable to think she might expect the same.

On 10 July 1819 Lister wrote in her diary that 'I must have someone who had the same authority in my house as a wife would have in her husband's house.'[23] The house must be Lister's, but not the wifely role. On 3 May 1820 she wrote: 'Musing on the subject of being my own master . . . Of going to Buxton in my own carriage with a man & a maidservant. Meeting with an elegant girl of family & fortune; paying her attention' and making a wife of her. Whether Lawton was on board or not, Anne Lister was still determined to obtain marital respectability. She must become a 'female husband'.

The term 'female husband' was brought to popular attention in Jen Manion's book *Female Husbands* (2020). The original term, however, can be traced to a broadside, *The Male and The Female Husband*, published in 1682. This relayed the 'shocking' true story of the nurse Mary Jewit, an intersex individual who had been brought up by a midwife at St Albans, England, having been abandoned at birth. Mary was raised female and, as an adult, eventually got another woman pregnant. Jewit was henceforth ordered by a judge to live as a man and marry the pregnant lover, terms to which Jewit agreed.[24] In that respect, the long tradition of the female husband was closely tied to gender non-conformity. In Lister's case, however, she wished to disrupt ideals of early-nineteenth-century patriarchy not by challenging it but by becoming part of it.

In January 1826, following instructions contained in the will of Anne's childless uncle, James Lister, Anne Lister inherited Shibden Hall along with part of the income from the lands, houses and estates that had once belonged to him. This fortuitous inheritance suddenly placed her amongst the most important Halifax landowners of the time and granted her a new kind of agency and power that few women commanded. It gave her the means to become financially independent, though the debts and financial burdens of running an ancient estate in decline became hers too.

Lister used her new-found status and riches to see something of the world. In fact she was one of the most prolific female explorers of her time. She lived in Paris, taking anatomy lessons under the tutelage of the elaborately coiffed naturalist Baron Georges Cuvier. In 1838 she conquered Vignemale, the highest of the French Pyrenean summits. She also visited Switzerland, the Low Countries, Germany, Scandinavia and Russia. A traditionalist, this was, for all intents and purposes, Lister's Grand Tour – another social marker of her masculinity.

Once back in Shibden, Lister ambitiously took control of her estates. From 1832 she set about putting together various teams of men who would redevelop 'shabby Shibden' under her instruction. Thus commenced a cacophony of digging, breaking, hammering and chiselling that echoed with glorious industry into the West Yorkshire sky. Lister's voracious intellect meant that she devoured the most up-to-date books on business, politics, geology, engineering and evolutionary biology. This appetite for knowledge helped inform her approach to managing her estate, particularly in the development of her coal mines to the north and south of the Hall. Vital rental income from the farms and cottages on the estate generated some of the funds that allowed Lister to develop her more ambitious projects, but she still needed more money.

With that in mind, what Lister had not yet managed to secure was a wife. Her pool of potential partners was somewhat smaller than that of the average landed Yorkshireman. Any prospective 'wife' would need to be unmarried (Lister had learnt her lesson with Mariana Lawton) and would, ideally, be the heiress to a large fortune. Lister had the additional burden that any potential match also needed to be willing to take another woman as her companion. That left Lister with a single eligible option: Miss Ann Walker.

Ann Walker began her adventures on 20 May 1803, two days after Britain declared war on France. The Napoleonic Wars would rage for the next ten years, claiming between 3 and 6 million military and civilian lives in the process. For context, the British census of 1801 indicates that the population of Britain at the time was approximately 10.5 million in total. So, by any metric, the loss of life in these wars was catastrophic. Against this harsh international backdrop little Miss Walker enjoyed a peaceful life in the West Riding of Yorkshire. Her very earliest years were spent at Cliffe Hill, near Halifax. Her father, John (1753–1823), was a very wealthy local merchant who married Mary Edwards (1763–1823), Ann's mother, the daughter of another wealthy businessman, in 1795. The Walkers were soon joined by little William (who died in childhood) in 1798, Mary in 1799, Elizabeth in 1801, Ann, and finally John in 1804.

When Ann was six years old her growing family abandoned Cliffe Hill for Crow Nest, a grand country seat in the Palladian style which her father inherited following the death of his brother. Crow Nest was newer than Lister's Shibden Hall and, to a modern eye, more genteel in appearance. But Lister, with the blood of an ancient lineage coursing through her veins, would have seen the Walkers as 'new money' and beneath her socially, despite their wealth.

Whilst Miss Walker's young life was materially comfortable, it was also marked by tragedy. On 1 February 1815, when she was just eleven, her sister Mary died. Miss Walker later lost both of her parents to illness in 1823, her father on 22 April followed by her mother on 3 November. This meant that her home, Crow Nest was inherited by her brother, John. However, when John was honeymooning in Naples in 1830 he too died, leaving Ann and her sister Elizabeth as sole inheritors of the Walker estate and its considerable associated wealth. Elizabeth had married Captain George Mackay Sutherland in 1828 and lived in Ayrshire so, at twenty-eight, Ann Walker became the de facto mistress of the Walker estate in Halifax. As she was now alone Miss Walker abandoned the too-large Crow Nest property (which would later be rented) and took up residence at Lidgate, a smaller home in her property portfolio, in 1831.

At Lidgate Walker endeavoured to cultivate a simple life for herself with the help of a servant, James Mackenzie, and a housekeeper, Sarah, who oversaw the rest of her staff. However, this domestic idyll was frequently interrupted by legal wranglings with her brother's widow, Fanny Penfold. John had died without leaving a will, so Fanny proceeded to claim part of the Walker estate by right of marriage. Though the matter was eventually settled, the stress of it left Miss Walker anxious and prone to 'hysteric' spiralling.

Walker's family were no strangers to her 'gloomy despondency' and she herself was only too aware that, at times, 'evils seem to increase upon me'.[25] To combat these evils, when she could, Walker lost herself at her piano and exorcised her mind through drawing and steady, confident sketching. She knitted and sewed too, measuring her thoughts in loops and stitches. From 1832, however, a year after she inherited her fortune, Ann Walker's life at Lidgate was upended, for better and worse, when she became reacquainted with Anne Lister.

The first meeting between Lister and Walker was neighbourly in nature; they lived two miles apart. 'Called on Miss Walker of

Lidgate & sat 1 ¾ hour with her – found her very civil & agreeable.'[26] The pair saw one another again on 17 August 1832, this time spending three hours together. Unbeknownst to Ann Walker, Anne Lister had already begun to seriously consider her as a possible wifely candidate. 'She little dreams what is in my mind,' Lister recorded in her diary, 'She has money and this might make up for rank.'[27] This is the first mention Lister makes of Walker's money, but it would not be the last.

Lister began her tactical courtship, proffering gifts and tokens that would endear her to Miss Walker. Things progressed rapidly and by 27 September Lister recorded that 'Miss W—& I very cozy & confidential . . . I can gently mould Miss W—to my wishes; & may we not be happy?'[28] Even at this early stage, it is clear that Lister would conduct her relationship with Walker on two levels. On the surface of it, the flirtatious interactions, gifting and promises were meant to sway Ann Walker towards her. Underneath that, however, were Lister's own private thoughts, recorded in her diary, which were altogether more calculated, more precise, and more focused. The very next day, 28 September, Lister noted: 'Bordering on love-making in the hut . . . Our liaison is now established.'[29] Wasting no time, on October 1, after about three months of knowing one another, Lister approached Walker about coming to live with her at Shibden Hall. We might interpret the invitation as an attempt towards the fulfilment of a sincere domestic dream based on a shared love and affection if it weren't for Lister's plotting prior to the suggestion. But, in response, Walker 'spoke of her great attachment' to the Walker estate and her reluctance to leave it, much to Lister's frustration.[30]

Lister's intense, determined attentions towards Ann Walker had stirred certain misgivings in the extended Walker family circles, many of whom saw Walker as vulnerable because of her wealth. Mrs Eliza Priestley, for instance, was Anne Lister's long-time friend but she was also married to Ann Walker's first cousin, William Priestley. The Priestleys lived at Lightcliffe, on the Walker estate, where they could inconspicuously monitor Lister's comings and goings. On 29 September 1832, for example, Mrs Priestley had seen Anne Lister arrive at Lidgate and, fuelled by her suspicions that Lister sought to exploit Walker, thought she might 'surprise' the women with an unannounced visit to ascertain the nature of their frequent meetings.

Priestley, known to Walker's household staff, easily gained access to the inner rooms at Lidgate whilst Lister and Walker were entangled in a passionate kiss, ignorant of their intruder's approach. Suddenly, on hearing someone at the door, Lister unwrapped herself from Walker and 'jumped up'. At the same time, Priestley entered the room. The colour drained from Lister's face. Ann Walker, who had come asunder somewhat, blushed, but did not move from her sofa. Mrs Priestley said not a word, merely observed the scene, 'looked vexed, jealous and annoyed' and made a dramatic exit, slamming the door behind her.[31]

If Mrs Priestley reported what she had seen that afternoon, she mentioned it only in the most trustworthy family circles, for Lister and Walker continued their affair unimpeded. Nonetheless, Walker herself had, likely due to her religious observances, struggled to come to terms with their same-sex intimacies. 'She thought it wrong to have connection with me,' Lister lamented. At such moments of acute feeling Miss Lister wondered what, exactly, she had begun, remarking, 'She [Walker] will not do for me.'[32]

By 14 December 1832, though, less than two weeks after she had lingered on the idea that they were not at all well suited, Lister was pressing Ann Walker to formalize their union once again. Lister played Walker's religious doubts to her advantage this time, arguing that 'without any tie between us [their relationship was] as wrong as any other transient connection'.[33] Walker, still unsure, eventually agreed with Lister that any union between them 'should be the same as a marriage'.[34] Lister seized on this opportunity to suggest that when the time came they ought to seal their union over a Bible and take the sacrament together to solemnize the occasion in the eyes of God. But when Walker showed no immediate signs of following Lister's orders, Lister became impatient once again. 'She wants my services & time and friendship, & to keep her money to herself.'[35] Amidst all this talk of grubbing (used throughout Lister's diary as a reference to sex), love, God and marriage, it is clear that it was Walker's fortune that predominantly occupied Lister's mind.

Ann Walker was soon presented with the opportunity to marry a blandly pleasant man named Mr Ainsworth. The match was broadly encouraged by the Walkers, the Priestleys and the Sutherlands alike. But in the face of such a prospect, Ann Walker's mood quickly deteriorated. She became unpredictable and low, and a gloom settled over Lidgate. Under the circumstances it was decided that Miss Walker would be best off in Scotland with her sister. This would give her time to recover and return to herself. Lister and the Priestleys agreed that Ann should go as she 'required a physician accustomed to mental suffering' and, it was felt, her sister could see to that. Walker herself did not want to leave Halifax.[36] Her feelings on the matter counted for little, however, and Lister recounts watching her depart for Scotland two days later, accompanied by her brother-in-law, Captain Sutherland, and his mother. Lister was not sorry to see the back of the woman she had, only a matter of weeks previously, proposed to make her wife. 'Heaven be praised,' she exclaimed later that night, once she had retreated to Shibden, 'I have got rid of her & am once more free.'[37] Lister and Walker continued to correspond but it was to be almost a year before their paths crossed in person again.

★

By January 1834, rumblings of Ann Walker's return south prompted Anne Lister to resume thinking on their match. Initially, Lister approached her friend Dr Steph Belcombe, brother of her former lover Mariana Belcombe (now Mrs Lawton), about securing lodgings for the pair in York. If Walker were to leave Scotland, Lister thought she should be taken away from the Walker estate. Some have argued that Lister was attempting to protect Walker from the interference of the wider Walker clan. Had they not, after all, contributed to her mental and emotional decline prior to her treatment in Scotland? But Lister betrays herself to her diary. On 5 January 1834 Lister complained that she had 'nothing serious to say to her [Walker] – she wants better manning than I can manage . . . Oh, that I may get well rid of her.'[38] The following day an exasperated Lister confessed, ''Tis well my care for her will not kill me.'[39]

Lister must have adopted a very different performance for Walker, though: flirting with her; pleasing her sexually; promising to take the burden of Walker's estate management under her own instruction, thus freeing Walker to indulge in the artistic pursuits she actually enjoyed. Eventually, Lister's graft paid off. On 7 January 1834 Ann Walker decided that Anne Lister would become the main beneficiary of her will. 'She seems quite decided to take me and leave me all for my life and I said then I would do ditto.'[40] Here at last was the financial promise Lister had worked so industriously towards. With access to Walker's money, Shibden Hall might properly reflect Lister's social and economic aspirations.

Though the promise had been made, Walker did not move at Lister's desired speed. Within twenty-four hours of Walker promising to name Lister as her executor, Lister griped, 'I can never make anything of her & why all this pother for nothing?'[41] The following day she lamented, 'I . . . wish myself out of the scrape. I am sick of the whole thing.' By 11 January, things had got personal. 'She snored so loud I could not sleep. "Why should [I] be so annoyed?" said I to myself and resolved to get rid of her as soon as I could.'[42] It was under this cloud of impatience that Anne Lister took her next, most questionable steps.

Having initially spoken to Dr Steph Belcombe about securing herself and Miss Walker lodgings in York when she returned from Scotland, Lister now pivoted. She wished Dr Belcombe to take Ann Walker under his medical supervision and to house her alone. Lister stipulated that Belcombe was to inform nobody of her instructions regarding Walker other than his wife. Walker was to be secretly placed in his care at York and receive treatment for her emotional and mental maladies. It is worth noting here that when Miss Eliza Raine, the orphan from India with whom Lister had conducted a secret adolescent affair at the Manor School, struggled to come to terms with the end of her intimacies with Lister, Lister had guided her towards the care of Dr Belcombe's father, William, in 1814. Dr William Belcombe ran an asylum in York at the time and Miss Raine would never leave supervised medical care again.

Almost two decades later, Dr Steph Belcombe quickly set about finding suitable lodgings in which to conceal another of Lister's lovers. On 14 January 1834 Lister inspected the property Belcombe had sourced at Heworth Grange, a mile or so beyond the city of York, and was 'sufficiently satisfied' with the proposed rooms. Lister arranged for Walker's baggage to be taken to the secret lodging house and assigned Walker a new lady's maid to ensure she was comfortably kept. Once again, on the surface of it, Lister's actions might be interpreted as all husbandly kindness and care. However, her decision to secretly enlist the help of a medical professional to hide Miss Walker away in York ultimately amounted to the orchestrated medical confinement of a 'troublesome' woman. This was not accepted practice for a late-Georgian or early-Victorian husband (or female husband), it should be noted.[43] Thus, in conceiving this plan with the help of Belcombe, Lister engaged in a rather extreme (though not unheard of) means of female, specifically wifely, control.[44] Allowing for this interpretation of events, an issue persists. Why? What did Lister have to gain by confining Walker in such a manner? As ever, her diary provides the answer. In the dying days of January 1834, as Lister prepared to return to Halifax, she asked for an appraisal of Walker's condition from Dr Belcombe. Lister records that, on 22 January, Dr Belcombe concluded that 'Miss W—[was] quite competent (perfectly so) to make a will.' Once again, Walker's money seems to have been the driving factor behind Lister placing Walker under Belcombe's care. Furnished with this vital piece of information, Lister returned home.

Back in Halifax, with Walker out of the way, Lister now quietly began to impose herself on Walker's finances where she could.[45] With the help of her agents, Lister financially assessed the Walker land, pits and rents and toyed with how best to manage the estate. Anticipating suspicion and resistance, she decided to undertake some damage control amongst the Walker family. She approached elderly Aunt Walker at Cliffe Hill first of all, in the hope of heading off questions that might arise about Ann. After some general chit-chat and more specific talk of Walker's poor mental health, Lister felt confident that she had convinced Aunt Walker that her niece ought to remain in York with Dr Belcombe. Then she disclosed that Miss Walker planned to change her will, making her, Lister, her executor. At this Aunt Walker blanched.

Surely, she enquired, if her niece was under such intensive medical care, she was in no fit condition to change her will? Lister countered that she 'was not like Mr Ainsworth [Walker's prospective male suitor], who would be glad to get hold of her whether

[Miss Walker] was able to decide for herself or not'.[46] Aunt Walker said nothing further on the matter but Lister had said too much. Rather than dispelling suspicions amongst the wider Walker clan she had instead succeeded in arousing them.

Thus, at the beginning of February 1834, the Priestleys, supported by the Walker family, thought it prudent to enquire directly of Dr Belcombe as to why it was that their cousin had been detained under his care. They wished to know Ann's exact whereabouts for she had, essentially, disappeared. Belcombe immediately reported this to Lister, stating that he had given nothing away, only that Miss Walker 'was here in lodgings, highly respectable, chosen by herself, and that her wish was to be more completely under my care than she had yet been, and for this purpose had resolved to come to York'.[47] Lister was pleased with this reply. She was 'anxious it should be considered and known that she [Walker] is entirely her own mistress in every way while here [in York]'.[48] Still, she was rattled.

Sensing that suspicions were growing, the following day, 5 February, Lister called once again on Aunt Walker at Cliffe Hill. Little did she know that Mrs Priestley had beaten her to it. Now, where Anne Lister was concerned, Aunt Walker would give little or nothing away. Aunt Walker said that it was her desire that her niece should now return to Halifax. Lister argued that Lidgate was not the place for Walker at this moment in time – she simply was not well enough to be there. She also assured Aunt Walker that she 'had nothing to do with the going to York beyond helping Miss W—', but proposed that when she did eventually leave York, Miss Walker would likely benefit from some time abroad under Lister's care. At that, Aunt Walker was startled once more. 'What [ought] she go abroad for?' she snapped. 'It would be very foolish.'

'Poor girl!' retorted Lister. 'I am sorry for her – she wants different management from that she has hitherto had.' A slight to the extended Walker and Priestley tribe, if ever there was one. They, Lister implied, had let Ann down; if it had not been for their carelessness, she would not be in this terrible condition at all. Lister left Aunt Walker with a warning: 'If you disapprove, you will only unsettle her and it is even now the toss up of a straw which way the thing turns.'[49] If the Walkers continued to interfere, Lister insinuated, it would destroy Ann's health for good and surely they would not wish for that? No, it was best that she remained away and that Lister alone continued to oversee her care.

Soon, however, on hearing that one of her close relatives was unwell (Ann was not short of relatives), Miss Walker thought it best she leave York and return to Halifax should the worst occur. This finally gave Aunt Walker a chance to see her niece face to face again, and when she did, she wasted no time in desperately bombarding Ann with questions regarding her absence. Where had she been? Why had she been there? Would she be returning to Lidgate for good? And what was all this she had heard from Anne Lister about a change of will? Walker quickly became overwhelmed by her interrogation, and more than a little irked when she found out that the Priestleys had gone to York to spy on her. Later, Walker instructed Lister 'never to name her [Ann] . . . again to old Miss W—[Aunt Walker] in future'. According to Lister's diary, Walker had had enough of her interfering family. This meant that she was increasingly isolated from them and that Lister had her right where she needed her.

To demonstrate their independence from the Walkers and the Priestleys, Lister and Walker planned a trip to France together. 'She [Walker] will pay,' Lister recorded, whilst Lister would make all the necessary arrangements.[50] Walker now leaned more readily into the relationship. Lister continued to press Miss Walker to place herself 'under no authority, but mine. To make her will

Geranium Sylvaticum

directly . . . to add a codicil leaving me a life estate in all she could and I would do the same for her.' Holiday plans continued apace, and it was soon arranged that rings were to be exchanged 'in token of our union'.[51]

Though it is difficult to decipher in Lister's diary, some form of ring exchange did eventually take place on 27 February whilst the women were travelling together in York. 'I asked her to put the gold wedding ring I wore [on] . . . she would not give it me immediately but . . . then put it on my left third finger in a token of our union – which is now understood to be confirmed for ever tho' little or nothing was said.'[52] Were two rings exchanged, as was customary? Or just Anne Lister's ring swapped between the two of them? It is difficult to say.

On Saturday, 8 March, with Walker still in York and Lister back at Shibden Hall, Anne Lister ruminated on this exchange of bands and, rather than recalling a profound coming together of two women in love, she found that the whole thing left her feeling rather flat in hindsight. Lister recalled that Walker had given her 'my ring languidly' without trace of delight or commitment. Had Walker just gone through the motions because Lister asked her to? Did it mean nothing to her? 'Does she mean to make a fool of me after all?' Lister questioned. 'I distrust her and feel as if the thing would again (and this time forever) go off between us.' As Lister scribbled, she became more and more incensed; 'I shall not be played with,' she insisted. She then questioned what we must too: 'Affront! Does this seem as if she really thought us united in heart and purse?'[53] Walker's money was never far from Lister's mind.

Amidst all this secrecy, tumult, distrust, fear and anger we return now to the celebrated 'wedding' day at York. We have already examined the plaque that commemorates this historic event. We have watched the loving dramatization of it in *Gentleman Jack*. But was the famous Lister–Walker ceremony at Holy Trinity Church in Goodramgate truly a heartfelt, groundbreaking, defiant queer marriage? What follows is the passage in Anne Lister's diary that inspired so much hope.

Sunday, 30 March 1834. 'At Goodramgate church at 10 35/'; . . . The first time I ever joined Miss W—in my prayers – I had prayed that our union might be happy – she had not thought of doing as much for me.'[54] And that, essentially, was that. No loving exchanges, no kisses in the carriage, no knowing looks as they walk up or back down the aisle. Anne Lister tells us that she had prayed for their union. She also tells us that Ann Walker had not thought to pray for their union. That's it, I'm afraid. This, surely, is no wedding. No marriage-like union was enacted here. If anything, that seems to have happened on 27 February, when Lister and Walker exchanged rings, and even then Lister was not convinced of Walker's true commitment. Walker certainly wasn't thinking about it a month later in Holy Trinity Church, as Lister was. As is so often the case, Ann Walker's intentions have all too easily been ignored or imagined, largely, it is safe to assume, because of the relative scarcity of material in her own hand. But sometimes, with enough patience and persistence, the past offers up a forgotten gem that goes some way towards revealing what was once obscured.

In October 2020, as archives across Britain slowly began to reopen their doors in the midst of the Covid-19 pandemic, Diane Halford, a founding member of the 'In Search of Ann Walker' research group, began her hunt for material relating to 'the Committeeship of Ann Walker after the death of Captain Sutherland' in the West Yorkshire Archives. If found, these documents would provide historians with details of how Walker's estate was managed after the death of her brother-in-law. Only a true enthusiast could find any great pleasure in such a document but Diane, determined to offer the world a more rounded picture of Ann Walker, knew that her work was important.

During her search, Diane spotted a document, WYC:1525/7/1/5/1, which had been classified as the 'Journal of Anne Lister, including travels in France and Switzerland with Ann Walker'. The journal in question was a 'blue marbled A6-ish size notebook', and Diane was intrigued. After a flick through the yellowing pages she quickly realized that this was no Lister journal. It was, in fact, a record of the words, thoughts, sights and sounds of Miss Ann Walker. Finally, Diane rushed to inform her collaborators and the archive about what she had found. Three days later she announced her findings to the world in a blog post entitled 'ANN'S DIARY: WE FOUND IT!!!'

Here, at last, was an insight into Ann Walker's mind, her private feelings, her perspective on the world. Within those pages, contrary to Anne Lister's description, we do not find a whimpering, unstable woman. Instead we discover a wonderfully erudite, charming person with whom one might be happy to spend some time. Walker had discerning taste, an advanced appreciation for art, particularly religious art, and a keen interest in the history she saw around her. She was sensitive, certainly, loving – particularly towards Anne Lister – and artistic. This new-found diary recounts Ann Walker's adventures abroad following what many have perceived to be her 'marriage' to Lister in York. The true gift of Walker's diary is that we can compare it to Lister's in order to get a more rounded picture of their relationship. In so doing, Lister emerges as a duplicitous, almost cruel companion, whilst Walker endears herself with gentle, caring sentiment. Lister, for example, complained about Walker throughout their European excursions: 'Never in my life saw such a fidget in a carriage – she was in all postures & places till at last she luckily fell asleep for about an hour.' Walker, however, was oblivious to Lister's secret frustrations and only writes, 'd[ea]r[es]t quite as fond & kind to me as ever'.[55]

On 16 June 1834, Walker records that she and Lister travelled through Tonnerre in France, the home of the Chevalier d'Éon, who had died alone and in poverty twenty-four years before their visit. Was Walker aware of the queer footsteps in which she trod? Unlike the Chevalier, Ann Walker's diary also shows that she loved her female apparel, took pride in her appearance and appreciated time alone to study the artistry and luxury of delicate silks and French fabrics.

As she travelled, we learn that she collected tokens from her journey, rummaging in bookshops and noting passages of particular interest to her. On 28 July, for instance, she 'went to Booksellers shop – bo[ugh]t prints of Savoy – read p[ar]t of [a] book giv[in]g advice to young . . . Ladies; "always to seek friends & comp[an]y of their own sex – & not to let their conversations with the other be too long or too freq[uen]t. She who courts danger is sure to perish by it."'[56]

It is clear, I think, that if, with the discovery of a portion of Walker's diary, readers hoped for a similarly in-depth and explicit offering as Lister had created, they would be sorely disappointed. Instead, Walker prefers to document events, places, people and things as she encounters them. Her writing, however, is precise and pleasantly staid. Her travel diary is a pleasure to read, in fact, and her descriptions of various pieces of art are, at times, utterly sublime. They may not be scandalous, but Ann Walker's words are important because they allow us to get closer than ever before to who she was, in her own terms.

Following their return to Halifax, the Lister–Walker household was finally formed in August 1834, nearly two years after Lister had first floated the idea. Once established at Shibden, Lister was keen that others perceive Walker in a wifely role, writing to Isabella Northcliffe, another former lover, on 14 October 1834 that Walker 'understands keeping house better than I do, so that I am better off than formerly'.[57] People in the locality viewed Lister and Walker as female husband and wife too, as a satirical announcement in the *Leeds Mercury* on Saturday, 10 January 1835 demonstrates. It read: 'Captain Tom Lister [Anne] of Shibden Hall to Miss Ann walker [*sic*], late of Lidgate, near the same place.'[58]

Once bound to Walker, Lister set about performing her 'husbandly' role as she had always planned. She took control of Walker's estate and its management, gaining considerably from the income it generated, which she then invested by way of loans into improvements to her own estate. Walker did not benefit in kind. For that, after all, was the contract of elite Georgian marriage: a husband gained further social, cultural, legal and financial agency through his union and a wife assumed domestic authority over their household. In this sense, Ann Walker might at least have expected to take over the day-to-day running of Shibden Hall as its mistress. However, it was Marian Lister, Anne's sister, who continued to oversee the domestic management at Shibden Hall.[59] As a result, Ann Walker's life with Anne Lister was 'very different from what she expected' and, Lister tells us, Walker 'fancies herself under restraint' in the household. Given Walker's feelings, by August 1835 Lister was once more expressing her regret at having tied herself to the heiress. Walker had 'a queer stupid temper', as Lister saw it, and was 'little-minded . . . I see she will be no companion for me. I shall be at large again.'[60] Lister had worked doggedly to secure Walker's place in her household, and her fortune. Now that she had it, she longed to play the field once more and be free of her! This, though, would not come to pass.

Anne Lister died unexpectedly a few years later, on Monday,

22 September 1840 whilst travelling in Georgia as part of another extensive European trip with Walker, leagues from her beloved Shibden. Lister had been thrown into a convulsive fever, possibly resulting from an insect bite, and died as a result six weeks later. Following Lister's death Walker returned to Shibden, where she undertook appropriate mourning for her 'late friend' and awaited the return of Lister's body for burial. Lister, it was reported in a local newspaper, was eventually laid to rest in the family vault 'at the Parish Church, Halifax . . . the vault in the interior of the church was beautifully finished. The coffin was of the most splendid description, bearing the coat of arms of the family.'[61] So many thousands gathered that day, Tuesday, 29 April 1841, that 'it was with the greatest difficulty the corpse could be got out of the hearse'.[62]

Walker would spend the majority of the next many years of her life in and out of psychiatric care, including stays in a number of asylums. Eventually, following old Aunt Walker's death, Ann returned to her family's estate and took up residence at Cliffe Hill, where she had been born. There she remained in domestic solitude until her own death, at the age of fifty, at about one o' clock in the afternoon on Friday, 25 February 1854. Her cause of death is recorded as 'Congestion of the Brain[,] Effusion[,] Certified'.[63] Following a relatively modest funeral, 'poor Miss Walker of Cliffe Hill' was buried under the reading pulpit inside Old St Matthew's Church, Lightcliffe.[64] The Walker estate therefore passed to Evan Charles Sutherland-Walker, Ann's nephew, who eventually sold it to the politician and philanthropist Sir Titus Salt in 1867. Salt is best known for having devised the self-contained model village of Saltaire near Shipley, West Yorkshire.

With Walker in mind, then, let's end this history where it began. Wander back with me to Goodramgate in York, heading north-west once more. Pass the bridal boutique on your right. Stop momentarily to consider the window of a local estate agent, then continue on past the row of artisans' cottages before taking a now-familiar right turn through the Georgian red-brick archway and into the grounds of Holy Trinity Church. Turn to your left and look at the plaque placed there following the success of *Gentleman Jack*. It was campaigned for and erected as a tribute to same-sex love, fidelity and hope. Sometimes, however, archival documentation insists we look at these things again. Despite knowing that it was done with the best of intentions, I am unconvinced that the complexities and cruelties of the Lister–Walker relationship can be summed up by a rainbow-encircled blue plaque. Nor am I convinced that this act of remembrance marks an actual historical event, rather than the hope of what might have been.

Often, when we imagine we have so little history of our own, there is an understandable impulse to stretch the boundaries of our archive to create a past we feel we deserve. By so doing we comfort ourselves, secure in the idea that we have always been here, that we will continue to resist and persist. But our history must reflect the past as it was, not as we wish it had been. For the truth is always more compelling in its complexity, is it not?

I anticipate that some readers will feel upset or cheated by the arguments I have presented here. These pages depict an Anne Lister whom many would not fully recognize, nor wish to claim. Nonetheless, the primary-source material is littered with examples of her coercive control, manipulation, greed and deceit, and when reading and rereading Lister's diary I felt compelled to confront these unsavoury elements directly. I did this, primarily, in the hope of helping to reveal a little more of Ann Walker from the shadows of her remarkable but often domineering companion. I also did it in the hope of pushing queer history beyond the simple act of 'finding the gays in the past' towards a more nuanced and complex approach which incorporates as many facets of the queer past as possible. But whatever your feelings are about Lister and Walker, I hope we can agree that the history presented here is no less exceptional, no less vital and no less queer for any of the debate and disagreement it might generate in our own time. Debate, after all, is what helps keep history alive.

CHAPTER TEN

A (Not So) Singular Case

H OPE, SWELLING ON PERPETUAL waves, carried George Wilson and his seventeen-year-old wife, Elizabeth, towards their new life. Beneath his excitement, however, George was ill at ease. The cause of his unrest was a secret, for sometimes it is our lot in life to keep secrets. But Wilson was resolved; he would not remain burdened. He would tell Elizabeth the truth. So, as the pair approached North America, Wilson gathered every ounce of his courage.

George Wilson and Elizabeth Cummins had been married only a few days previously, on Friday, 6 April 1821, in the Barony parish of Glasgow, Scotland. George attended alone but Elizabeth's family had turned out in force to bless their union. Indeed, the newlyweds had been introduced by Elizabeth's father, James Cummins, who was superintendent at the Glasgow factory where George worked.

Almost 80,000 Glaswegians, out of a population of 150,000, were employed in the city's cotton industry, which boomed thanks to an ever-growing Atlantic trade. Most of these employees were women and children. Factory hours were long and the working environment treacherous, with the loss of appendages, limbs and lives far from uncommon. Of course, if factory conditions were tough, it was nothing compared to the conditions in which enslaved people toiled to procure the raw cotton wool across the Atlantic. This was then imported by Scottish merchants and eventually spun in Scottish factories, just like the one James Cummins oversaw.[1]

When Cummins had learnt that Wilson had no family of his own, he must have taken pity on the young man and seen fit to introduce him to his wife, Margaret, and their many children. They enjoyed dinners together and played cards on several occasions. Whether Cummins had ever intended Wilson to become his son-in-law is unclear, but once Elizabeth Cummins met George Wilson sparks led to flutters and vows were soon exchanged. The newlyweds would soon leave Glasgow bound for a new life. They knew that they would never see Scotland again, but the promise and opportunity of North America had proved too alluring.

The Wilsons will have undertaken their voyage on a packet ship. Whilst steamships were not unheard of, the wind-powered packet still dominated Atlantic travel in the early nineteenth century. The packets were so named because they transported letters and packages throughout the British Empire, but they might transport other goods, including paying passengers too. As a result, packet ships had the innovative distinction of operating under a regulated and advertised departure schedule, though they were designed with sturdiness and the threat of an Atlantic storm in mind, rather than speed.

We do not know exactly which packet ship Elizabeth and George made their voyage of hope on as records for that year are incomplete. But it is thought that they left Glasgow within a couple of days of being married and likely set sail from a Scottish port two or three days after that.[2] It is possible, therefore, that they made their way south to Dumfries where, on 12 April 1821, six days after the Wilsons had married, the *Thompson* packet was scheduled to set sail for Pictou, Canada with Captain Lookup at the helm. On board were eighty passengers, whose names are now lost to time. We know that the journey took thirty days and was recorded as having reached its final destination around 12 May. Whether or not Elizabeth and George had boarded the *Thompson* specifically, their journey across the Atlantic would have been much the same on any scheduled departure from Britain.

On board their packet, George and Elizabeth would have travelled steerage, the cheapest option available. A ticket for steerage passage cost about £5 (£460), but despite being a lucrative commodity, the number of steerage tickets assigned to each ship

Figure 23. The 'Patrick Henry', a packet ship typical of the first half of the nineteenth century.

was strictly limited. To regulate potential excess, custom house men tallied the overall measurement of each boat and designated passenger numbers accordingly. Provisions for the journey would then be inspected to ensure that they were sufficiently plentiful and of decent enough quality to last the projected length of the voyage. Elizabeth and George will also have been inspected for lice, or other signs of contagious disease, before departure, as an outbreak at sea could lead to catastrophic outcomes for passengers and crew alike. Despite these seemingly civilized precautions (which in any case were not always observed), contemporary accounts of transatlantic steerage travel tell us that a month aboard a packet ship was akin to living in 'a floating hell'.[3]

To access steerage, the Wilsons would have climbed down a ladder through the hatchway, often the only source of light for their quarters. If the sea was particularly high and waves sprayed violently across the deck, the hatchway (and the steerage passengers beneath) would be contained and kept dry by placing a lid over it. During such times, which were not rare in the tempestuous North Atlantic, steerage was plunged into utter darkness. Thus, confined in a space eighteen feet square and seven feet high, passengers blinked back the blackness and held on for dear life.

Steerage passengers typically slept in bunk beds. One account tells us that 'passengers crept night and morning' in and out of their berths, like ants about their business. Around them, from the ceiling, hung the stuff of life: 'hats and hams . . . bonnets, onions, and frying pans; boots and red-herrings'. Everything swayed with the interminable, nauseating metronome of the sea. Boxes and other containers were nailed to the floor to secure them in place. These were filled with valuables, but also acted as 'chairs and tables, as well as cupboards'.

A crossing was not a silent affair either. Outside, the sea hammered and rolled, 'thundering at our wooden walls for admittance'.

The creaking of the ship's wood might have gone unnoticed at first given the fear and excitement that ensued once the packet initially set sail, but as the voyage went on each creak, groan, squeak and yawn from the timber world around them bored deeper into the brain. Children wept, pots and kettles clanked, and the crew above caused a ruckus with their 'hallooing at the forecastle every four hours'.

George and Elizabeth kept a daily diet of rice pudding, as it easily withstood the length of the journey. This they would have boiled on deck when the weather was good enough. Otherwise the Wilsons and their like had to content themselves with 'crunching hard biscuits' in the dark depths of steerage.

However, 'no sooner did clouds clear off, and the sun break through . . . than all troubles were forgotten' on board the trusty packet. In those golden moments, George and Elizabeth were permitted to explore the deck. They may have taken walks together round the 'jolly-boat' looking at 'the cow, or sheep, or pigs, or poultry' the packets transported. They may have read, or simply looked up into to the great blue skies overhead. That is not to say that steerage passengers had free rein on deck. George and Elizabeth's movements will have been curtailed by chalk lines that designated areas for the exclusive use of first- and second-class passengers. It was whilst aboard their packet ship (maybe on one of those pleasant, sunny days) that George Wilson offered the story of his old life up to his new wife, and to the sea, so that he might be free of it and begin again. That day, surrounded by the vast Atlantic Ocean, he told Elizabeth that he had not always been a man.

Historian Jen Manion has identified George Wilson, given his marital status and gender performance, as 'the first designated female husband found living in the United States'.[4] Female husbands, as we saw in the last chapter, might include many variants of gender non-conforming people, but the vast majority that made international headlines were 'people assigned female who transed gender, lived as men, and married women', as Manion details.[5] The term was common in print media during the eighteenth and nineteenth centuries on both sides of the Atlantic, and indeed contemporary newspaper reports would eventually come to refer to Wilson as a female husband too, as we shall see.[6] We do not know how Elizabeth reacted to George's news; we only know that when the Wilsons finally reached Canada, they disembarked and continued on together.[7]

The Wilsons were but two of the many millions of people who emigrated to North America from Northern and Western Europe across the next century. From 1820 to approximately 1957, 13 million people travelled to the United States alone, for example. The vast majority of them came from Ireland (4.6 million) and Great Britain (4.5 million), for various and often overlapping reasons including desperate necessity, economic opportunity and the perceived religious and political tolerance available at the end of their voyage. But in the context of this book, it is clear that they also travelled for another, overlooked, reason; some migrants went to America because their queerness compelled them to. We have already seen how William Courtenay, 9th Earl of Devon, absconded to New York in 1811 when his same-sex attraction drew unwanted legal attention back in England. Here too, bridging the queer class divide, George Wilson ventured west in search of an identity he felt he might not fully realize in Scotland. This is no coincidence.

In the seventeenth century, the American colonies inherited a version of English law regarding the regulation of sodomy, namely the Buggery Act of 1533. However, following independence, nineteenth-century American legalese had, effectively, tongue-tied itself into silence on the matter. Sodomy was illegal, make no mistake, but it was also seen as an act 'not fit to be named amongst Christians'. If you could not name it, you could not prosecute it. This perceived legal loophole also extended to other ideas relating to gender non-conformity more broadly, which, in turn, 'marginalized sexuality beyond the jurisdiction of criminal enforcement. For a moment in time, [in America] sodomy law regulated itself into extinction.'[8] This was that time. And this is why George Wilson, Kitty Courtenay and others deliberately made their way to the United States in moments of potential crisis.

Were they on board the *Thompson*, the Wilsons would have arrived at Pictou, a picturesque port town in Nova Scotia, on 12 May 1821. The region had been given its settler name (meaning New Scotland) by the Scottish explorer Sir William Alexander, who was awarded the land by King James VI of Scotland and I of England in 1621, with little regard for the naming customs and homesteads of the Indigenous Mi'kmaq peoples who had inhabited and cultivated the land for countless generations previously. Many Scots settled there, and George and Elizabeth would have been comforted by the lilt and rhotic 'R's of the familiar accent as soon as they disembarked.

Although we know they arrived in Nova Scotia, it is difficult to track the Wilsons' whereabouts for the next several years. Various later accounts would claim that they settled in New Limerick, Canada or New Harmony, Indiana.[9] We do know that during this time Elizabeth's father, James, joined them and that the industrious trio set up home together under the same roof in Nova Scotia. It isn't until 1827 that the Wilsons re-emerge in the archive, this time in Paterson, New Jersey. James and George found themselves back in the cotton factories, working at the Clark & Robinson cotton mill. Soon, however, the pair would lose their jobs and the three of them would make for New York, where they settled at 47 Forsyth Street. Forsyth was one of a set of streets on the Lower East Side named for heroes from various American military and naval conquests. These also included Christie, Eldridge and Ludlow. I can't imagine, though, that George, Elizabeth and James spent much time thinking of this legacy when they settled there in the 1820s, if they knew about it at all. It was the promise of work that had drawn them there.

George found employment at Joseph Barron's factory at 171 Water Street, a half-hour walk from Forsyth. Whilst the genteel classes could afford a comfortable life far from the noise and dirt of industry, the labouring classes lived close to where they worked for ease of access. Barron was a furrier, so George would have been employed in the making of fur goods. That was, however, until a fire broke out one December night in 1835 at 173 Water Street and decimated the surrounding businesses, including Barron's fur factory.[10] We cannot say with certainty what the immediate impact of the fire was for George, but it appears that Barron got himself and his employees back on their feet again quickly, because by the summer of the following year George was still employed by him.

Back on Forsyth, 'modest but decent' accommodation had been raised by speculative builders to accommodate a growing number of journeymen and factory labourers.[11] But whilst the Wilsons may have found relatively good accommodation there, conditions were still far from ideal. Behind the street lay 'a maze of alleyways . . . crowded with industrial workshops'.[12] The two- to four-storey (mostly) wooden houses that lined the street were still multi-occupancy. The area near the Bowery nearby stank of dead flesh from slaughterhouses and tanning yards, whilst more and more stinking bodies crammed into the streets around them on a weekly basis. Pigs roamed free, defecating and copulating hither and thither. Meanwhile, modern conveniences such as 'coal stoves, gas lights, ice boxes, and other improvements' were reserved for the classes above the Wilsons.[13] Instead, after the workday was done, Forsyth was illuminated by candlelight and community.[14]

Women hollered from windows to one another, passing information and gossip above the din of the street below. Local residents called on their neighbours unannounced and looked after their friends' children, or, rather, assigned their own children to look after their friends' children, in the streets with the pigs. The women sewed, and laundered, and cooked, and fought, and did what they could to get by, sometimes supplementing their husbands' income with work of their own. They survived because the alternative was unthinkable.

The men, like George, when not working, 'liquored'. Whisky was provided by employers to factory men in order to spur them on through the often-hopeless monotony of their daily grind, and a refreshing beer might be offered in the summer months to cool the rising heat. The cost for their employers was less than a cup of tea or coffee, so it was a worthwhile expense.[15] Outside of work, George will have enjoyed the brotherhood of his New York co-workers at one of the thousands of taverns or saloons that had been approved by the city, alongside others that had not. Here men drank whilst exchanging stories of their domestic frustrations and learnt about the availability of new work opportunities.[16] George was very much welcomed into this manly fold. His contemporaries saw no reason not to include him in their homosocial bonding. We know that he partook in this everyday act of male bonding because it was 'liquoring' that eventually brought him to the attention of the authorities one summer night in 1836.

The corner of Pearl Street and Chatham, one Friday night (likely the 5th, but records differ), August 1836. The night air was warm and frivolity was high. A local policeman kept his beat. Buildings on this block had been destroyed in a revolutionary skirmish on 20 September 1776. However, by the first decades of the nineteenth century the scorched remains of Pearl Street had risen, phoenix-like, from the rubble and the street was now lined with sturdy, brick-faced Federal-style homes and businesses. Pearl and Chatham was a busy and popular intersection and business owners and residents slept somewhat more soundly knowing that their neighbourhood was worth protecting.

At an unrecorded hour, as he approached the corner of Pearl and Chatham, our policeman happened across what he thought was a drunken sailor slumped on the ground. George Wilson had 'liquored' particularly hard that night and the pavement must have seemed the most restful spot on which to gather his strength for the walk home. He was only a couple of streets over from Water Street, where he worked, so he had likely been out with the boys from work. As the constable approached George, he had no idea that the 'sailor' he'd stumbled across was about to make headline news right across America.

Vagrancy laws in New York sought to rid the city of individuals who were found inexplicably loitering or 'out of place', just as George had been that night. These laws were purposely vague. In attempting to enforce them, authorities sought to avoid social disturbances and reinforce class hierarchies as and when they saw fit. Public drunkenness was a fine example of an offence that could get you arrested under this legislation in New York in 1836. Interestingly, these same vagrancy laws were often applied to individuals suspected of gender or sexual non-conformity, but in George Wilson's case it was his drunkenness and not his gender that inspired our policeman to scoop him up and escort him to the nearest 'police office', as it was termed, that night. There the 'sailor' could sober up and, if this was his first offence, would be on his way soon enough.

By the time George arrived at the police office, he had realized the potential extent of his troubles. In a desperate attempt to avoid questioning that might expose his former identity, and to avoid implicating Elizabeth, he had decided to lie. Initially, he told the processing magistrate, Mr Lowndes, that his name was 'James Walker' and said that he was Irish, not Scottish. 'Walker' claimed that he was thirty years old, though it was observed that 'care and trouble have left the furrows of more advanced age' across his face.[17] 'Walker' also gave his address as Tillary Street, Brooklyn, another misdirection.[18]

Despite his obfuscation, the arresting officer and Lowndes suspected that all was not as it seemed with prisoner 'Walker''s backstory. One report claimed the magistrate had become suspicious because of 'the softness of [the prisoner's] voice', leading the authorities to believe that 'Walker' might not be the man he claimed. Whatever the case might have been, they soon suspected 'that [they] had caught a female in man's attire, although she was sunburnt and appeared somewhat masculine'.[19]

Faced with their continued probing, George soon felt that his former self was too precarious a thing to hide. To throw Lowndes and the arresting officer off the scent, 'Walker' admitted that he had, indeed, been lying. He confessed that his 'real name was Jane Walker'.[20] This was another invention, but George quickly concocted an elaborate backstory for 'Jane' in the hope that she might elicit pity from the magistrate and ensure a speedy release.

Jane's 'story was one of disappointed love'.[21] She had been on a promise from a young man back in Ireland. This young man had, apparently, left Ireland's shores, like so many did, and arrived in Quebec. Eventually, after about two years, he sent Jane the money he had promised so that she could join him there. This she did diligently, George revealed, but when she got to Quebec her old flame was nowhere to be found! 'Jane', wishing to maintain her dignity and fend for herself in this new land, set upon 'assuming the garb of a man' in order to survive. This she had accomplished by working on the docks in the hope of one day stumbling across her lost love amongst the other labourers there. It was quite the romantic yarn, heroic even. Despite this, Lowndes could hardly just release 'Jane Walker' now. She had lied before; was she lying again?

Lowndes therefore summoned either a female prisoner or a surgeon, depending on your source, in order to carry out an inspection that would attempt to establish the 'facts' behind 'Walker''s latest confession.[22] It was swiftly concluded that 'Jane Walker' was a woman. Lowndes gave 'Walker' a firm talking to about the evils of 'throwing aside her feminine dress', and placed her back in the cell overnight.[23] And that might have been that. 'Jane Walker' might otherwise have spent the night in the cells and, having been directed to readopt female attire, been released. 'Jane Walker' might have become nothing more than a lovelorn footnote in the annals of American immigration. But all chance of that vanished when, on the next morning, Saturday, 6 August, Mrs Elizabeth Wilson approached Mr Lowndes, magistrate, in search of her missing (presumed drunk) husband Mr George Wilson.

Mr Lowndes was, by all accounts, slightly baffled by the appearance of this 'decently dressed' Scottish immigrant.[24] He had not detained any man called George Wilson the previous night, he said, but having spoken with Elizabeth a little longer, it dawned on Lowndes that the prisoner Elizabeth wished to see was none other than 'Jane Walker'. If Lowndes had understood correctly, Elizabeth had been legally married to his 'Jane' for over fifteen years. 'On receiving this information, the magistrate ordered the prisoner to be brought up for a second examination.'[25]

George is recorded as having been 'quite confused' when

confronted with his wife in the magistrate's office.[26] One can imagine the wave of anxiety that overtook him momentarily and then the frustrated anguish when Elizabeth looked at him in 'vexation and rage . . . on hearing her husband's sex was discovered', refused to speak to him, 'and went away'.[27] Lowndes then informed his prisoner that Elizabeth had furnished him with additional details concerning the prisoner's real name and their marriage. George, sensing there was nowhere left to hide now, told the magistrate that he was not Irish but had been born to Scottish parents at No. 20 Atherton Street, Liverpool.[28] George stated that the name he had been given at birth was 'George Moore Wilson, and that George is a name commonly given to females in England'. George elaborated that 'in consequence of being ill-treated by her friends', after George's mother had remarried, 'she ran away from them, put on boys' clothes, and made her way to Scotland'.[29]

Wilson had spun so many tales that Lowndes asked for proof that this version of his life contained some truth, and so a marriage certificate was produced. This the prisoner already had secreted about his person, if contemporary newspaper reports are to be believed. According to these reports the document read:

Glasgow, 2d April, 1821.
 CERTIFICATE. – That George Wilson, cotton spinner, of Brighton, and Elizabeth Cummins, residing there, have been three Several Sabbaths lawfully proclaimed in the BARONY CHURCH, in order to marriage, and no objection has been offered.
 The above parties were lawfully married by me, JOHN MARFORTAINE, Minister.[30]

When the story inevitably leaked, as all good stories do eventually, hacks were suspicious of this certificate. 'Wilson, has told two stories,' they observed, 'it would not be at all surprising if this marvellous marriage should turn out to be a sham affair got up within a few days past.'[31]

The details of the certificate quoted in *The Pennsylvanian* remain curious. The first question has to be why did a labourer carry confirmation of his marriage on him? Had George and Elizabeth agreed on this as a strategy should George's identity ever be questioned? But the details of the document are sketchy too. For instance, Wilson and Cummins are thought to have married on 6 April 1821, not 2 April as stated here. 'Brighton' should read Bridgeton, formerly a 'quoad sacra' parish and part of the larger parish of Barony, in the suburbs of Glasgow.[32] That was a far cry from Brighton in the south-east corner of England. And here's the other thing: there is no record of a Minister 'John Marfortaine' administering to his Glaswegian flock at this or any time in the National Records of Scotland. And so even I began to worry about the authenticity of their marriage.

George Wilson had understandably lied to Magistrate Lowndes to protect his gender identity and his family. But in lying he has muddied the archival waters. Where had this 'certificate' come from? Who had issued it? Perhaps he and Elizabeth Cummins had not married at all, as people suspected? For some reason, the prospect that they had not married irked me. The Wilsons owed me nothing, obviously, but I needed to know if they had duped the heteroregulated system, surreptitiously inserting themselves within it. So much we know about George and Elizabeth comes from disparaging third-party accounts that I'd felt that their marriage certificate was the one piece of archival evidence which actually reflected them, on their own terms, simple and all as it was. So for their marriage certificate to suddenly emerge as bogus felt like we were losing the one concrete piece of evidence in their archive. The reality was, though, that this document, as it appeared in *The Pennsylvanian*,

A (Not So) Singular Case

could not be trusted as proof of their marriage. I would have to dig a little deeper. If George and Elizabeth had legally married, there would be one readily available document lying in a Scottish archive waiting to confirm it, an entry in the Barony parish papers from 1821. And so I returned to the archive once more.

Initial searches threw up nothing. Plenty of Wilsons, but no *George* Wilson, and not a trace of Elizabeth Cummins at all. I persevered, training my eyes on the spider-like writing scribbled across each of the pages. Finally, I came to 2 April 1821, the date when they had supposedly married according to *The Pennsylvanian*. I checked each entry for that day and can confirm that there was no Wilson–Cummins wedding. Maybe it was not altogether surprising, I told myself as I disappointedly continued examining the entries for the next day, and the next. Maybe it was too much to hope that they had truly succeeded in infiltrating the system. It was then that I found them! There they were, in black and white: on 6 April 1821, not the 2nd, George Wilson married Elizabeth Cummins. They *had* been married. They had fooled the system!

Their entry in the Old Parish Registers (662 ref 160/23) of Barony is straightforward and to the point, but it corrects some misinformation that has been passed down to us over these last 200-odd years. The reported date of their marriage was out by four days, and in place of the elusive 'John Marfortaine' they had instead been married by John Mcfarlane. The entry in full reads: 'George Wilson Cotton spinner Bridgeton and Elizabeth Cummin residing there married 6th. April by the Revd. John Mcfarlane.'[33] It still didn't explain the inconsistencies of the 'marriage certificate' printed in *The Pennsylvanian*, but their marriage really had been legally formalized in April 1821.

As Magistrate Lowndes attempted to get to grips with the interweaving elements of Wilson's stories, George sat calmly, 'perpetually taking snuff . . . attired in striped pantaloons, a plaid stock, and a grey roundabout'.[34] The life he and Elizabeth had worked so hard to build together over the last fifteen years had come tumbling down about him in less than fifteen hours. Wilson worked the snuff between his fingers before sharply inhaling it. He rubbed the residue across his teeth and into his gums. What more could he do?

The Pennsylvanian tells us that when it came to George Wilson's trial, Justice Hopson caused considerable 'merriment' during the proceedings when he asked, 'How many children they had since their marriage?' Despite these jibes, Elizabeth Cummins, who had been summoned to attend, is recorded as having 'treated the affair with the greatest nonchalance'.[35] If these proceedings fazed her, she would not show it. Ultimately, George was found guilty under the Vagrancy Act, which covered both his drunkenness and his gender misdirection, and 'was again remanded'.[36] It is not known for how long he was held (though such sentences tended to be mercifully short for first-time offenders), if he was released, or if he ever saw Elizabeth again. And that's it. That's all we know. It is here that we must abruptly take our leave of the tenacious George Wilson and the resourceful Elizabeth Cummins as they slip out of the primary-source material. That is how it sometimes goes, with history: we are bound to the information that has survived.

Regardless of where their lives took them next, and despite contemporary claims to the contrary, it should be noted that there is nothing singular about the case of George Wilson. There were 'George Wilsons' across America and the world, each working in his factory, labouring at his dock, taking himself a wife, just as our George had done. The only difference is that our George Wilson had come to the attention of the authorities and, as a result, made it into the headlines. Though, in truth, not even his discovery marks him out as unique, as the later queer histories of

A (Not So) Singular Case

Charles Hamilton, similarly tried under English Vagrancy Laws, and John Smith, a New York tinsmith who also fell prey to New York's Vagrancy Laws, demonstrate.[37] But there's a frustration in this ending nonetheless, is there not? This history feels somewhat unresolved, as if the Wilsons ought to have provided us, for some unknown, petulant reason, with a happy ending. It was whilst thinking on this that I suddenly realized that maybe that was exactly what they had left us with.

Remember: George and Elizabeth had never wanted to make headlines. They never wanted to endure the media scrutiny that followed George's arrest. They had wanted to avoid the jibes, the debate and the deeply personal and intimate intrusion that followed. They had simply wanted to get on with their invisible, everyday lives. To work, earn money and exist in the world on their own terms. Though we can never know for sure unless new evidence comes to light, it is my hope that their sudden archival departure denotes their happy return to that sought-after obscurity, a return to the mundanity of their lives before George had had a little bit too much to drink that August night in 1836. That's my hope for them, and what's history without a little hope?

CHAPTER ELEVEN

The Amalgamationist[1]

IN 1836, MR PETER Sewally was serving three (or five) years' hard labour for grand larceny – theft, essentially – at Sing Sing Prison in New York State.[2] Sing Sing, or the House of Fear as it was known, had opened its gates eight years previously, on 26 November 1828. It sat on a piece of land known to Indigenous Americans as Ossining, meaning 'stone upon stone'. This was fitting, for Sing Sing was a four-floor stone building containing 800 cells measuring three feet three inches wide, seven feet deep and six feet seven inches high. It had, by 1836, expanded to include a hospital and a place of worship and was the largest prison in the world.

As an inmate, Sewally would have been subject to the 'Auburn System' of correction. This meant that officers controlled the movement of inmates by keeping them in 'lockstep' with one another. Inmates travelled in lines, one behind the other, each with his arm locked under that of the inmate in front of him, making acts of aggression and escape less likely. During the day, Sewally and his fellow inmates' shackles would be loosened so that they might work silently outside in groups. Together they laboured in open-air quarries, extracting the stone and marble that would be used to construct landmark buildings across the great city of New York. All the while prisoners were monitored by guards and whipped with the lacerating cat-o'-nine-tails in order to hasten their productivity.[3] Then, as night fell, they marched once more in lockstep back to the 'Big House'. Once back inside, each inmate was, in theory, confined to a single cell of their own at night. In practice, however, we know that it was not uncommon for multiple prisoners to share these suffocatingly small spaces. With such supposedly exemplary and modern systems of confinement in place, city officials and prison administrators alike had deemed 'Ossining's pride' a colossal success. Those subject to correction behind its imposing walls would have strongly disagreed.

Since his incarceration, Peter Sewally had gained quite the public reputation. His portrait, by the noted satirist H. R. Robinson, had spread right across New York in the wake of his trial, a notoriety most inmates could not boast. In it Robinson describes Sewally as a 'Man-Monster', though not on account of his crimes. But despite his gothic intentions, there is nothing in the least bit monstrous about the person in Robinson's rendering. Neither is it a likeness of Peter Sewally, as it happens. In fact, it is not even a man.

Instead, Robinson introduces us to a striking Black woman. Her dignified face looks confidently towards us, soft but resolute and framed by her classically styled wig. Pearls dangle from her ears like milky teardrops and a delicate, crisp white capelet, fastened with a diamond-shaped brooch, protects her from a chill. The volume and frill of her day dress, decorated with a floral pattern and cinched at the waist, lends a fashionable air of romance, whilst her white gloves speak of respectability and innocence. This was Mary Jones, Peter Sewally's alias. Mary's history, alongside Peter's, begins thirty-one miles south of Sing Sing, in the congested streets of Manhattan which, in June 1836, must have felt like the very centre of the world. Many of those who lived and worked on these streets would likely have been familiar with Miss Mary Jones; others, like Mr Robert Haslem, came there with the express purpose of seeking Miss Jones, or one of her colleagues, out.

Robert Haslem was a master mason, which meant that he would have been only too familiar with the ongoing cause of the General Trades Union of the City of New York (GTU). The GTU was composed of representatives from various professional crafts, including the masons. Their cause highlighted the growing disparity between the employer and those he employed, the master and the journeyman.[4] Between 1833 and 1835 the GTU backed several strikes across their respective crafts, much to the chagrin of

Figure 24. Mary Jones as she is said to have appeared in court in 1836.

masters like Robert Haslem. One of the significant gripes of the journeyman masons was their stagnant wage levels, owing in part to the competition mounted against them by 'felons and scum'. They meant the marble and stone that had been cut by the inmates of Sing Sing Prison.[5] However, on the night of 14 June 1836, Robert Haslem had left his work worries behind and met Miss Mary Patterson 'at the corner of Bowery and Bleecker Street'.[6] Patterson skilfully negotiated the fee for her company, time and expertise that evening and obliged Haslem by following him to the Vauxhall Gardens, 'as Gay a Place' as New York had known.[7]

The Vauxhall pleasure gardens were named in honour of their London counterpart and fulfilled much the same function: pleasure in all its forms. The New York gardens had been established the century previously and, having moved from Greenwich Village to Broome Street, eventually settled between Lafayette to the west and the Bowery to the east, in what is now Astor Place. The gardens' crunchy gravel paths wove in between and around luscious shrubbery. Lamps swung from branches, bearing soft flames, whilst a full orchestra was secreted here and there amongst the trees, giving 'to the band of music and singing voices, a charming effect on summer evenings'.[8] Patrons might expect theatre and fireworks and all fashion of merry-making. The gardens were a space for love, too. So, hidden within the privacy of a specially hired box, something akin to a private theatre box, Robert Haslem got to know Mary Patterson a little better. Later, in 1855, *The Herald* would reminisce that many 'couples still . . . remember Vauxhall Gardens as the place where their first vows were made!'.[9] Neither Haslem nor Patterson had any such intentions that night, however. Their coming together was a matter of commerce.

Similar economic models were employed by a significant body of sex workers across New York. The sale of sex in the city was, almost exclusively, geared towards the male customer and grew in

The Amalgamationist

tandem with the entertainment industry.[10] The sale of sex in early-nineteenth-century New York was a blatant and public activity. Some women and girls were attached to certain bawdy houses, of which there were over 200 at this time, whilst others, known as 'street-walkers', staked a claim to a specific area or street. Others achieved the status of 'courtesan' and worked predominantly around the theatres, hotels and other mid-to-upmarket venues in the city.

Mary Patterson was known as a street-walker.[11] The area she patrolled, around Bleecker Street, was thought to be one of the more polite neighbourhoods in the city and furnished her with the possibility of earning up to $50 ($1,790) per week for her labour. Not a bad haul; in contrast, a schoolteacher might have expected to make $10 ($359) per week.[12] It might be assumed, however, that schoolteachers would not have exposed themselves to the same level of abuse and exploitation that Patterson and her colleagues did, whether street-walker, courtesan or madam.

Later that night, once her business with her master mason had been concluded, *The Herald* reported that Haslem, in gentlemanly fashion, returned Patterson to 'where he had found her, i.e. on the same corner'.[13] Haslem then made for home sometime between 10 p.m. and 11 p.m. He cannot have walked very far, as soon 'he came up with this dingy representation of the female sex' also employed in Mary Patterson's line of business.[14]

'Good evening,' she called to Haslem in a 'sweet' voice. Haslem, despite his earlier dalliance with Patterson, was intrigued by the potential of this new prize.

'Where are you going my pretty maid?' he enquired.

His new companion said that she was bound for her aunt's house and Haslem, sidetracked, offered to accompany her there. As they walked together, Haslem asked after his new paramour's name and was informed that he walked in step with Miss Mary Jones. Jones also sometimes went under the sobriquets 'Miss Ophelia . . .

Miss Jane . . . [and] Eliza Smith' to safeguard her reputation.[15] *The Herald* reports that 'These delicate preludes having ended, they proceeded onwards, until they arrived at an alley in Green street.'

Jones, as it happened, rented one of the upper rooms at No. 108 Greene Street, which is believed to have been a brothel.[16] Greene Street was one of the working-class areas of New York into which 'free Blacks' had moved following the state's abolition of slavery in 1827, though a significant community of free Black people had already settled there before this legislative milestone.[17] At the tail end of the eighteenth century, for instance, New York was home to one free Black American for every two enslaved people, but by 1810 it is estimated that there were seven free Black Americans for every one person who remained enslaved.[18] Areas that became home to a significant majority of free Black Americans at this time included Greenwich Village and Seneca Village, the land on which a portion of Central Park now stands.[19] Although the presence of this free Black community represented a form of progress, the high concentration of free Black men and women in certain poorer neighbourhoods was partially due to their exclusion elsewhere. Further, there was a limited range of 'acceptable' occupations available to them in antebellum New York.[20] Free Black men could be found predominantly in the 'dining rooms and kitchens of the great hotels and restaurants';[21] free Black women often took in washing to earn money; whilst either might work as a fruit peddler.[22] Mary Jones, however, had found her calling in another of the city's most established professions.

On the night in question (14 June 1836) we are told that Mary Jones had, by now, 'conceived a violent liking' for Haslem and soon set upon him.[23] Haslem welcomed her advances and the two tumbled into an alley wherein they had more privacy, 'which having entered * * * * * * * *'. Those eight asterisks, which appeared in *The Herald* to describe what happened next, tell you everything you need to know, which this journalist could not explicitly tell his readers on 17 June, when the story was printed.[24] Thus doubly reduced, Haslem finally ventured homewards.

Setting down his possessions at home, Haslem soon discovered that he had been relieved of his 'pocket book, which contained $99'. Bizarrely, in its place was another wallet that 'he had never seen before, which contained an order for $200 on a person he had never heard of'.[25] We might safely assume that the bamboozled Haslem did not sleep soundly that night.

The next day, Wednesday, 15 June, armed with the name of the man on the bank order, Haslem decided to seek him out, hoping that if he could return this gentleman's $200 order he might also locate their shared 'Houri' (an ironic term used by newspapers to describe sex workers) and, in turn, have his own pocket book and money back. So Haslem approached a local police officer, one Constable Bowyer. Though the police could and often did arrest 'common prostitutes', the sex trade was not properly regulated at this time, and Haslem would have been very confident that by approaching Bowyer no legal proceedings would be brought against him.[26] Bowyer immediately set about finding the man whose pocket book Haslem had in his possession. Presumably Bowyer asked after the name in local inns, taverns and from the odd sex worker upon whom he could rely. Eventually the man they sought was located, but he denied any knowledge of a thieving sex worker or of having been robbed. However, after a little coaxing from Bowyer, the unnamed man admitted to suffering the same misfortune that had befallen Haslem. Within hours Bowyer had concocted a plan to ensnare this deceitful double thief and so he waited for the cover of darkness to fall.

That night Bowyer recruited the help of his brother-in-law. Together the men 'went on a cruise' of the Bowery in order to locate the woman Haslem had described.[27] They wandered 'up and down town' and it wasn't until 11 p.m. that one particular Black woman caught Bowyer's eye. Maybe it was her hair, or the meticulous nature of her dress that matched the description Haslem had given him; but when he looked deep into her face, 'he made up his mind that he was right'. Feigning interest in her wares, Bowyer struck up a conversation.

'Where are you going at this time of night?' he asked.

Jones, skilled in the nuances of conversation, replied, 'I'm going home,' then followed up boldly with 'Will you go too?'

Bowyer agreed and they set off in the direction of Greene Street together. Once they reached the door of her lodging house, Mary Jones courteously invited the undercover constable inside. We only have Bowyer's word for this, but he tells us that upon receipt of this invitation he declined and, expressing deep regret, took his leave of her. Jones then went indoors whilst Bowyer crossed the road and secreted himself in an alleyway with a clear view of her lodgings. For the following thirty minutes, Bowyer recalled, he watched Jones's house 'with exemplary patience' until she appeared again.[28]

Bowyer then followed Mary Jones and presented himself to her once more. As before, he asked Jones where she was off to. She responded, exactly as she had to Robert Haslem, by telling him that she was headed 'To my aunt's.'[29] Bowyer walked along with Jones once more until they came to the same alley where she had been with Haslem the night before. Together they turned into the alley and Jones propositioned Bowyer in much the same way that she had Haslem. Bowyer was backed into a corner. Where was his brother-in-law? Surely he was somewhere hereabouts and would jump out to save him any moment now?

The brother-in-law failed to appear. Bowyer, attempting to stall, sent Jones to the lot at the end of the alley to make sure they were truly alone before they commenced their transaction. Jones undertook the investigation and all too soon, as far as Bowyer was concerned, returned to her patron and 'proceeded to be very affectionate'. Bowyer shrank from her again, however, saying he still couldn't be sure that they were alone and begged Jones to investigate one more time. Jones embarked 'on a voyage of discovery, and her answer was the same'.[30]

By this time, Bowyer had given up on the intercession of his brother-in-law. Rather than let the intimacies between himself and Jones develop any further, Bowyer decided now was the time to 'unmask' himself and claim his prize. Suddenly, he seized Mary Jones and a struggle ensued. In their desperate skirmish Bowyer noticed that Jones took 'something from her bosom and threw [it] into an area close by'.[31] Jones tried to run, but Bowyer gave quick chase and caught her easily. Once Jones had been secured, Bowyer sought out the items he had seen Jones throw off and discovered two pocket books, one of which belonged to Mr Robert Haslem. Bowyer had captured his thief.

Mary Jones was subsequently taken to the local Watch house, one of a network which served New York's newly formed professional police force, established in 1829. At this time, Watch houses were still mainly wooden buildings, the interiors of which were conveniently divided to facilitate the interrogation and temporary restraint of prisoners. Thus contained, Mary Jones underwent the customary body search. This might have been conducted by another female prisoner, if one were to hand, and if not by a male member of the Watch. During this routine search Mary's house key was found and confiscated. Bowyer eventually took the key, returned to her lodgings and located 'a number of pocket books, which had doubtless come in to her possession in the same manner' as Haslem's.[32]

Altogether more revelatory, however, was the discovery that Mary Jones had not been born a woman. Instead, it was found that Jones had fashioned herself a '*sexus femineus, fabrefactus fuerat portio bovillis, (cara bubulu) terebratus at apertus similis matrix muliebris, circumligio cum cingulum*'.[33] Partially censored by its use of broken Latin, *The Sun* newspaper informed its readers that Mary had fashioned herself a vagina using a cut of beef that had been 'drilled' to form an entry point through which her male clients might enter. It was, *The Sun* disclosed, bound and held in place with a girdle.[34] *The Herald* was not so bold when describing what the body search had uncovered and stated simply, 'It matters not what means he [Sewally] used to prevent detection of his sex, suffice it to say he did, and most effectually.'[35] Both *The Sun* and *The Herald* explicitly stated that prior to this discovery, neither Haslem, Bowyer nor the unnamed man who also had his pocket book stolen had any suspicions that Mary Jones's gender and sex did not align as they might have expected. This revelation, the details of which spread like wildfire in a matter of hours, meant that Jones's case had already captured the imaginations of New Yorkers, even before the story appeared in print or she had set foot in court.

The following day, Robert Haslem formally accused Mary Jones of stealing from him. Bowyer recorded the accusation in Police files thus:

Thursday June 16th 1836

WATCH RETURNS[36]

| Robert Haslem | Peter Sewally alias Mary Jones B | G[rand]. L[arceny] stealing a pocket wallet cont[aining] $90 |

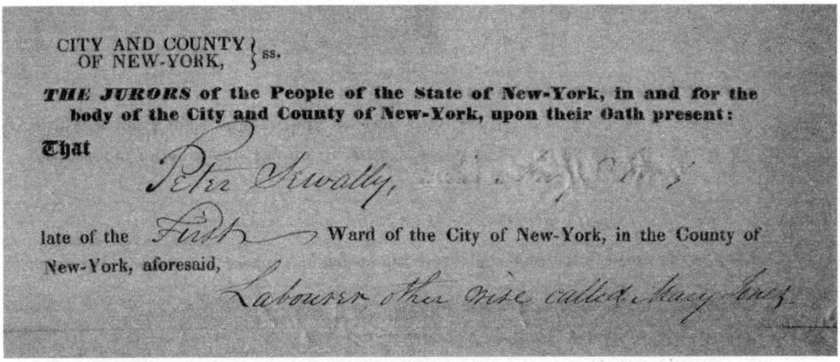
CITY AND COUNTY } ss.
OF NEW-YORK,

THE JURORS of the People of the State of New-York, in and for the body of the City and County of New-York, upon their Oath present:

That Peter Sewally,

late of the First Ward of the City of New-York, in the County of New-York, aforesaid,

Labourer other wise called Mary Jones

Figure 25. Jury Indictment for 'Peter Sewally, alias Mary Jones'. Look closely and you can see that an attempt was made to erase the original entry of her name.

The details of Jones's crime and identity were laid bare, in simple terms. But if Peter Sewally stood accused, so too did Mary Jones. In fact, Haslem exclusively referred to 'Mary Jones' throughout his testimony, never mentioning Peter Sewally at all.[37] The name Mary Jones is also entered on the Court of General Sessions Minutes regarding the case.[38] Likewise, when Jones's testimony was offered to the court it was officially recorded as 'Mary Jones being examined' rather than Peter Sewally.[39] Jones is named on her jury indictment too, dated 14 June 1836.[40]

But take a closer look at the 1836 indictment in Figure 25. On the same line as the 'Peter Sewally' entry, the faint outline of another name is decipherable. It originally read 'alias Mary Jones'. However, at some point in this document's history someone has tried to erase all trace of Mary Jones from the archive.

This erasure demonstrates, in the simplest possible terms, a deliberate attempt to expunge gender non-conforming people from history. It obligates modern historians of gender and sexuality to work all the harder to identify and explore similar hidden or obscured queer experiences in the past. But by so doing we take valuable steps towards countering arguments in our own time that queerness, gender non-conformity and transness in particular are somehow exclusively a modern preoccupation.

Until now, it has been assumed that New York's legal system, as it stood in 1836, had no formal mechanism through which the 'transing' of one's gender identity could be legally acknowledged. It is generally accepted that it was not until 1968 that a New York court ruled in favour of allowing a trans person to have their 'chosen name' recognized in court. However, as we can see, Mary Jones's female name *was* legally recognized in 1836, albeit alongside her male one.[41]

Thus processed, Mary Jones's trial took place on 16 June 1836, the day after she had been arrested. Mr John A. Morrill was her defence attorney, having attached himself to the case with very little preparation time. Morrill hoped to have Jones/Sewally's conviction reduced to 'petit larceny', if not to have her fully acquitted.

The defendant entered a packed courthouse. She was dressed as she had been the previous night when she had been taken up. Despite her equanimity, *The Herald* tells us, the courthouse around her rumbled with laughter; even 'the sedate grave Recorder laughed till he cried'.[42] Curious New Yorkers had gathered in the gallery, where they taunted Mary Jones. Amidst their tittering, someone 'snatched the flowing wig from the head of the prisoner', which in turn 'excited a tremendous roar of laughter throughout the room'.[43]

To those gathered in the court that day, Mary Jones was to be denied her humanity. Not because she was a thief, but because of the perceived disparity between her gender and her sex. They may have legally recorded this fluidity, as we have seen above, but they did not approve of it. They were determined to tear strips from Mary Jones to 'expose' Peter Sewally. And yet she stood resolute, and her testimony was offered to the court.

The Amalgamationist

'What is your age, place of birth, business and residence?' she was asked.

'I will be thirty-three years of age on the 12th day of December next,' Mary answered. '[I] was born in this City, and get a living by Cooking, waiting &c and live [at] No. 108 Green Street.' Mary's date of birth, then, was 12 December 1803, which means she may well have been the first member of her family not to have been born into slavery.

In his questioning of the defendant, the examiner came quickly to the heart of the matter, if not the crime.

'What is your right name?'

This is what they had come for.

'Peter Sewally,' Mary answered. 'I am a man.'

If Mary's womanhood was a vital component of her identity, then Peter's manhood mattered too for, as we shall soon see, 'Peter Sewally' was used as a personal identity marker alongside 'Mary Jones' and other female names throughout her life. For Jones/Sewally, Mary and Peter were two sides of the same coin.

'What induced you to dress yourself in Women's Clothes?' the examiner went on.

'I have been in the Practice of waiting upon Girls of ill fame and made up their Beds and received the Company at the door and received the money for the Rooms &c,'[44] Mary explained, carving out a first-hand account of her day-to-day business with some of New York's sex workers. It was these sex workers, Jones went on, who had inspired her to adopt female dress. 'They induced me to dress in Women's Clothes, saying I looked so much better in them.' Through this rare and precious testimony, Jones reiterated what we have long known about queer working-class communities in large cities: look for the sex workers and you will find the queers.

But Mary did not confine her womanhood to New York's brothels. She went on: 'I have always attended parties among the people of my own Colour dressed in this way – and in New Orleans I always dressed in this way.'[45] The idea that Mary 'always' dressed in female clothing is countered by *The Sun*, which reported that it was Peter who 'generally promenades the street in a dashing suit of male apparel' during the day, whilst Mary emerged to 'prowl' street corners at night.[46] Context is key here, and one might easily interpret *The Sun*'s contribution as an artistic flourish, written to heighten the 'panic' it wished to associate with Jones's supposed emergence into the city after night fell. However, in her own statement Mary wished to make it clear that she had succeeded in carving out a place for herself in her various Black communities where her womanhood was widely acknowledged. That Mary specifically chose to mention that she was accepted 'among the people of my own Colour' is particularly evocative.

It is worth remembering that Jones/Sewally was not actually on trial for gender non-conformity, despite this line of questioning. She had broken no laws by transing her gender identity. Instead, she stood accused of grand larceny. Once the court's attention turned to that crucial matter, it quickly became clear that Sewally/Jones was doomed. There was plenty of damning evidence to suggest that she had stolen Robert Haslem's pocket wallet as he had claimed, despite her denials. Constable Bowyer had even seen her throw it from her dress. Once all the evidence had been presented, 'after consulting a few moments, [the jury] returned a verdict of guilty of grand larceny as charged'. Thus it was, following the humiliation of the trial, that Peter Sewally was sent to Sing Sing, where we first encountered him at the beginning of this chapter.[47]

Mary Jones and George Wilson were both arrested in 1836. They lived within minutes of one another, one in lodgings on Greene Street, the other on Forsyth. Would George have recognized Mary as one of the girls who frequented the corner of Bowery and

Bleecker Street? Or, as Mary set out to work one night, might she have locked eyes with George as he passed on his way home from drinking with the boys? A whole hidden world might have passed between them then. Unlike Wilson, however, Jones/Sewally's story does not end with incarceration. She refuses to disappear.

Peter Smally (Sewally) appeared more than five years after his first trial in the Police Watch Returns for Friday, 31 December 1841, this time for an 'encounter' with a man named Henry Clark.[48] In March 1842 Constable Bowyer recognized 'the waddling, mincing gait of a strapping she darky, whose appearance excited suspicions that she was of "no good"'.[49] Still dressing in female attire, Jones had earned herself a new nickname in the intervening years, 'Beefsteak Pete'. This was inspired, no doubt, by Sewally's first name and the comestible modifications found attached to Mary Jones when she was arrested in 1836.[50] On this occasion, citing vagrancy laws, Bowyer grabbed Jones and attempted to restrain her. She fought back, however, almost freeing herself until Bowyer beat and subdued her with his billy club. Sewally was subsequently imprisoned in Blackwell Prison, this time for six months. It was hoped that another prison sentence would 'tame him before his time was out'.[51] Reader, I'm glad to report that it did not.

Two years later, in December 1844, Sewally made headlines once more following another arrest for vagrancy. This time, however, he was arrested alongside 'a genteel looking fellow' named John Williams, alias Joseph Lyness (or Liness). Lyness was, according to the article, himself a noted character 'who had not stuck very rigidly to the paths of honesty'.[52] His criminal record included stealing from his employers, but on this occasion he was taken up for stealing 'Moffat's Life Pills, worth $1'.

Moffat's 'pills' had been introduced on to the growing but unregulated New York pharmaceutical market in the mid-1830s and claimed to cure 'Scrofula, Ulcers, Scurvy, or Eruptions of the Skin, and all diseased [sic] arising from impure blood Bilious and Liver complaints'. The thief Lyness was found in the company of 'the notorious Beefsteak Pete', who was sentenced to yet another six months' imprisonment. When Sewally was searched, the most 'singular' document was reportedly found in his possession which the *New York Herald* referred to as 'An Oath of Allegiance' or a 'Love Correspondence'. It read:

> I Joseph Liness Do Hereby certify that I have taken an oath in the presence of Theodore Augustus Jackson that I will be a friend to Peter Sewarly till Death Separates us[.] He giving me the privilege to marry the girl of my choice provided She is beyond doubt virtuous I also Swear to tell him everything of the least moment that transpires concerning either of us through Life and this I do voluntarily Swear before God & man[.]
> Signed
> Joseph Lyness
> Oct 3rd 1844[53]

It is interesting that this oath was supposedly undertaken by Lyness and Sewally, not between Lyness and Jones. Lyness swore that their relationship would endure 'till Death Separates us', evoking the language of marriage to solemnize the union between them. In this way, Sewally and Lyness are seen to participate in the very long tradition of queer marriages that took place across the eighteenth and nineteenth centuries, as we have encountered throughout this book.

In a particularly queer turn, Sewally authorizes Lyness to take a legal wife so long as she is 'virtuous'. That being the case, Sewally and Lyness demonstrate that they understood their relationship alongside, and not in opposition to, heteroregulated unions. The oath determined that should Lyness indeed take a wife, it was the intimacy and transparency between the two men, and their joint blessings from God, that bound them together 'through Life'.

However, it appears that things between Sewally and Lyness had soured. For simultaneously discovered in Joseph Lyness's pocket when he was searched was another document. This piece of paper was 'signed' by Sewally, which threatened Lyness 'with officers Hathwaite and Ruckle, unless he gave up all claims to some clothing [presumably belonging to Sewally] he had in his possession'. Was this male or female clothing? We do not know. But clothing was a valuable commodity, particularly to the likes of Jones/Sewally, whose appearance mattered in their work, so it was no wonder he wanted the items back.

The origins of both the oath found on Sewally and the threat found on Lyness ought to be questioned, however. For we know from the 1836 legal documents that Sewally was not literate and could not sign his own name, as *The Herald* article suggests he had in 1844.[54] It is not beyond the realms of possibility that the industrious Sewally had learnt to write by this time. Or, perhaps, that Sewally had had someone else write to Lyness on his behalf? But then, why were the men taken up together if they had been arguing, as Sewally's threat indicated? The figure of the unknown 'Theodore Augustus Jackson' is curious too, especially as he shared his latter two names with the famous Black American Augustus Jackson (1808–52), former White House chef and, by the 1840s, a Philadelphian entrepreneur who had acquired a sizeable fortune through his skill for innovating ice-cream recipes.

Alongside Sewally's threat, Lyness was also found to be carrying a letter from his *'inamorata . . . Almyra C'*, dated 11 June 1843.[55] Was Almyra the source of Sewally's bitterness? Or, maybe, all three documents had been invented by *The Herald* to make for a better story? Certainly, questions remain regarding their authenticity, as the only trace of them that exists now are the extracts that were printed in the paper in December 1844. But, whether they were real or invented, Sewally and Lyness now faced yet another six months behind bars.

In early August 1845, 'Beefsteak Pete' was once more arrested under the Vagrancy Act for 'perambulating the streets in woman's attire'.[56] Then, on 15 February 1846, the *New York Herald* reported that 'Pete Sevanley, alias beef steak Pete; a notorious black rascal, who dresses in female attire and parades about the street', had been arrested yet again for 'playing up his old game, sailing along the street in the full rig of a female'.[57] Back to prison Sewally went for yet another six months.

On Sunday, 23 August 1846 the Police Watch Returns tell us that Sewally, having been released just days previously, was back behind bars once more for 'vagrancy'.[58] The *Newark Daily Advertiser* reported that when Jones/Sewally was arrested this time she was 'tricked out in female apparel of the most fashionable style and cut, and sporting the newest shaped hat'. It appears that despite her several visits to Blackwell's Island and her first, longer stretch at Sing Sing, as the *Daily Advertiser* concluded, Mary Jones's 'ruling passion appears too strong for punishment to subdue'.[59] She was who she was, and she would live her life accordingly.

Despite her penchant for theft and the administrative chaos she heaped on the state of New York – or because of these things, actually – I greatly admire Mary/Peter. There was no fall so great that Peter Sewally could not pick himself up again. No jokes, jibes or bullying so harsh that Mary Jones could not rise above them. To persevere in such a determined manner must have been exhausting, galling even, but time after time Jones defied authority to serve her 'ruling passion'. For Sewally, despite the repeated interventions of the state and the cruelty and danger he will have experienced during several spells of incarceration, his passion meant that he was determinedly unwilling or unable to sacrifice his womanhood. We can but conclude that it was too precious and too valuable a thing to give up.[60]

And so we take our leave of the indomitable Mary Jones as she returns to her usual beat on that warm summer evening in 1846, before she is taken up again. In that moment she stands amongst her fellow New Yorkers, a free queer Black woman, dressed in her finery, sporting a striking new hat. She struts about West Broadway, triumphant, despite the turmoil that has gone before. One foot in front of the other, she keeps on keeping on. Because that, my dear reader, is sometimes all it takes to make history.

Epilogue

On 4 March 1837, Martin Van Buren was inaugurated as the eighth President of the United States, overseeing a financial crisis that would shape the following decade. Across the Atlantic, on 20 June 1837, the eighteen-year-old Princess Alexandrina Victoria was divinely appointed Victoria, Queen of the United Kingdom of Great Britain and Ireland. This was a period of rapid technological and scientific innovation across much of the world. The 1830s saw the invention of what would become the modern refrigerator, for example. In the 1840s Dr William Morton became the first in his field to use anaesthesia for a tooth extraction. In 1862 Louis Pasteur perfected his process of pasteurization, and in 1868 Károly Mária Kertbeny 'invented' homosexuality. The French philosopher and historian Michael Foucault later proposed that our understanding of what it meant to be 'homosexual' should not predate Kertbeny. Foucault suggested that this was 'the precise moment when the "homosexual" created a radical rupture in western understandings of [sexual identity]', and that from there broader notions of queerness emerged.[1]

However, having spent more than five years in various archives in Europe and America, I have concluded that Foucault's theory is no more than a clever exercise in semantics and offers very little in the way of meaningful historical insight or analysis. In fact, I believe it has hindered it, as this idea has since been co-opted to deliberately conceal queer histories before the late nineteenth century.

Certainly, John Chute, Horace Mann and Antonio Cocchi would never have referred to themselves as 'homosexual' or 'gay' or 'queer', but they very much understood the personal, social and legal complexities of same-sex desire. These men placed their intimacies with other men above traditional marital unions, and they understood that this set them apart from much of the rest of male society. They also articulated an acute understanding of the potential physical and verbal violence they faced as a result of their minority status. In that way, though they may not have used the precise language to describe themselves as we do today, we might yet recognize something of ourselves in them.

Words and their meanings change. Labels and classifications date, identities modify, shift and revise themselves to suit each individual and each moment in time. They are changing, even now. When I first 'came out' in 2002 I told people I was gay because that was the word I had to hand. Now, if I have to choose something, queer feels more appropriate. To me, at least, both markers still very much feel like a continuation of the same history, a history that leads back to the mollies at Mother Clap's and beyond. We may not share the same words to describe ourselves, but we share in the same history nonetheless. Whilst investigating this history across the various archival collections that inform this book, I have identified four intersecting areas through which queer histories in the long eighteenth century can be interrogated, beyond identity markers. These are homes, marriage, community and the law.

Epilogue

Homes

The existing historiography on same-sex domestic life in the long eighteenth century, such as it is, has tended to focus on women's relationships, and not always satisfactorily. Amanda Vickery's brief analysis of Anne Lister's home life in *Behind Closed Doors*, for instance, concluded that she was a 'mannish lesbian romantic . . . the exception that proves the rule'.[2] The rule being that eighteenth-century homes were the refuge of those who could successfully heteroregulate. By contrast, it is the premise of this book that exceptions do not, in fact, prove the rule. Instead they offer scholars an opportunity to examine the rule again.

Concurrently, histories of (predominantly male) same-sex desire have tended to focus on the public locations where 'sodomites' met and had sex with other men: the streets, the alleyways and the latrines. Identifying and tracking these locations was an important step in uncovering the queer past, but it was only the first step. Combined with the idea that a fulfilling home life was reserved for heteroregulated intimacies, alongside what was previously understood to be the very public nature of same-sex activity between men, experts have concluded that queer intimacy in the eighteenth century was a very public affair; that queer Georgians could not be, and therefore were not, concerned with domestic lives. This research proves that that was not the case.

Mother Clap's, for example, was not only a place where men like Gabriel Lawrence could meet other men, though that was a vitally important function it fulfilled. It was also where his fellow mollies, William Griffin and Thomas Phillips, lived for more than two years. It was their home. At the other end of the social scale, John, Lord Hervey and his companion Ste Fox also made a home at No. 31 Great Burlington Street. Having discussed, in their letters, the possibility of one day living together, Hervey eventually oversaw the redecoration of the magnificent London town house so that it might better accommodate their companionship. Once complete, Hervey confessed, all the house required was Fox to make it a home.

John Chute's home, The Vyne, both in the collaborative nature of its interior design and in the naming of certain rooms, was a true reflection of his queer friends, the Strawberry Committee. In the comfort of their homes they could relax together, solidifying their friendships with mysterious, quasi-religious ceremonies. In contrast, Eleanor Butler and Sarah Ponsonby possessed the ability to both disrupt and create domestic space based on the needs of their relationship. For so long as the Butler and Fownes families tried to keep them apart, Butler and Ponsonby would continually threaten and upset their respective home lives by running away, breaking in and hiding in closets. However, once established at Plas Newydd in Llangollen, the ladies succeeded in making a home which so perfectly honoured their relationship that it attracted national attention. What's more, it provided other queer women, like Anne Lister, with a queer template which they hoped to replicate in their own home lives.

But if Butler and Ponsonby's house attracted attention for the ways in which it appeared unique, Lister wished to create something altogether more traditional at Shibden Hall. The Hall conferred upon her, as a landowner, a conventional type of respectability which in turn afforded her power and agency beyond what most contemporary women could have imagined. Shibden became the bricks and mortar wherein she imagined a perfectly queer household headed by herself and, eventually, a wife. Others, on the other hand, enjoyed the privilege of not having to care quite so much about domestic convention.

Behind the high walls at Fonthill Abbey, for instance, William Beckford and Gregório Franchi set about creating a decadent queer space wherein they could indulge their every fantasy, including, as this book has revealed, sex with other men. With its winding Gothic stairways and fairy-tale towers, however, the house never achieved a homely aspect. Instead it became something more like to a Studio 54-type mansion, 'a useless, amoral, and sensual space that lives only in and for experience. It is a space of spectacle, consumption . . . a space of pure artifice.'[3] Ultimately, Fonthill Abbey haunted its owner, leading to its eventual sale and the dissolution of the Beckford–Franchi companionship altogether.

For many queer people in the long eighteenth century, then, it is clear that the house, and more particularly the *home*, played a pivotal role in their lives and in shaping their identities. As we have seen, the home incorporated experiences of comfort, joy, companionship, 'perfect friendship' and sex. In that way, this book insists on the importance of domestic sites in order to more completely explore and understand queer lives in the pre-modern age.

Marriage

Some readers might be surprised at the extent to which marriage and marriage-like vocabulary weaves its way through these chapters. Certainly, the importance of the trope has escaped the attention of historians. But, as we have seen, marriage and traditions associated with it have long been used by queer people to signal the importance of queer relationships. Likewise, ideas of marriage were upended or subverted to satisfy queer expectations. For instance, the mollies at Mother Clap's disappeared into rooms together, by twos, to 'marry' one another, according to Ned Ward in 1709. This was backed up by later testimony provided by the spies for the Society for the Reformation of Manners, Samuel Stephens and Jospeh Sellers, as discussed in Chapters

One and Two. It is unclear exactly what 'marrying' meant to the mollies of the early eighteenth century, but both Ward and Stephens insinuate that it related to sex. In the eyes of the Society, therefore, the mollies' mockery was seen to undermine and threaten a cornerstone eighteenth-century institution. Despite this, it was to the language of marriage specifically that the mollies turned when they wanted to recognize their intimacies in a way that distanced what they did (and who they were) from ideas of legal retribution.

At the other end of the social scale, John, Lord Hervey deliberately used heteroregulated marriage to conceal his relationship with Ste Fox by matching him with a thirteen-year-old wife. This marriage, Hervey knew, would invest Fox with the privileges associated with mature Georgian masculinity, whilst Elizabeth Fox's age would ensure that they had to live apart, thus securing the Hervey–Fox intimacies for some time to come. The friendship group of John Chute and Francis Whithed went one step further, conferring a blended joint surname on the men, the Chuteheds. This naming ritual represented not only their closeness but also the familial implications of Chute having adopted Whithed.

None of our queer protagonists were more blatantly occupied with forming a marriage-like match than Anne Lister. Lister deliberately set out to find herself 'a wife'. She hoped, as we saw in Chapter Nine, that taking a wife would further bolster the power she exercised in and around Halifax as a landowner. Plus she needed some cash, a consideration in many well-planned gentry marriages in Georgian England. In hoping to secure herself a wife, Lister performed many of the recognizable customs associated with the institution too: the exchange of rings, prayers in a church, the signing of wills and so on. Though, as I have shown, it remains unclear if the women she performed such ceremonies with, particularly Ann Walker, viewed their exchanges in exactly the same way.

George Wilson, the Englishman in New York who had previously transed his gender identity in Scotland, married his boss's daughter, Elizabeth. The Wilsons' Barony marriage record demonstrates the simple ways in which blatantly queer histories might go unnoticed, where there are no clear indicators of queerness in sight. It is a tantalizing hint at other 'George Wilsons' who may have managed to dupe a system that sought to exclude them. Once he was discovered, many, even in his trial for vagrancy, were more intrigued by the ins and outs of his marriage with Elizabeth than with the details of his actual crime. Their union became a joke.

It is worth remembering too that Wilson seems to have carried some form of marriage certificate with him, as an insurance of sorts, should he ever find himself in the situation he did that summer in 1836. Wilson's document is reminiscent of the one reportedly found on Joseph Lyness in December 1844. The language is distinctly marital and insinuates that a formalized and witnessed union had taken place between himself and Peter Sewally, also known as Mary Jones.

So when commentators say that the history of same-sex marriage begins in the twentieth century with the fight for marriage equality, or with the legalization that emerged in 2001 (the Netherlands), 2013 (the United Kingdom) or 2015 (Ireland and the United States), they are woefully short-sighted in their analysis. For, as the Chuteheds, Lister and the mollies at Clap's establishment demonstrate, this history extends to the beginning of the eighteenth century at the very least. Marriage is, therefore, and always has been, a very queer institution indeed.

Community

The historical analysis of queer communities is, almost exclusively, the preserve of the twentieth century. Language, once again, plays a significant role in this. The notion of a queer community is, further, strongly tied to the history of the gay rights movement and the increased visibility this brought with it. Over time, our understanding of the tensions and intersections that influence the communities we belong to has led to a fracturing of old ideas of a monolithic queer community. This notion has been replaced by a greater appreciation for the many queer communities that exist and the ways in which they overlap and inform one another. But these queer communities did not miraculously emerge from nowhere in the twentieth century.

The *Oxford English Dictionary* defines 'community' as a shared 'social intercourse; fellowship, amity' (a meaning in use since the sixteenth century), or 'a group of people distinguished by shared circumstances of nationality, race, religion, sexuality, etc.' (since 1713).[4] Many of the protagonists we've encountered in this book belonged to just such a community. Therefore, we might now confidently state that the history of queer communities can be traced back to the eighteenth century, at the very least. The men at Clap's, including Gabriel Lawrence and Orange Deb, gathered there in joyful fellowship and amity in the run-up to the raid. They had coded maiden names for one another, could reveal a part of themselves otherwise hidden and had an awful lot of craic: a life enriched by their association with others like themselves.

The same can be said for Chute, Whithed, Walpole, Mann, Gray, Cocchi and their friends. Together, these committed bachelors forsook convention and embraced a life more befitting 'literary men'. Their sense of community was solidified in their 'catholic enjoyment' of secret rituals undertaken at The Vyne, but also in the peace and comfort they offered one another. When Walpole wanted to unburden himself of the fear of taunting from the boys at Westminster, or Gray wished to demonstrate that he no longer felt ashamed in public, they each turned to other members in their wider homosocial community because they knew, based on their shared experiences and identities, that they would empathize.

Beckford and Franchi cultivated their own all-male household at Fonthill Abbey, but a select few, whom Franchi names as part of their 'buggering' community, might also be invited into the relative privacy of the Abbey in order to mingle and have sex with other men. Beckford also hints at a wider community still when he suggests that *every* 'bugger' has been captivated by the beauty of the circus performer Saunders, for example.

These archivally supported histories remind me of the delightfully camp Mr Maiden, a character from Thomas Baker's hugely successful 1703 play *Tunbridge-Walks*. In it Maiden describes his little community who, he wants to make clear, do not meet in coffee houses or other public settings, preferring each other's homes as the location of their communes. Once there, Maiden and his friends enjoy a 'Bowl of Virgin-Punch' together, which they make themselves, demonstrating their domestic aptitude:

> We never make it with Rum nor Brandy – like your Sea-Captains, but two Quarts of Mead to half a Pint of White-Wine, Lemon-Juice, Burridge, and a little Perfume; then we never read Gazettes, nor talk of Menlo and Vigo like your Coffee-house Fellows, but play with Fans, and mimick the women; scream, hold up our Tails, make Curt'sies, and call one another Madam.[5]

Sounds like a good night out, if you ask me.

The law

Such gatherings, however, particularly those which took place in public at venues like Mother Clap's or at the White Swan on Vere Street, were not without their dangers. During the period under examination in this book, should they have been uncovered, under the Buggery Act (1533) it might well have meant death. Such was the fate that tragically befell Gabriel Lawrence and some of his comrades.

The entire history of the Chevalier d'Éon's gender identity was, I have argued in Chapter Six, the result of legislation imposed on him by the French king to punish him for his betrayal of France. The impetus for this royal enforcement, as the Chevalier understood it, was her sexuality. Subsequently, the ways in which modern historians and Chevalier enthusiasts alike have interpreted this singular queer history has been shaped by the lasting impact of this legislation and not the Chevalier's own drive to realize her true identity.

Both William Beckford and Kitty Courtenay were denied the comforts of their respective homes when the law threatened to pursue them for their same-sex sexual activity. This forced Beckford to leave for Europe in 1785 and Courtenay to flee in 1811 after he was indicted for buggery, after which he was forced to live in New York as it was perceived that the laws there had so tongue-tied themselves with regard to sex between men, it was a safe place to retreat to.

The laws of New York did not provide much escape for George Wilson and Mary Jones, however. Though both were arrested in 1836 for vagrancy and theft respectively, they each made headlines within hours once their gender non-conformity was discovered. This then became the focus of the police and judges who processed them through their various legal battles. And, for Mary Jones in particular, those battles were many. However, the subsequent archival trail that her encounters with the law has left has inadvertently provided us with a wealth of material with which we might attempt to piece together a coherent picture of an extraordinary queer life.

One note of caution on this point. A significant portion of the evidence examined throughout this book is derived from legal proceedings, be they the documents relating to Gabriel Lawrence's trial at the Old Bailey in London or the New York Police Watch Reports detailing the arrest and rearrests of Mary Jones/Peter Sewally. But when queer Georgians were thus arraigned, the slews of documents produced as a result are inherently set against them. The perspective they offer is skewed. So whilst official paper trails are an essential part of piecing these histories together, we must be critical of their agenda.

It would be remiss of me not to mention the modern iterations of these eighteenth-century anti-queer laws. After decades of what felt like progress, we are beginning to see the erosion of hard-won LGBTQIA+ legal rights and social recognition across the globe. In Oklahoma, for example, current 'AIDS prevention education shall specifically teach students that: 1. engaging in homosexual activity . . . is now known to be primarily responsible for contact with the AIDS virus'.[6] In Texas, emphasis is placed on the idea that 'homosexuality is not a lifestyle acceptable to the general public'.[7] In Colorado, despite same-sex marriages having become legal nationwide in the United States in 2015, the state Constitution still dictates that 'Only a union of one man and one woman shall be valid or recognized as a marriage in this state.'[8] And in Florida, Governor Ron DeSantis has become so hysterical in his pursuit of transgender youth that he has put in place laws governing their toileting habits and prohibiting the use of pronouns in classrooms beyond those they were assigned at birth.

Literally hundreds of similarly intrusive and restrictive laws are currently being proposed in Republican-leaning states across the United States. On top of that, the current incumbent at the White House has rabidly begun erasing federal nondiscrimination protections for LGBTQIA+ people, and, more specifically, introduced mandates that target transgender people, who make up less than 1 per cent of the population of the United States.

England, Scotland, Wales and Ireland are, despite relatively favourable legislation, increasingly unsafe places for LGBTQIA+ people too, with hate crime targeted towards the community on the rise. According to the charity Stonewall, 41 per cent of trans people in Britain have experienced a hate crime linked to their gender identity; 58 per cent of gay men refrain from holding hands with their partner in public for fear of violent retribution, and 34 per cent of queer people with global-majority heritage living in Britain have been the victim of a hate crime due to their sexual and/or gender orientation.[9]

Elsewhere, in March 2023, Uganda imposed the Anti-Homosexuality Act, which will see severe punishments for engaging in same-sex relationships, discussing your queer identity or even renting or selling a property to a queer person. In July 2023 a Bill banning all gender-affirming care for trans Russians was passed in the upper house of parliament. This follows a 2022 law which prohibits the discussion or promotion of LGBTQIA+ relationships.

Following this litany of legally enforced oppression across centuries, it feels increasingly difficult to find what we have determinedly sought, where possible, in this book: inspiration and hope. But it is my belief, as a historian, that in the face of these aggressions our queer past matters now more than ever. For the people who promote these laws are the same people who would deny us our histories. And why would they deny them us? Because these histories are powerful.

*

Epilogue

Presented with these, our queer ancestors, queer people today might now situate themselves in a once-forgotten history and, in so doing, claim their place in society with even more determination and expectation. These histories prove that LGBTQIA+ identities were categorically *not* invented by twenty- and twenty-first-century 'liberal elites' with a 'woke mind virus', as certain billionaires have suggested.[10] Instead our roots run deep and our resilience knows no bounds; the centuries have shown it. Thus, where once you felt isolated or downtrodden, I hope you find companionship in the pages of this book. Not fictional renderings of an imagined better way, but proof of our persistence.

Gabriel Lawrence's determined insistence on keeping the company of men like himself, despite the associated dangers, offers us an example of everyday courage, does it not? Margaret Clap's allyship is exuberantly uplifting. The simplicity of John, Lord Hervey and Ste Fox's homemaking at No. 31 Great Burlington Street (aided, to be fair, by their healthy budget) emerges here as a triumphantly quotidian display of same-sex devotion. A simple thing. A revolutionary thing. The Chuteheds and the Ladies of Llangollen demonstrate how the benefits and intimacies of marriage did not, in fact, exclude same-sex-attracted people in the eighteenth and nineteenth centuries. At the same time, Beckford, Franchi and Courtenay prove the value of alternative queer households. Both George Wilson and Mary Jones demonstrate the long tradition of transing one's gender identity. Together, these histories remind us that even when the odds are stacked against us we survive (d'Éon), and that given our tenacity (Lister) we may thrive yet. Each one of us, shoulder to shoulder with the other; nobody left behind.

Notes

AUTHOR'S NOTE

1 Anthony Delaney, 'Cotqueans: Queer Domesticity in Eighteenth-Century England', PhD Thesis (University of Exeter, 2003). See also Lauren Berlant and Michael Warner, 'Sex in Public', *Critical Inquiry* 24, no. 2 (1998), pp. 547–66, 549.
2 William Dorland, *Dorland's Illustrated Medical Dictionary* (Philadelphia, 1901), Webster's *New International Dictionary* (G. & C. Merriam: Springfield, 1923).
3 Eve Kosofsky Sedgwick, *Tendencies* (Durham, NC: Duke University Press, 1993), pp. 8–9.

PROLOGUE

1 Though it should be noted that the Georgian period (1714–1837) is technically shorter than the long eighteenth century (c.1680–1837).
2 Amanda Vickery, *Behind Closed Doors: At Home in Georgian England* (London: Yale University Press, 2009), p. 193.
3 *Oxford English Dictionary*, cotquean, n., June 2022, https://www.oed.com/view/Entry/42446?redirectedFrom=cotquean (accessed 4 September 2020). Barbara Dancygier, *The Cambridge Handbook of Cognitive Linguistics* (Cambridge: Cambridge University Press, 2017), p. 5. Richard Hogarth's *Gazophylacium Anglicanum* (London, 1689) provided

the following etymological explanation: 'Cockquean, or Cotquean, q. d. Cook quean, one that playeth the Cook among women: Or from the Teut. Kochin, a she-Cook', ff. 5v–6r.
4   Samuel Johnson, *A Dictionary of the English Language* (London, 1755), p. 485.
5   Ibid., pp. 31–2.
6   Joseph Addison, *The Freeholder: Numb. XXXVIII Monday, April 30* (London, 1716), Martin Parker, *The Figure of Five* (London, 1645).
7   Anon., *Satan's Harvest Home: Or the Present State of Whorecraft* (London, 1749), p. 49.
8   Erin Blakemore, 'The Revolutionary War Hero Who Was Openly Gay', www.History.com 14 June 2018, updated 22 June 2023, https://www.history.com/news/openly-gay-revolutionary-war-hero-friedrich-von-steuben (accessed 16 May 2024).
9   Josh Trujillo and Levi Hastings, *Washington's Gay General: The Legends and Loves of Baron von Steuben* (New York: Surely, 2023).

CHAPTER ONE: A HOUSE ON FIELD LANE

1   Emily Cockayne, *Hubbub: Filth, Noise & Stench in England, 1600–1770*, new edn (London: Yale University Press, 2021).
2   milkman, n.s., Samuel Johnson, *A Dictionary of the English Language* (London, 1773), https://johnsonsdictionaryonline.com/1755/milkman_ns 'man who sells milk' (accessed 22 February 2023).
3   Trial of Martin Mackintosh, July 1726, *Old Bailey Proceedings Online*, https://www.oldbaileyonline.org/browse.jsp?id=t17260711-53&div=t17260711-53&terms=Martin_mackintosh#highlight, 28 March 2023, t17260711-53.
4   Ibid.
5   Walter Thornbury, 'Holborn: The Northern Tributaries', in *Old and New London: Volume 2* (London, 1878), pp. 542–52, British History Online, http://www.british-history.ac.uk/old-new-london/vol2/pp542-552 (accessed 10 February 2023). Charles Dickens, *Oliver Twist* (London, 1837).
6   John Strype, *Survey of the Cities of London and Westminster* (London, 1720).
7   Trial of Gabriel Lawrence, 20 April 1726, *Old Bailey Proceedings Online*, https://www.oldbaileyonline.org/browse.jsp?id=t17260420-64&div=

t17260420-64&terms=Gabriel_Lawrence#highlight (accessed 6 March 2023).

8 Daniel Maudlin, 'The Urban Inn: Gathering Space, Hierarchy and Material Culture in the Eighteenth-Century British Town', *Urban History* 46, issue 4 (November 2019), pp. 617–48.

9 It was the linkboy's job to carry a torch to light the way for pedestrians at night.

10 Trial of Margaret Clap, 11 July 1726, *Old Bailey Proceedings Online*, https://www.oldbaileyonline.org/browse.jsp?id=t17260711-54&div=t17260711-54&terms=Derwin_Margaret_clap#highlight (accessed 6 March 2023).

11 Nick Levine, 'Mother!: A Queer Term Centuries in the Making', *Gay Times*, 22 February 2023, https://www.gaytimes.co.uk/originals/mother-a-queer-term-centuries-in-the-making/ (accessed 19 April 2023).

12 Edward Ward, *The Secret History of Clubs* (London, 1709), p. 284.

13 Ibid.

14 'Isaac Bickerstaff', *The Tatler*, vol. 1, issue 26 (London, 7–9 June 1709).

15 Anon., Societies for the Reformation of Manners, *Proposals for a National Reformation of Manners* (London, 1693), pp. 1–5.

16 Ward, *The Secret History of Clubs*.

17 The information gathered in the following section has been brought together from first-hand accounts of eighteenth-century prisoners at Newgate. They include Batty Langley (c.1696–1751), the eccentric English garden designer who was held at Newgate for debt in 1724, and the notorious robber John Hall, who published his own 'lively representation of Newgate' in 1708. Alongside these first-hand prisoner accounts, specific details from Ordinaries at Newgate that emerged following Lawrence's trial help to accentuate the queerer elements at this notorious London gaol.

18 Stephen Halliday, *Newgate: London's Prototype of Hell* (Stroud: Sutton, 2007).

19 John Hall, *Memoirs of the Right Villainous John Hall*, 4th edn (London, 1714).

20 Batty Langley, *An Accurate Description of Newgate* (London: printed for T. Warner, at the Black Boy in Pater-Noster-Row, 1724), https://link-gale-com.uoelibrary.idm.oclc.org/apps/doc/CW0102668682/ECCO?u=exeter&sid=ebsco&xid=0e83e542&pg=1.

Notes to pp. 27–46

21 Hall, *Memoirs of the Right Villainous John Hall*.
22 Langley, *An Accurate Description of Newgate*.
23 Hall, *Memoirs of the Right Villainous John Hall*.

CHAPTER TWO: THE DEADLY NEVERGREEN

1 Walter Thornbury, 'The Old Bailey', in *Old and New London: Volume 2* (London, 1878), pp. 461–77.
2 Thomas Pennant, *Some Accounts of London*, 2nd edn (London, 1793).
3 Bernard de Mandeville, *An Enquiry into the Causes of the Frequent Executions at Tyburn* (London, 1725), p. 17.
4 John H. Langbein, 'The Prosecutorial Origins of Defence Counsel in the Eighteenth Century: The Appearance of Solicitors', *The Cambridge Law Journal* 58, no. 2 (1999), pp. 314–65.
5 Trial of Gabriel Lawrence, April 1726, *Old Bailey Proceedings Online*, https://www.oldbaileyonline.org/browse.jsp?id=t17260420-64&div=t17260420-64&terms=Margaret_clap#highlight (accessed 10 July 10 2023).
6 Ibid.
7 Trial of George Whytle, 20 April 1726, *Old Bailey Proceedings Online*, https://www.oldbaileyonline.org/browse.jsp?id=t17260420-68&div=t17260420-68&terms=George_Whytle_sodomy#highlight (accessed 10 July 2023).
8 Joanne Bailey, *Unquiet Lives: Marriage and Marriage Breakdown in England, 1660–1800* (Cambridge: Cambridge University Press, 2003), p. 2. Fraser Easton has written about the laws which were 'linked to the social regulation of the poor' in 'Gender's Two Bodies: Women Warriors, Female Husbands and Plebian Life', *Past & Present* no. 180 (2003), pp. 131–74, 135–6.
9 Martin Madan, *Thoughts on Executive Justice with respect to our Criminal Law*, 2nd edn (London, 1785), p. 26.
10 De Mandeville, *An Enquiry*, p. 21.
11 In 1725 de Mandeville observed: 'WHEN the Day of Execution is come, among extraordinary Sinners, and Persons condemned for their Crimes, who have but that Morning to live, one would expect a deep Sense of Sorrow, with all the Signs of a thorough Contrition, and the utmost Concern; that either Silence, or a sober Sadness, should prevail; and that all, who had any Business there, should be grave and serious, and behave

themselves, at least, with common Decency, and a Deportment suitable to the Occasion. But the very Reverse is true.'
12 Ibid.
13 James Boswell, 'The Execution of Gibson and Payne', *The Public Advertiser*, 26 April 1768.
14 Trial of Margaret Clap, *Proceedings of the Old Bailey Online*, https://www.oldbaileyonline.org/browse.jsp?id=t17260711-54&div=t17260711-54&terms=margaret_clap#highlight (accessed 19 July 2023).
15 César De Saussure quoted in Robert Shoemaker, *The London Mob: Violence and Disorder in Eighteenth-century England* (London: Bloomsbury, 2004), p. 82.

CHAPTER THREE: SEDITION AND DEFAMATION DISPLAY'D

1 R. Halsband, *The Life of Lady Mary Wortley Montagu* (Oxford: Oxford University Press, 1961), p. 118.
2 John, Lord Hervey, *Lord Hervey and His Friends, 1726–38, Based on Letters from Holland House, Melbury, and Ickworth*, ed. the Earl of Ilchester (London: John Murray, 1950), p. 16.
3 Ibid., p. 257. Hervey to Fox, 4 December 1736.
4 Susan Whyman, *The Pen and The People: English Letter Writers 1660–1800* (Oxford: Oxford University Press, 2009), p. 20.
5 honey-moon, n.s., Johnson, *A Dictionary of the English Language*, https://johnsonsdictionaryonline.com/1773/honey-moon_ns (accessed 14 January 2025).
6 Hervey, *Lord Hervey and His Friends*, Hervey to Fox, 1 June 1727, p. 16.
7 BL Add 51345, f. 28, Hervey to Fox, 18 November 1729.
8 See Prologue, pp. 2–4.
9 Horace Walpole, *Horace Walpole's Correspondence*, vol. 33, 'Walpole to Lady Ossary, 7 August 1778' (Yale University: The Lewis Walpole Library), p. 37.
10 Ibid.
11 See Hervey, *Lord Hervey and His Friends* and John, Lord Hervey, *The Collected Verse of John, Lord Hervey (1696–1743)*, ed. Bill Overton (Cambridge: Cambridge University Press, 2016).
12 John, Lord Hervey, *Some Materials Towards Memoirs of the Reign of King George II*, ed. Romney Sedgwick, 3 vols (London, 1931), p. xv.

13 Frederick Augustus followed in 1730, William in 1732, Amelia Caroline Nassua in 1734 and Caroline in 1736.
14 Robert Halsband, *Lord Hervey: Eighteenth-Century Courtier* (Oxford: Oxford University Press, 1973), p. 58.
15 Ibid., p. 59.
16 Anon., *Satan's Harvest Home*, p. 51.
17 BL Add MS 51345, f. 15, Mary Hervey to Stephen Fox, 9 December 1728.
18 Ibid., f. 13, Mary Hervey to Stephen Fox, 20 September 1728.
19 Ibid., f. 15, 9 December 1728.
20 Ibid., ff. 89–90, 26 July 1741.
21 Ibid., f. 118, lines 212–15.
22 Harrowby MS, ff. 66r–66v, Hervey to Henry Fox, Florence 1729.
23 See Chapter Five.
24 See John, Lord Hervey, *The Collected Verse of John, Lord Hervey (1696–1743)*.
25 For details of the duel see Hervey, *Lord Hervey and His Friends*, and Lucy Moore, *Amphibious Thing: The Life of Lord Hervey* (London: Viking, 2000), pp. 112–18.

CHAPTER FOUR: NO. 31 GREAT BURLINGTON STREET

1 Suffolk Record Office 941/47/4, f. 120, Hervey to Fox, 21 August 1730.
2 Denotes a small dwelling in this context.
3 Mary Douglas, 'The Idea of a Home: A Kind of Space', *Social Research* 58, no. 1 (1991), pp. 287–307, 289.
4 Hervey, *Lord Hervey and His Friends*, p. 58.
5 Halsband, *Lord Hervey*, p. 120.
6 Hervey, *Lord Hervey and His Friends*, p. 137.
7 Ibid., p. 232, Hervey to Mrs Digby, 13 November 1735.
8 Catamite is another word for sodomite.
9 Halsbrand, *Lord Hervey*, p. 189.
10 Henry French and Mark Rothery, *Man's Estate: Landed Gentry Masculinities, 1660–1900* (Oxford: Oxford University Press, 2012), p. 192.
11 Tanya Evans, 'Women, Marriage and the Family', in Hannah Barker and Elaine Chalus, *Gender in Eighteenth-Century England: Roles, Representations and Responsibilities* (Harlow: Longman, 1997), pp. 57–71.

12 Mark Searle and Kenneth W. Stevenson, *Documents of the Marriage Liturgy* (New York: Pueblo Publishing, 1992), p. 217.
13 Eve Kosofsky Sedgwick, *Between Men: English Literature and Male Homosocial Desire* (New York: Columbia University Press, 1985), p. 26.
14 Hervey, *Lord Hervey and His Friends*, pp. 274–5.
15 For more on queer family romance see Witney Davis, 'Queer Family Romance in Collecting Visual Culture', *GLQ* 17, no. 2–3 (2011), pp. 309–29. For a more in-depth analysis of *Lord Hervey and His Friends* see Jill Campbell, 'Politics and Sexuality in Portraits of John, Lord Hervey', *Word & Image* 6, no. 4 (1990), pp. 281–97.
16 Halsband, *Lord Hervey*, p. 199.
17 Ibid., pp. 198–203.
18 Don K. Nakayama, 'Queen Caroline's Umbilical Hernia', *The American Surgeon* 89, issue 1 (2023), pp. 5–8.
19 BL Add MS 51337, f. 6, Elizabeth Fox-Strangways to Stephen Fox-Strangways, 3 October 1736.
20 Ibid., f. 9.
21 Ibid., f. 13.
22 BL Add MS 51345, f. 100, Mary Hervey to Lord Ilchester, 3 December 1743.
23 BL Add MS 51337, f. 73, Ilchester to Lady Ilchester, 26 April 1755.
24 Helen Berry and Elizabeth A. Foyster, *The Family in Early Modern England* (Cambridge: Cambridge University Press, 2007), p. 181.

CHAPTER FIVE: OUR LITTLE COMMUNITY

1 Hampshire Record Office 31M57/942, f. 1.
2 Thomas Gray to John Chute, October 1746, and see Figure 10, National Trust, https://www.nationaltrustcollections.org.uk/object/718711 (accessed 11 October 2023).
3 Raymond Bentman, 'Horace Walpole's Forbidden Passion', in *Queer Representations: Reading Lives, Reading Cultures*, ed. Martin Dubeman (New York: New York University Press, 1997), p. 277.
4 Ibid., Horace Walpole to Horace Man, 4 November 1746.
5 GBR/1058/GRA/3/4/44, Gray to Walpole, 13 May 1748.
6 Horace Walpole, *The Letters of Horace Walpole: Earl of Orford*, vol.1, ed. John Wright (Philadelphia: Lea and Blanchard), p. 532; Horace Walpole,

The Letters of Horace Walpole: Earl of Orford, vol. 2, ed. John Wright (Philadelphia: Lea and Blanchard), p. 202.

7 Walpole, *Horace Walpole's Correspondence*, vol. 9, Walpole to Montagu, 18 May 1748, p. 54.

8 Ibid., Walpole to Mann, 1 April 1751.

9 Ned Ward, 'Of the Mollies Club', in *Satyrical Reflections on Clubs*, vol. 5 (London, 1709).

10 *Select Trials at the Sessions-House, in the Old-Bailey*, vol. 2 (London, 1742), pp. 362–4.

11 Sharon Marcus, *Between Women: Friendship, Desire, and Marriage in Victorian England* (Princeton: Princeton University Press, 2007), p. 104. See also Stephen G. Hague and Karen Lipsedge (eds), *At Home in the Eighteenth Century: Interrogating Domestic Space* (New York: Routledge, 2022) and Freya Gowrley, *Domestic Space in Britain, 1750–1840: Materiality, Sociability and Emotion* (New York: Bloomsbury Academic, 2022). In both instances Hague and Lipsedge and Gowrley attempt a highly valuable 'queering' of the domestic space as opposed to demonstrating the archival potential to support queer domestic practice.

12 Vickery, *Behind Closed Doors*, p. 77.

13 French and Rothery, *Man's Estate*, p. 4.

14 Vickery, *Behind Closed Doors*, p. 82.

15 William Seymar, *Marriage Asserted, in Answer to a Book Entitled Conjugium Conjugium* (London, 1700), p. vii.

16 celibate, n.s., Johnson, *A Dictionary of the English Language*, https://johnsonsdictionaryonline.com/1755/celibate_ns (accessed 12 October 2003).

17 Quoted in John Nichols, *Literary Anecdotes of the Eighteenth Century*, vol. 1 (London, 1812), p. 347.

18 Antonio Cocchi, *Del matrimonio discorso di Antonio Cocchi Mugellano* (Pisa, 1762). Published in English as Antonio Cocchi, *The Grand Question, Is Marriage Fit for Literary Men?*, trans. Paul Heffernan (London, 1769).

19 Cocchi, *The Grand Question*, p. ii.

20 Ibid., pp. 88–9. A coxcomb was a flashy Georgian man who aggressively pursued multiple women.

21 Clorinda Donato, 'Where Reason and the Sense of Venus Are Innate in Men: Male Friendship, Secret Societies, Academies, and Antiquarians in Eighteenth-Century Florence', *Italian Studies* 65, no. 3 (November 2010), pp. 329–44, 344. Although Donato's research looks specifically at Cocchi's

native Italy, Heffernan's relatively speedy translation, its subsequent reprints, and Cocchi's associations with Mann, Walpole and Chute are testament to the relevance of his words to a network of bachelors in England too.

22   Ibid., p. 154.
23   Hampshire Record Office 31M57/637, 'Bill of Frederick Kandler to John Chute', 1756–8. 'Nurling' or knurling meant the item had been impressed *à la française* with a series of fine serrations.
24   Ibid.
25   See Markman Ellis, 'Tasting Eighteenth-Century Tea', *Tea in Eighteenth Century Britain*, History of Tea Project, Queen Mary University of London, 2 September 2013, https://qmhistoryoftea.wordpress.com/2013/09/02/tasting-eighteenth-century-tea/ (accessed 31 May 2024).
26   Hampshire Record Office 31M57/637, f. 4.
27   Ibid.
28   Walpole, *Horace Walpole's Correspondence*, vol. 14, Gray to Walpole, 21 September 1756, p. 96, https://libsvcs-1.its.yale.edu/hwcorrespondence/page.asp (accessed 18 February 2021).
29   Ibid., vol. 9, Walpole to Montagu, 25 August 1757, p. 216, https://libsvcs-1.its.yale.edu/hwcorrespondence/page.asp (accessed 18 February 2021).
30   Chute was forced to sell his London house in 1760 for £3,000 in order to facilitate work at The Vyne. In 1762 the house and its estates were mortgaged to provide further financial relief, though by 1765 his fortunes had stabilized enough for him to purchase another London residence close to Berkeley Square. Ibid., 20 August 1758.
31   Walpole quoted in Maurice Howard, *The Vyne, Hampshire* (Corsham: National Trust, 2018), p. 58.
32   Thomas Gray, *Correspondence of Thomas Gray*, ed. Paget Toynbee, Leonard Whibley and H. W. Starr, vol. 1 (Oxford: Clarendon Press, 1971), p. 184.
33   His sentiments call to mind Irish drag queen Panti Bliss's (Rory O'Neill) viral 'Noble Call' of 2014 when she declared, 'Sometimes I hate myself. I f*cking hate myself, because I check myself when I stand at pedestrian crossings.' Rory expressed fear that he might be violently targeted in public because of his queerness.
34   Walpole, *Horace Walpole's Correspondence*, vol. 35, Walpole to Chute, 4 August 1753, p. 71, https://libsvcs-1.its.yale.edu/hwcorrespondence/page.asp?vol=35&seq=109&type=b (accessed 5 July 2022).
35   Ibid.

CHAPTER SIX: THE SPECULATION

1. Louis XV had died in 1774.
2. Charles d'Eon de Beaumont, *The Maid of Tonnerre: The Vicissitudes of the Chevalier and Chevalière d'Eon*, ed. and trans. Roland A. Champagne, Nona Ekstein and Gary Kates (London: Johns Hopkins University Press, 2001), pp. 58–61.
3. Jono Namara, 'The Chevalier d'Éon: The 18th Century Transgender Spy', BBC reel, 7 April 2022, https://www.bbc.co.uk/reel/video/pobzwxqy/the-chevalier-d-on-the-18th-century-transgender-spy
4. Charles d'Eon de Beaumont, *Memoirs of the Chevalier d'Eon: Louis XV's favourite spy required by Versailles and St James's never to dress as a man*, trans. Antonia White (London: Anthony Blond, 1970), p. xvi.
5. Gary Kates, *Monsieur d'Éon is a Woman: A Tale of Political Intrigue and Sexual Masquerade* (London: Johns Hopkins University Press, 2001), p. 94.
6. Nivernais to the Comte de Choiseul, 2 October 1762, in *Lettres, mémoires, et négociations particulières du Chevalier d'Éon*, 3 vols (London, 1764), 1, 2:2.
7. Anna Clark, 'The Chevalier d'Éon and Wilkes: Masculinity and Politics in the Eighteenth Century', *Eighteenth-Century Studies* 32, no. 1 (Fall 1998), pp. 19–48, 19.
8. Joseph Addison, *The Freeholder: Numb. XXXVIII Monday, April 30* (London, 1716).
9. 'The trial of M. D'Eon by a jury of matrons', British Museum, https://www.britishmuseum.org/collection/object/P_1886-1221-6 (accessed 31 May 2024).
10. D'Éon, *Memoirs*, pp. xv–xvi.
11. Karen Harvey, *The Impostress Rabbit Breeder: Mary Toft and Eighteenth-Century England* (Oxford: Oxford University Press, 2020).
12. 'A Celebrated Hoax', *Tungamah and Lake Rowan Express and St. James Gazette*, 23 June 1892.
13. 'Brewer-Street', *Morning Post*, 13 November 1775.
14. '18 November 1776', *Kentish Gazette*, 19 July 1777.
15. D'Éon, *The Maid of Tonnerre*, p. 28.
16. 'The SEX of D'EON *Determined*', *Derby Mercury*, 4 July 1777.
17. Ibid.
18. Ibid.
19. 'Lord Mansfield', *Caledonian Mercury*, 5 July 1777.

20 'The SEX of D'EON *Determined*', *Derby Mercury*, 4 July 1777.
21 'Brewer-Street', *Kentish Gazette*, 20 August 1777.
22 'Yesterday', *Derby Mercury*, 15 August 1777.
23 D'Éon, *The Maid of Tonnerre*, p. 61.
24 Ibid., p. 28.
25 'Madame D'Eon', *Oxford Journal*, 3 December 1785.
26 Hannah More, *Percy: A Tragedy* (London, 1784), Prologue.
27 James Boswell, *Boswell, the English Experiment, 1785–1789*, ed. Irma S. Lustig and Frederick A. Pottle (New York: McGraw-Hill, 1986), p. 48.
28 'George IV', *Britannica*, https://www.britannica.com/biography/George-IV (accessed 3 June 2024).
29 *Ipswich Journal*, 21 April 1787.
30 *Kentish Gazette*, 2 November 1787.
31 D'Éon, *The Maiden of Tonnerre*, p. 18.
32 Cynthia Cox, *The Enigma of the Age: The Strange Story of the Chevalier d'Eon* (London: Longmans, 1966), p. 132.
33 *Staffordshire Advertiser*, 20 June 1795.
34 *Chester Chronicle*, 27 February 1795.
35 *Caledonian Mercury*, 10 August 1795.
36 *Gloucester Journal*, 31 August 1795.
37 Ibid.
38 'Mademoiselle D'EON Fencing Here', advertisement for d'Éon's appearance at 'the lower rooms, Bath', issued December 1795. See Kates, *Monsieur d'Éon is a Woman*, p. 275.
39 *Reading Mercury*, 5 September 1796.
40 *Cumberland Pacquet*, 16 January 1798.
41 D'Éon, *The Maid of Tonnerre*, p. 6.
42 Kates, *Monsieur d'Éon is a Woman*, p. xviii.
43 'Anatomical drawing of the penis and emaciated thighs of Charles Genevieve Louis Auguste Andree Timothee D'Eon de Beaumont (called the Chevalier D'Eon)', British Museum, 1868, 0808.7947, c.1810, https://www.britishmuseum.org/collection/object/P_1868-0808-7947 (accessed 3 June 2024).
44 *The Sun*, 24 May 1810.
45 *Pilot London*, 25 May 1810.
46 *General Evening Post*, 26 May 1810.

47 John V. Grombach to Alfred C. Kinsey, 20 May 1953.
48 Alfred C. Kinsey to John V. Grombach, 28 May 1953.
49 D'Éon, *Memoirs*, p. xxi.
50 J. M. J. Rogister, 'D'Éon de Beaumont, Charles Geneviève Louis Auguste André Timothée, Chevalier D'Éon in the French nobility', *Oxford Dictionary of National Biography*, 4 October 2012, https://www.oxforddnb.com/display/10.1093/ref:odnb/9780198614128.001.0001/odnb-9780198614128-e-7523?rskey=QqmM4G&result=1 (accessed 3 June 2024).
51 Hugh Ryan, 'How This 18th Century French Spy Came Out as Trans', them, 9 April 2018, https://www.them.us/story/chevalier-d-eon-trans-woman (accessed 3 June 2024). 'The Chevalier d'Éon: The 18th Century Transgender Spy', BBC, 7 April 2022, https://www.bbc.com/reel/video/pobzwxqy/the-chevalier-d-on-the-18th-century-transgender-spy (accessed 3 June 2024).
52 Gary Kates, 'The Transgendered World of the Chevalier/Chevalière d'Eon', *The Journal of Modern History* 67, no. 3 (September 1995), pp. 558–94, 599.
53 D'Éon, *The Maiden of Tonnerre*, p. 3.
54 Ibid., p. 16.
55 Ibid., p. 17.
56 University of Leeds, Brotherton Collection box 7, file 20, p. 120.

CHAPTER SEVEN: THAT FEVERISH DREAM CALLED YOUTH

1 It's thought that this idea was coined by Francis Plowden in 1803 and infers the 'Gaelicization' of the early Anglo-Norman settlers in Ireland.
2 *Reminiscences of Mrs Caroline Hamilton*, MS. 4811, National Library of Ireland.
3 Ibid.
4 Ibid.
5 Ibid.
6 Ibid.
7 Ibid.
8 Ibid.
9 Ibid.
10 Ibid.
11 Lady Betty Fownes to Lucy Goddard, NLI Wicklow MS.

12 Eugene Coyle, 'The Irish Ladies of Llangollen: "the most celebrated virgins in Europe"', *History Ireland* 23, issue 6 (November/December 2015).
13 Hamwood Papers, 29. See also Elizabeth Mavor, *The Ladies of Llangollen: A Study in Romantic Friendship* (London: Moonrise Press, 2011), pp. 38–9.
14 Hamwood Papers, f. 29.
15 Ibid., f. 30.
16 Ibid.
17 Ibid.
18 Ibid.
19 Ibid.
20 Ibid.
21 Ibid.
22 Ibid.
23 Ibid., f. 36.
24 Ibid., f. 38.
25 Mavor, *The Ladies of Llangollen*, p. 47.
26 *Reminiscences of Mrs Caroline Hamilton*, MS. 4811, National Library of Ireland.
27 Ibid.

CHAPTER EIGHT: INFLAMMABLE MATERIALS

1 'Kitty' was an affectionate name used by his family when writing to him and, as a result, the current Courtenays, or so I've been told by members of the household, don't encourage the use of Kitty beyond the family. However, in the tradition of molly maiden names outlined in Chapter One, I think the name Kitty has significant historical meaning and inferences. Likewise, in the canon of historical queerness, I would argue that Kitty belongs to a wider, queerer family too. As such, I use Kitty in this chapter where I can.
2 Letter from Charles Greville to Sir William Hamilton, 25 December 1784, https://william1768courtenay.com/scandal-of-1784-texts-from-the-time/
3 *Morning Herald*, London, 27 November 1784.
4 See *Morning Herald*, 30 December 1784, and letter from Charles Greville to Sir William Hamilton, 25 December 1784. See https://william1768courtenay.com/ for transcripts and further details of letters.

5   Letter from Beckford at Fonthill to Samuel Henley, 13 October 1784.
6   Ibid.
7   Diary entry by Hester Piozzi, 3 January 1791.
8   Letter from Lady Margaret Gordon to Lady Gower, 22 November 1784.
9   Letter from Beckford to Lady Craven, c.1790.
10 See Boyd Alexander (trans. and ed.), *Life at Fonthill 1807–1822 with Interludes in Paris and London from the Correspondence* (London: R. Hart-Davis, 1957), p. 28 and Rictor Norton, 'Dearest Impresario; The Gay Love Letters of William Beckford', in *Gay History and Literature: Essays by Rictor Norton*, 1998, http://rictornorton.co.uk/beckford.htm (accessed 5 October 2021).
11 Boyd Alexander, *Lisbon to Baker Street: The Story of the Chevalier Franchi, Beckford's Friend* (Lisbon: British Historical Society Portugal, 1977), pp. 8–9.
12 Ibid., p. 10.
13 Ibid., p. 29.
14 Ibid., p. 23. 'Stupid, stupid, stupid, it makes me tremble.'
15 Meg Kobza, unpublished PhD thesis, Newcastle University, p. 18.
16 *Public Advertiser*, 7 August 1790.
17 Bridget Purling-Stream to Miss Diana Paleface, *The Times*, 7 August 1790. The names used are pseudonyms.
18 Rictor Norton, 'Oddities, Obituaries and Obsessions: Early Nineteenth-Century Scandal and Social History Glimpsed through William Beckford's Newspaper Cuttings', *The Beckford Society Annual Lectures 2004–2006*, ed. Richard Allen, 2008, p. 19.
19 *Morning Post*, 4 August 1790.
20 Whitney Davis, 'Queer Family Romance in Collecting Visual Culture', *GLQ Journal of Lesbian and Gay Studies* 17 (2–3), pp. 309–29.
21 Alexander, *Life at Fonthill*, p. 55.
22 'Visit to Fonthill', *Literary Gazette* (1822), p. 527.
23 William Beckford, *Life at Fonthill 1807–1822 with Interludes in Paris and London from the Correspondence*, ed. Boyd Alexander (London: R. Hart-Davis, 1957), p. 74.
24 Ibid., p. 25.
25 Ibid., p. 43. The letter, originally in Italian for security, has been edited here by Alexander, who omitted the word 'bugger's'.

26 Ms. Beckford c.13, f. 47. Italian (vulgar): *cresce il vento, nunca l'arte, e si faran tuttes buggerar*. A series of code names appear to have been used to conceal the identity of those referred to in Franchi's letter.
27 Tim Flight, 'You Won't Believe the Architectural Vision of a True English Eccentric', *History Collection*, 12 April 2018, https://historycollection.com/you-wont-believe-the-architectural-vision-of-a-true-english-eccentric/2/ (accessed 3 June 2024).
28 Alexander, *Life at Fonthill*, p. 98.
29 Ibid., p. 114.
30 Ibid., p. 110.
31 *The Star*, 11 January 1811.
32 Alexander, *Life at Fonthill*, p. 92.
33 *Oxford English Dictionary*, s.v. sod (*n.3*), sense 2.a, June 2024, https://doi.org/10.1093/OED/1184979940
34 *The Diary of Joseph Farington*, 1810, Royal Collections Trust, RCIN 1047069.
35 *Morning Chronicle*, 25 February 1811.
36 Norton, 'Oddities, Obituaries and Obsessions: Early Nineteenth-Century Scandal and Social History Glimpsed through William Beckford's Newspaper Cuttings', pp. 53–72.
37 Dr Jonathan Parker Fisher, Sub-Dean of Exeter cathedral, recorded in *The Diary of Joseph Farington* (London: Paul Melon Centre, 1983), entry for 17 May 1811.
38 Ibid.
39 Robert Day, *The Diary of Robert Day*, ed. Gerald O'Carroll (Kerry: Polymath Press), entry for 9 September 1811.
40 *The Freeman's Journal*, 1 October 1813.
41 *Bath Chronicle & Weekly Gazette*, 23 May 1811.
42 *Morning Chronicle*, 24 June 1818.
43 *New York Evening* Post, 23 April 1813.
44 'A Return to the Department of State Alien Enemies who have reported themselves to the Marshal of the District of New York from the twentieth to the twenty fifth day of July 1812'.
45 Letter from William Courtenay to US Department of State in Philadelphia, 19 March 1814.
46 *Boston Daily Advertiser*, 27 October 1814.

47 Alexander, *Life at Fonthill*, p. 128.
48 Ibid.
49 Ibid., pp. 103 and 117.
50 Ibid., p. 173.
51 Ibid., Beckford to Franchi, 11 November 1807, p. 57.
52 John Britton, *Graphical and Literary Illustrations of Fonthill Abbey* (London: Longman, Hurst, Rees, Orme, Brown, and Green, 1823), p. 15.
53 Alexander, *Life at Fonthill*, p. 340.
54 'Earl banned from holding weddings at his 600-year-old castle for refusing to allow a gay marriage', *Daily Mail*, 30 May 2008, https://www.dailymail.co.uk/news/article-1023037/Earl-banned-holding-weddings-600-year-old-castle-refusing-allow-gay-marriage.html (accessed 21 May 2024).
55 Ben Miller and Huw Lemmey, *Bad Gays: A Homosexual History* (Verso: London, 2023).

CHAPTER NINE: GERANIUM SYLVATICUM

1 Kittredge Cherry, 'Anne Lister Had Historic Lesbian Church Wedding in 1834', *QSpirit*, 11 January 2024, https://qspirit.net/anne-lister-historic-lesbian-church-wedding-new-tv-series/ (accessed 1 February 2024).
2 This plaque was added following amendments to an earlier version of a similar plaque erected in 2018.
3 Fiona Brideoake, 'Extraordinary Female Affection: The Ladies of Llangollen and the Endurance of Queer Community', in *Queer Romanticism* no. 36–37 (November 2004, February 2005), p. 18.
4 Anne Lister, 25 December 1816.
5 Helena Whitbread (ed.), *The Secret Diaries of Miss Anne Lister* (London: Hachette, 2010), p. 7.
6 5 April 1820.
7 William Van Reyk, 'Christian Ideals of Manliness in the Eighteenth and Early Nineteenth Centuries', *The Historical Journal* 52, no. 4 (December 2009), pp. 1053–73.
8 They may well have referred to her (privately, of course) as a 'robin', a contemporary term for a masculine woman who interfered too much with 'masculine concerns'. See Anon., *The Reflector; a Selection of Essays*

Notes to pp. 205–220

      on *Various Subjects of Common Life from Original Papers*, vol. 2 (London: W. Lane, 1788), p. 31.
9   28 June 1818.
10 15 September 1823.
11 28 May 1817 – written in Anne's journal (SH:7/ML/E/1)
12 22 July 1821.
13 Ibid.
14 28 July 1821.
15 Stéphanie Félicité Genlis, *Memoirs of the Countess de Genlis*, vol. 6 (London: Henry Colburn, 1825), pp. 185–6.
16 A supposed letter from Princess Caroline to an unnamed recipient, c.May 1814, in John Galt (ed.), *Diary Illustrative of the Times of George the Fourth interspersed with Original Letters from the Late Queen Caroline* (London: Henry Colburn, 1839).
17 13 July 1822.
18 14 July 1822.
19 23 July 1822.
20 Ibid.
21 17 July 1822.
22 Ibid.
23 10 July 1819.
24 Later, in 1746, Henry Fielding's *The Female Husband* provided a fictionalized account of the 'diabolical tricks of Miss M. Hamilton, alias Mr. G. Hamilton', which was based on the true story of Mr Charles Hamilton, who had been born to another name and gender and had legally married a woman in 1746.
25 *In Search of Ann Walker*, p. 12, https://insearchofannwalker.com/ann-walker-booklet/ (accessed 3 June 2024).
26 Jill Liddington, *Female Fortune: The Anne Lister Diaries, 1833–36: Land, Gender and Authority* (London: Manchester University Press, 2022), p. 59.
27 17 August 1832.
28 27 September 1832.
29 28 September 1832.
30 1 October 1832.
31 8 October 1832.
32 6 December 1832.

33   14 December 1832.
34   Ibid.
35   22 December 1832.
36   16 February 1833.
37   18 February 1833.
38   5 January 1834.
39   6 January 1834
40   7 January 1834.
41   'pother' infers an argument or a heated debate. Walker, despite modern speculation, had a will of her own.
42   8–11 January 1834.
43   C. Tasca, M. Rapetti, M. G. Carta and B. Fadda, 'Women and Hysteria in the History of Mental Health', *Clinical Practice Epidemiology Mental Health* 8 (2012), pp. 110–19.
44   Elizabeth Foyster, 'At the Limits of Liberty: Married Women and Confinement in Eighteenth-Century England', *Continuity and Change* 17 (2002), pp. 39–62.
45   22–26 January 1834.
46   28 January 1832.
47   4 February 1834.
48   Ibid.
49   5 February 1834.
50   9 February 1834.
51   10 February 1834.
52   27 February 1834.
53   8 March 1832.
54   30 March 1834.
55   Lister, 21 July 1834. Walker diary, 28 July 1834, WYC:1525/7/1/5/1, f. 35.
56   Walker diary, 28 July 1834.
57   14 October 1834.
58   *Leeds Mercury*, 10 January 1835.
59   20 January 1835
60   14 August 1835.
61   *Leeds Times*, 1 May 1840.

Notes to pp. 232–243

62 Ibid.
63 Diane Halford and Leitner Daleen, 'In Search of Ann Walker: The Last Days of Ann Walker', 2023, https://insearchofannwalker.com/the-last-days-of-ann-walker/ (accessed 13 October 2024).
64 Charles Musgrave to Abraham Horsfall, 3 March 1854, WYK1581/1/145.

CHAPTER TEN: A (NOT SO) SINGULAR CASE

1 Anthony Cooke, *The Rise and Fall of the Scottish Cotton Industry 1778–1914* (Manchester: Manchester University Press, 2010).
2 'A Singular Case and A Female Husband', *The Pennsylvanian*, 16 August 1836.
3 Details of early-nineteenth-century transatlantic steerage travel in the following section are collected from D. Griffiths Jr, *Two Years' Residence in the New Settlements of Ohio, North America: with Directions to Emigrants* (London: Westley and Davis et al., 1835), pp. 9–22.
4 Jen Manion, *Female Husbands: A Trans History* (Cambridge: Cambridge University Press, 2020), p. 151.
5 Ibid., p. ii.
6 See 'A Singular Case and A Female Husband', *The Pennsylvanian*, 16 August 1836, and 'Extraordinary Cause of a Female Husband', *The North Carolina Standard*, 1 September 1836, for example.
7 'A Singular Case and A Female Husband'.
8 Jason Anthony Brown, 'The Jurisdiction of Silence: Sodomy Law in 19th Century Law and Culture', unpublished MA thesis, University of California, Irvine, 2021.
9 See, for example, 'Extraordinary Cause of a Female Husband'.
10 *The Evening Post*, 16 December 1835.
11 Edwin G. Burrows and Mike Wallace, *Gotham: A History of New York City to 1898* (Oxford: Oxford University Press, 1998), p. 476.
12 Ibid., p. 745.
13 Ibid., p. 746.
14 Ibid.
15 Ibid., p. 485.
16 Ibid.

17 Just as Wilson had given Lowndes a false name, he seems to have given a false age too, for had he been thirty in 1836 he would have been fifteen in 1821 when he married Elizabeth and left Scotland.
18 Burrows and Wallace, *Gotham*, p. 485.
19 'A Female Husband', clipping, 1836, *Digital Transgender Archive*, https://www.digitaltransgenderarchive.net/files/js956f94r (accessed 26 March 2024).
20 'A Singular Case and A Female Husband'.
21 'A Discovery', *Evening Star*, 13 August 1836.
22 'A Singular Case and A Female Husband'.
23 'A Discovery'.
24 'New York Police Office', *Maine Farmer and Journal of the Useful Arts* 4, issue 30, 26 August 1836, p. 238.
25 'A Singular Case and A Female Husband'.
26 Ibid.
27 'New York Police Office', p. 238.
28 Ibid.
29 Ibid. Pronouns as they appear in the primary-source material.
30 'A Singular Case and A Female Husband'.
31 'A Female Husband'.
32 A parish for sacred purposes only.
33 '1821 WILSON, GEORGE', National Records of Scotland, Old Parish Registers Marriages 622/Barony, f. 23.
34 'A Singular Case and A Female Husband'.
35 'The Man Woman Again', *Alexandria Gazette*, 18 August 1836.
36 'New York Police Office', p. 238.
37 Manion, *Female Husbands*, pp. 152–71.

CHAPTER ELEVEN: THE AMALGAMATIONIST

1 'Amalgamation' was used in the nineteenth century to describe, amongst other race-related topics, sex between different races. See Jonathan Ned Katz, *Sex Between Men Before Homosexuality* (Chicago: University of Chicago Press), p. 83. It is used here to hint at qualities that might be most closely aligned to 'gender fluidity' today.

Notes to pp. 253–259

2. *The Sun*, 17 June 1836, gives Sewally's sentence as three years. *The Herald*, 17 June 1836, reports that he was sentenced to five years.
3. Burrows and Wallace, *Gotham*, p. 506.
4. Ibid., p. 604.
5. Ibid., pp. 604–5.
6. *The Herald*, 17 June 1836.
7. Ibid.
8. Ann Haddad, 'Vauxhall Garden: The Coney Island of Its Day', *Merchant's House Museum*, 16 January 2018, https://merchantshouse.org/blog/vauxhall-garden/ (accessed 3 June 2024).
9. 'Improvements in the City', *The Herald* (morning edition), 24 March 1855.
10. Timothy J. Gilfoyle, *City of Eros: New York City, Prostitution, and the Commercialisation of Sex, 1790–1920* (New York: W. W. Norton & Company, 1992), p. 18.
11. Ibid.
12. Ibid., p. 287.
13. *The Herald*, 17 June 1836.
14. Ibid. 'Dingy', at this time, was used to denote a person of colour, but also meant 'dirty' or 'unclean'. This reference to cleanliness relates to her profession rather than her appearance.
15. 'Court of Sessions', *The Sun* (morning edition), 17 June 1836.
16. Ibid. See also Gilfoyle, *City of Eros*, p. 136.
17. Leslie M. Harris, *In the Shadow of Slavery: African Americans in New York City, 1626–1863* (Chicago: University of Chicago Press, 2003), p. 72.
18. Ibid., p. 74.
19. Burrows and Wallace, *Gotham*, p. 854.
20. Harris, *In The Shadow of Slavery*, p. 79.
21. Ibid.
22. Ibid., p. 80.
23. Ibid.
24. Details extracted from 'General Sessions, A good one', *The Herald*, 17 June 1836.
25. Ibid. A bank order was an instruction by a bank to pay a specified payee a stated amount.
26. Timothy J. Gilfoyle, 'The Whorearchy', in *City of Eros*, pp. 55–75.

27 Ibid.
28 Ibid.
29 Ibid.
30 Ibid.
31 Ibid.
32 Ibid.
33 'Court of Sessions', *The Sun* (morning edition), 17 June 1836.
34 Ibid.
35 *The Herald*, 17 June 1836.
36 'Police Watch Return', 16 June 1836. NYDA Case Files, NYC Municipal Archives.
37 'Testimony of Robert Haslem, against the defendant Mary Jones, 1836', NYDA Case Files, NYC Municipal Archives.
38 'The People vs. Peter Sewally alias Mary Jones, Trial on Indictment for Grand Larceny', Court of General Sessions Minutes, 1836, NYC Municipal Archives.
39 'Testimony of Mary Jones, 1836', NYDA Case Files, NYC Municipal Archives.
40 'Grand Jury Indictment of Peter Sewally alias Mary Jones, 1836', NYDA Case Files, NYC Municipal Archives.
41 Matter of Anonymous, 57 Misc. 2d 813, 293 N.Y.S.2d 834 (1968).
42 *The Herald*, 17 June 1836.
43 'Court of Sessions', *The Sun* (morning edition), 17 June 1836.
44 'Testimony of Mary Jones, 1836', NYDA Case Files, NYC Municipal Archives.
45 Ibid.
46 'Court of Sessions', *The Sun* (morning edition), 17 June 1836.
47 *The Herald*, 17 June 1836.
48 'Police Watch Returns', 31 December 1841, NYDA Case Files, NYC Municipal Archives.
49 'An Amalgamationist In Limbo For The Second Time', *The Herald*, 9 March 1842.
50 Ibid.
51 Ibid.
52 Ibid.
53 'Singular Case', *The Herald*, 21 December 1844.

54 Ibid.
55 Ibid.
56 *Commercial Advertiser*, 9 August 1845.
57 *The Herald*, 15 February 1846.
58 'Police Watch Returns', 23 August 1846, NYDA Case Files, NYC Municipal Archives.
59 'Caught Again', *Newark Daily Advertiser*, 25 August 1846.
60 Peter Sewally would be arrested in 1848 in similar circumstances, this time using the name Julia Johnson; see 'Testimony of Julia Johnson', 6 April 1848, NYDA Case Files, NYC Municipal Archives. See also 'Peter Savori, alias Julia Johnson, alias Beef Steak Pete', 10 May 1848, NYDA Case Files, NYC Municipal Archives.

EPILOGUE

1 Robert Beachy, 'The German Invention of Homosexuality', *The Journal of Modern History* 82, no. 4 (2010), pp. 801–38.
2 Vickery, *Behind Closed Doors*, p. 124.
3 Aaron Betsky, *Queer Space: Architecture and Same-Sex Desire* (New York: William Morrow & Co., 1997), p. 5.
4 *Oxford English Dictionary*, s.v. community (n.), sense I.5.a & II.12, September 2024, https://doi.org/10.1093/OED/4399690008
5 Thomas Baker, *Tunbridge-Walks: Or, The Yeoman of Kent* (London, 1703), p. 47.
6 70 Oklahoma Statutes § 11-103.3. Homosexual activity is listed alongside other 'known causes' including drug use. See also '2023 Oklahoma Statutes', www.law.justia.com/codes
7 Texas Health & Safety Code § 163.002
8 Lindsey Toomer, 'Repeal of State Constitution's Same-sex Marriage Ban Heads to Voters with Gov. Polis' Signature', *Colorado News Online*, 8 May 2024, https://coloradonewsline.com/2024/05/08/repeal-same-sex-marriage-ban-colorado/ (accessed 10 May 2024). At the time of writing, Democratic Governor Jared Polis hopes to eradicate this prohibition.
9 Chaka L. Bachmann and Becca Gooch, *LGBT In Britain: Hate Crime and Discrimination* (Stonewall, 2017), pp. 6–7.
10 Tim Higgins, 'Why Elon Musk Won't Stop Talking About a "Woke Mind Virus"', *The Wall Street Journal*, 23 December 2023.

Select Bibliography

Archives

<u>Beinecke Library, Yale University</u>
GEN MSS 102, William Beckford Collection

<u>Bodleian Library, Oxford</u>
MS Beckford

<u>British Library</u>
The Holland House Papers are held in the British Library Manuscripts Collections: Add MS 51318-52254

<u>Hampshire Record Office</u>
Chute of The Vyne Papers 31M57/118-119
120A03/45/1, Office extract of the administration of the goods and chattels of Anthony Chute of The Vine, Sherborne St John, granted to John Chute, his brother
5M50/2089-2096, Papers and vouchers of Thomas Puckridge, agent for Richard Whithed and Francis Thistlethwayte Whithed

<u>National Archives, Kew</u>
PROB, 11/1745/181, Gregório Franchi (Will)

<u>National Library of Ireland</u>
Tighe, Hamilton and Howard Papers, 1749–1919

Select Bibliography

National Library of Wales
The Hamwood Papers

New York City Municipal Archives
Peter Sewally alias Mary Jones Papers

Suffolk Archives
HA507 The Hervey Papers
941/5/2, Papers and correspondence of John, Lord Hervey

West Yorkshire Archives
Lister Diaries
Walker Diary

Primary Sources: Modern Compilations of Manuscript Sources

Beckford, William, *The Life and Letters of William Beckford of Fonthill*, ed. Lewis Melville and James Storer (London: William Heinemann, 1910).

——*Life At Fonthill 1807–1822 with Interludes in Paris and London from the Correspondence*, trans. and ed. Boyd Alexander (London: R. Hart-Davis, 1957).

De Beaumont, Charles d'Eon, *Memoirs of the Chevalier d'Eon: Louis XV's favourite spy required by Versailles and St James's never to dress as a man*, trans. Antonia White (London: Anthony Blond, 1970).

——*The Maid of Tonnerre: The Vicissitudes of the Chevalier and Chevalière d'Eon*, trans. and ed. Roland A. Champagne, Nona Ekstein and Gary Kates (London: Johns Hopkins University Press, 2001).

Gray, Thomas, *Correspondence of Thomas Gray*, ed. Paget Toynbee, Leonard Whibley and H. W. Starr, vol. 1 (Oxford: Clarendon Press, 1971).

Lister, Anne, *The Secret Diaries of Miss Anne Lister*, ed. Helena Whitbread (London: Hachette, 2010).

Lord Hervey, John, *Lord Hervey and His Friends, 1726–38, Based on Letters from Holland House, Melbury, and Ickworth*, ed. the Earl of Ilchester (London: John Murray, 1950).

——*Some Materials Toward Memoirs of the Reign of King George II*, ed. Romney Sedgwick. Reprint of the 1931 edn, 3 vols (New York: AMS Press, 1970).

Select Bibliography

———*The Collected Verse of John, Lord Hervey (1696–1743)*, ed. Bill Overton (Cambridge: Cambridge University Press, 2016).

Thrale Piozzi, Hester, *Thraliana: The Diary of Mrs. Hester Lynch Thrale (Later Mrs. Piozzi) 1776–1809*, ed. Katharine C. Balderston, 2nd edn, 2 vols (Oxford: Clarendon Press, 1951).

Primary Sources: Online Editions of Published Manuscript Sources

Old Bailey Proceedings Online, https://www.oldbaileyonline.org/

The Yale Edition of Horace Walpole's Correspondence, ed. W. S. Lewis, 48 vols (New Haven: Yale University Press, 1937–83), http://images.library.yale.edu/hwcorrespondence/default.asp (accessed 20 February 2020).

Primary Sources: Printed

Anon., *Mundus Foppensis: Or, The Fop Display'd* (London, 1691).

———*Proposals for a National Reformation of Manners* (London, 1693).

———*The Batchellors Fore-Cast, or, Cupid Unblest* (London: R. Burton, 1697).

———*The Sodomites Shame and Doom, Laid before Them with Great Grief and Compassion* (London, 1702).

———*Satan's Harvest Home: Or the Present State of Whorecraft* (London, 1749).

Baker, Thomas, *Tunbridge-Walks: Or, The Yeoman of Kent* (London, 1703).

Beckford, William, *Vathek and the Episodes of Vathek*, ed. Kenneth W. Graham, trans. Sir Frank T. Marzials and Kenneth Graham (Peterborough, Ontario: Broadview Press, 2001).

Booker, John, *The Dutch Fortune-Teller: Discovering Thirty Six Several Questions* (London, 1766).

Cocchi, Antonio, *Del matrimonio discorso di Antonio Cocchi Mugellano* (Pisa, 1762).

———*The Grand Question, Is Marriage Fit for Literary Men?*, trans. Paul Heffernan (London, 1769).

Gordon, Thomas, *The Conspirators, or, The Case of Catiline* (London, 1721).

Gouge, William, *Of Domesticall Duties*, 3rd edn (London, 1634).

Holloway, Robert, *The Phoenix of Sodom, or the Vere Street Coterie* (London, 1813).

Select Bibliography

Lancaster, Nathaniel, *The Pretty Gentleman: Or, Softness of Manners Vindicated from the False Ridicule Exhibited under the Character of William Fribble, Esq.* (London: M. Cooper, 1747).

Langley, Batty, *An Accurate Description of Newgate* (London: printed for T. Warner, at the Black Boy in Pater-Noster-Row, 1724).

Pope, Alexander, *An Epistle from Mr. Pope, to Dr. Arbuthnot* (London: printed by J. Wright, 1734).

Pulteney, William. *A Proper Reply to a Late Scurrilous Libel; intitled, Sedition and Defamation display'd* (London, 1731).

Seymar, William, *Marriage Asserted, in Answer to a Book Entitled Conjugium Conjugium* (London, 1700).

Ward, Edward, *The Secret History of Clubs* (London, 1709).

Primary Sources: Newspapers and Periodicals

Addison, Joseph, *The Free-Holder. Or Political Essays* (London: J. & R. Tonson, 1761).

Anon., *The Reflector; a Selection of Essays on Various Subjects of Common Life from Original Papers*, vol. 2 (London: W. Lane, 1788).

Blackwood's Edinburgh Magazine, vol. 17, January–June, Edinburgh and London, 1825

Crackenthorpe, Mrs (pseud. Thomas Baker), *The Female Tatler*, nos 18, 19, 25, 31, London, 1709.

Gray, Thomas, *Correspondence of Thomas Gray*, ed. Paget Toynbee, Leonard Whibley and H. W. Starr, vol. 1 (Oxford: Clarendon Press, 1971).

Manners, George and Jerdan, William (eds), *The Satirist: Or Monthly Meteor*, vol. 4 (London, 1809).

The Spectator, in Eight Volumes, vols 7 and 8 (Glasgow: David Diven, 1791).

Secondary Sources: Monographs

Alexander, Boyd, *England's Wealthiest Son: A Study of William Beckford* (London: Centaur Press, 1962).

Amussen, Susan, *An Ordered Society: Gender and Class in Early Modern England* (Oxford: Oxford University Press, 1988).

Arnold, Dana, *The Georgian Country House: Architecture, Landscape and Society*, 2nd edn (Stroud: Sutton, 2003).

Select Bibliography

Bailey, Joanne, *Unquiet Lives: Marriage and Marriage Breakdown in England, 1660–1800* (Cambridge: Cambridge University Press, 2003).

——— *Parenting in England, 1760–1830: Emotion, Identity, and Generation* (Oxford: Oxford University Press, 2012).

Barker, Hannah and Chalus, Elaine, *Gender in Eighteenth-Century England: Roles, Representations and Responsibilities* (Harlow: Longman, 1997).

Begiato, Joanne, *Manliness in Britain, 1760–1900: Bodies, Emotion, and Material Culture* (Manchester: Manchester University Press, 2020).

Berry, Helen and Foyster, Elizabeth A., *The Family in Early Modern England* (Cambridge: Cambridge University Press, 2007).

Betsky, Aaron, *Queer Space: Architecture and Same-Sex Desire* (New York: William Morrow & Co., 1997).

Bobker, Danielle, *The Closet: The Eighteenth-Century Architecture of Intimacy* (Princeton: Princeton University Press, 2020).

Bray, Alan, *Homosexuality in Renaissance England* (London: Gay Men's Press, 1982).

——— *The Friend* (Chicago: University of Chicago Press, 2003).

Brideoake, Fiona, *The Ladies of Llangollen: Desire, Indeterminacy, and the Legacies of Criticism* (Lewisburg: Bucknell University Press, 2017).

Brown, Roger Lee, *The Fleet Marriages: A History of Clandestine Marriages* (Welshpool: Tair Eglwys Press, 2007).

Burrows, Edwin G. and Wallace, Mike, *Gotham: A History of New York City to 1898* (Oxford: Oxford University Press, 1998).

Burton, Elizabeth, *The Georgians at Home* (London: Arrow Books, 1976).

Bushman, Richard L., *The Refinement of America: Persons, Houses, Cities* (New York: Knopf, 1992).

Butler, Judith, *Gender Trouble: Feminism and the Subversion of Identity* (London: Routledge, 1990).

Chapman, Guy, *Beckford*, 2nd edn (London: R. Hart-Davis, 1952).

Cockayne, Emily, *Hubbub: Filth, Noise & Stench in England, 1600–1770*, new edn (London: Yale University Press, 2021).

Cohen, Michèle, *Fashioning Masculinity: National Identity and Language in the Eighteenth Century* (Oxford: Routledge, 1996).

Colley, Linda, *Britons: Forging the Nation, 1707–1837* (London: Pimlico, 1994).

Connell, R. W., *Masculinities*, 2nd edn (Cambridge: Polity, 2005).

Select Bibliography

Cook, Matt, *London and the Culture of Homosexuality, 1885–1914* (Cambridge: Cambridge University Press, 2003).

——— *Queer Domesticities: Homosexuality and Home Life in Twentieth-Century London* (London: Palgrave Macmillan, 2014).

Cox, Cynthia, *The Enigma of the Age: The Strange Story of the Chevalier D'Eon* (London: Longmans, 1966).

Dabhoiwala, Faramerz, *The Origins of Sex: A History of the First Sexual Revolution* (London: Allen Lane, 2012).

Dakers, Caroline, *Fonthill Recovered: A Cultural History* (London: UCL Press, 2018).

Fletcher, Anthony, *Gender, Sex and Subordination in England, 1500–1800* (London: Yale University Press, 1995).

Fone, Byrne R. S., *Homophobia: A History* (New York: Metropolitan Books, 2000).

Fothergill, Brian, *Beckford of Fonthill* (London: Faber & Faber, 1979).

French, Henry and Rothery, Mark, *Man's Estate: Landed Gentry Masculinities, 1660–1900* (Oxford: Oxford University Press, 2012).

Gemmett, Robert J., *William Beckford's Fonthill: Architecture, Landscape, and the Arts* (Croydon: Fonthill Media, 2016).

Goldsmith, Sarah, *Masculinity and Danger on the Eighteenth-Century Grand Tour* (London: University of London Press, 2020).

Gowrley, Freya, *Domestic Space in Britain, 1750–1840: Materiality, Sociability and Emotion* (New York: Bloomsbury Academic, 2022).

Guilfoyle, Timothy J., *City of Eros: New York City, Prostitution, and the Commercialisation of Sex, 1790–1920* (New York: W. W. Norton & Company, 1992).

Haggerty, George E., *Men in Love: Masculinity and Sexuality in the Eighteenth Century* (New York: Columbia University Press, 1999).

——— *Queer Gothic* (Urbana: University of Illinois Press, 2006).

——— *Horace Walpole's Letters: Masculinity and Friendship in the Eighteenth Century* (Lewisburg: Bucknell University Press, 2011).

——— *Queer Friendship: Male Intimacy in the English Literary Tradition* (Cambridge: Cambridge University Press, 2018).

Halliday, Stephen, *Newgate: London's Prototype of Hell* (Stroud: Sutton, 2007).

Halperin, David M., *How to Do the History of Homosexuality* (Chicago: University of Chicago Press, 2002).

Select Bibliography

Halsband, Robert, *The Life of Lady Mary Wortley Montagu* (Oxford: Oxford University Press, 1961).

——*Lord Hervey: Eighteenth-Century Courtier* (Oxford: Oxford University Press, 1973).

Harknett, Polly, Heffernan, Caitlin and Smith, Matt (eds), *Unravelling The Vyne* (Basingstoke: National Trust, 2013).

Harris, Leslie M., *In the Shadow of Slavery: African Americans in New York City, 1626–1863* (Chicago: University of Chicago Press, 2003).

Harvey, Karen, *The Little Republic: Masculinity and Domestic Authority in Eighteenth-Century Britain* (Oxford: Oxford University Press, 2012).

Herrup, Cynthia B., *A House in Gross Disorder: Sex, Law, and the 2nd Earl of Castlehaven* (Oxford: Oxford University Press, 2001).

Higgs, David, *Queer Sites: Gay Urban Histories Since 1600* (London: Routledge, 1999).

Howard, Maurice, *The Vyne, Hampshire* (Corsham: National Trust, 2018).

Janes, Dominic, *Picturing the Closet: Male Secrecy and Homosexual Visibility in Britain* (Oxford: Oxford University Press, 2015).

Kates, Gary, *Monsieur d'Eon is a Woman: A Tale of Political Intrigue and Sexual Masquerade* (London: Johns Hopkins Univeristy Press, 1995).

Kelly, Jason M., *The Society of Dilettanti: Archaeology and Identity in the British Enlightenment* (New Haven: Yale University Press, 2009).

Lewis, Brian (ed.), *British Queer History: New Approaches and Perspectives* (Manchester: Manchester University Press, 2013).

Liddington, Jill, *Female Fortune: The Anne Lister Diaries, 1833–36: Land, Gender and Authority* (London: Manchester University Press, 2022).

Malatino, Hilary, *Queer Embodiment: Monstrosity, Medical Violence, and Intersex Experience* (Lincoln: University of Nebraska Press, 2019).

Manion, Jen, *Female Husbands: A Trans History* (Cambridge: Cambridge University Press, 2020).

Marcus, Sharon, *Between Women: Friendship, Desire, and Marriage in Victorian England* (Princeton: Princeton University Press, 2007).

Marinucci, Mimi, *Feminism Is Queer: The Intimate Connection between Queer and Feminist Theory* (London: Zed Books, 2010).

Mavor, Elizabeth, *The Ladies of Llangollen: A Study in Romantic Friendship* (London: Moonrise Press, 2011).

McFarlane, Cameron, *The Sodomite in Fiction and Satire, 1660–1750* (New York: Columbia University Press, 1997).

Select Bibliography

McNeil, Peter, *Pretty Gentlemen: Macaroni Men and the Eighteenth-Century Fashion World* (New Haven: Yale University Press, 2018).

Moore, Lucy, *Amphibious Thing: The Life of Lord Hervey* (London: Viking, 2000).

Morgan, Kenneth, *Slavery, Atlantic Trade and the British Economy, 1660–1800* (Cambridge: Cambridge University Press, 2000).

Mounsey, Chris and Gonda, Caroline (eds), *Queer People: Negotiations and Expressions of Homosexuality, 1700–1800* (Lewisburg: Bucknell University Press, 2007).

Norton, Rictor, *Mother Clap's Molly House: The Gay Subculture in England, 1700–1830* (London: Gay Men's Press, 1992).

O'Donnell, Katherine and O'Rourke, Michael (eds), *Love, Sex, Intimacy and Friendship between Men, 1550–1800* (Houndmills: Palgrave Macmillan, 2003).

Oliver, John Walter, *The Life of William Beckford* (Oxford: Oxford University Press, 1932).

Pilkey, Brent, Scicluna, Rachael M., Campkin, Ben and Penner, Barbara (eds), *Sexuality and Gender at Home: Experience, Politics, Transgression* (London: Bloomsbury, 2018).

Probert, Rebecca, *Marriage Law and Practice in the Long Eighteenth Century* (Cambridge: Cambridge University Press, 2009).

Reeve, Matthew, *Gothic Architecture and Sexuality in the Circle of Horace Walpole* (University Park, Pennsylvania: Pennsylvania State University Press, 2020).

Scott, Joan Wallach, *Gender and the Politics of History*, rev. edn (New York: Columbia University Press, 1999).

Sedgwick, Eve Kosofsky, *Between Men: English Literature and Male Homosocial Desire* (New York: Columbia University Press, 1985).

———*Tendencies* (Durham, NC: Duke University Press, 1993).

———*Epistemology of the Closet*, rev. edn (London: University of California Press, 2008).

Trumbach, Randolph, *Sex and the Gender Revolution* (Chicago: University of Chicago Press, 1998).

Vickery, Amanda, *Behind Closed Doors: At Home in Georgian England* (London: Yale University Press, 2009).

Williamson, Gillian, *Lodgers, Landlords, and Landladies in Georgian London* (London: Bloomsbury, 2021).

Select Bibliography

Secondary Sources: Articles, Chapters and Essays

Bailey, Joanne, ' "A Very Sensible Man": Imagining Fatherhood in England *c.* 1750–1830', *History (London)* 95, no. 3 (2010), pp. 267–92.

Baydar, Gülsüm, 'Sexualised Productions of Space', *Gender, Place & Culture* 19, no. 6 (2012), pp. 699–706.

Beachy, Robert, 'The German Invention of Homosexuality', *The Journal of Modern History* 82, no. 4 (2010), pp. 801–38.

Begiato, Joanne, 'A "Master-Mistress": Revisiting the History of Eighteenth-Century Wives', *Women's History Review*, 17 January (2022), pp. 1–20.

Berlant, Lauren and Warner, Michael, 'Sex in Public', *Critical Inquiry* 24, no. 2 (1998), pp. 547–66.

Berry, Helen, 'Queering the History of Marriage: The Social Recognition of a Castrato Husband in Eighteenth-Century Britain', *History Workshop Journal* 74, no. 1 (Autumn 2012), pp. 27–50.

Campbell, Jill, 'Politics and Sexuality in Portraits of John, Lord Hervey', *Word & Image* 6, no. 4 (1990), pp. 281–97.

Chow, Jeremy, 'Eighteenth-Century Queer Studies, Revisited', *Literature Compass* 18, no. 7 (1 July 2021), e12643.

Clark, Anna, 'The Chevalier d'Eon and Wilkes: Masculinity and Politics in the Eighteenth Century', *Eighteenth-Century Studies* 32, no. 1. (Fall 1998), pp. 19–48.

Cohen, Michèle, 'The Grand Tour. Language, National Identity and Masculinity', *Changing English* 8, issue 2 (2001), pp. 129–41.

——— ' "Manners" Make the Man: Politeness, Chivalry, and the Construction of Masculinity, 1750–1830', *Journal of British Studies* 44, no. 2 (2005), pp. 312–29.

Coyle, Eugene, 'The Irish Ladies of Llangollen: "the most celebrated virgins in Europe" ', *History Ireland* 23, issue 6 (November/December 2015).

Davis, Whitney, 'Queer Family Romance in Collecting Visual Culture', *GLQ* 17, no. 2–3 (2011), pp. 309–29.

Douglas, M., 'The Idea of a Home: A Kind of Space', *Social Research* 58, no. 1 (1991), pp. 287–307.

Drescher, Jack, 'From Bisexuality to Intersexuality: Rethinking Gender Categories', *Contemporary Psychoanalysis* 43, no. 2 (2007), pp. 204–28.

Easton, Fraser, 'Gender's Two Bodies: Women Warriors, Female Husbands and Plebian Life', *Past & Present* 180 (2003), pp. 131–74.

Select Bibliography

Finn, Margot, 'Men's Things: Masculine Possession in the Consumer Revolution', *Social History* 25, no. 2 (2000), pp. 133–55.

Gavroche, Julius, 'Queering Straight Space: Thinking Towards a Queer Architecture', *Anatomies* (blog), 2016, https://autonomies.org/2016/10/struggles-for-space-queering-straight-space-thinking-towards-a-queer-architecture-4/ (accessed 2 March 2021).

Halberstam, Jack, 'Unbuilding Gender', *Places Journal*, October 2018, https://doi.org/10.22269/181003 (accessed 2 March 2021).

Halperin, David, 'How to Do the History of Homosexuality', *Sexuality Research and Social Policy* 2, no. 3 (2005), pp. 71–3.

Harvey, Karen, 'Men Making Home: Masculinity and Domesticity in Eighteenth-Century Britain', *Gender & History* 21, no. 3 (2009), pp. 520–40.

Klein, Lawrence E., 'Gender and the Public/Private Distinction in the Eighteenth Century: Some Questions about Evidence and Analytic Procedure', *Eighteenth-Century Studies* 29, no. 1 (1995), pp. 97–109.

Lemmings, David, 'Marriage and the Law in the Eighteenth Century: Hardwicke's Marriage Act of 1753', *The Historical Journal* 39, no. 2 (June 1996), pp. 339–60.

Lepine, Ayla, 'Queer Gothic: Architecture, Gender and Desire', *The Architectural Review*, 20 January 2015, https://www.architectural-review.com/essays/gender-and-sexuality/queer-gothic-architecture-gender-and-desire (accessed 5 March 2021).

Marsh, Christopher, 'The Woman to the Plow; And the man to the Hen-Roost: Wives, Husbands and Best-Selling Ballads in Seventeenth-Century England', *Transactions of the Royal Historical Society* 28 (2018), pp. 65–88.

Reeve, Matthew, 'Gothic Architecture, Sexuality, and License at Horace Walpole's Strawberry Hill', *The Art Bulletin* 95, no. 3 (2013), pp. 411–39.

Rosenheim, James, 'The Pleasures of a Single Life: Envisioning Bachelorhood in Early Eighteenth-Century England', *Gender & History* 27, no. 2 (1 August 2015), pp. 307–28.

Scott, Joan W., 'Gender: A Useful Category of Historical Analysis', *The American Historical Review* 91, no. 5 (1986), pp. 1053–75.

Tadmor, Naomi, 'The Concept of the Household-Family in Eighteenth-Century England', *Past & Present* 151, no. 1 (1 May 1996), pp. 111–40.

Tague, Ingrid, 'Love, Honour and Obedience: Fashionable Women and the Discourse of Marriage in the Early Eighteenth Century', *Journal of British Studies* 40, no. 1 (January 2001), pp. 76–106.

Acknowledgements

The initial idea for *Queer Georgians* came as a result of my PhD research on cotqueans at the University of Exeter. As such, it would be remiss of me to forget to extend my gratitude to colleagues in the Department of History there for their support and insight throughout that project which has, in turn, significantly informed this book. Sincere thanks must go to Professor Henry French and Professor Sarah Toulalan, who both provided encouragement and feedback throughout and on the final thesis. Most impactful of all, though, has been the superlative guidance of my supervisor Professor Helen Berry, whose expert direction and sharp critical eye has generously continued into this project too.

The insights and contributions of the wider research community have been vital in piecing together this research. Professor Jason Kelly (Indiana University) kindly insisted that my PhD research should find its way into book form; I hope this meets the mark. I am also particularly indebted to the work of Diane Halford and her colleagues at insearchofannwalker.com and to David Whitfield for his tireless dedication to and enthusiasm for uncovering material relating to the life of William 'Kitty' Courtenay, 9th

Acknowledgements

Earl of Devon. Dr Katie Edwards provided a great sounding board for late-night discussions about the 9th Earl and his material culture, whilst the current archivists and house staff at Powderham Castle could not have been more welcoming, accommodating or enthusiastic about my research. My thanks too to the current earl, Charlie Courtenay, and his family for allowing me to stay at Powderham whilst I pored through the archive there. Dr Amy Frost has been a great go-to regarding Beckford and his foibles, whilst Dr Selina Patel Nascimento's translation skills helped me rediscover Gregório Franchi's lost voice.

Beyond the archives, my literary agent, Charlotte Merrit, has guided me through this entire process whilst somehow remaining effortlessly chic. Would that you all had a Charlotte. Further thanks to the wider team at Andrew Nurnberg Associates. Without the expertise and vision of the editorial teams in the UK and US there would be no *Queer Georgians*. It is difficult to account for the ways in which Alex Christofi at Transworld has helped shape this book; his belief in the project and tireless dedication to it has been remarkable. That passion and enthusiasm has been on display throughout the wider team at Transworld too, and my sincere thanks extend to Sharika Teelwah, Izzie Ghaffari Parker, Rosie Ainsworth, Katherine Cowdrey, Viv Thompson and Linden Lawson to name but a few. Across the pond, Amy Hundley's enviable attention to detail has been an inspiration and helped to chisel something altogether more polished from the rough terrain of earlier drafts. The wider team at Grove Atlantic have also continually upheld their infectious enthusiasm for this project and that, as any writer will tell you, is no small matter!

Never underestimate the power of an encouraging voice note and many have been exchanged with wonderful friends who are also traversing the early stages of their own writing careers including my *After Dark* co-host Dr Maddy Pelling, who has been

Acknowledgements

a patient beacon of experience throughout, and Dr Meg Kobza, who has been relentless in her encouragement and positivity.

And finally, to my family. My parents, Bridget and George, and my siblings Michelle and Shane, for showing me what it is to persevere. Darragh and Danny, who remind me that the past only matters if we keep one eye on the future. My dogs, Kip and Molly, for daily remembrances regarding the vital importance of belly rubs, naps, stretches and treats. And to Shane, my husband. For everything.

Picture Acknowledgements

Every effort has been made to contact copyright holders. Any who have not been acknowledged here are invited to get in touch with the publishers.

Page 16: John Rocque: A Plan of the Cities of London and Westminster, and Borough of Southwark, London, John Pine & John Tinney, 1746, Library of Congress, Geography and Map Division

Page 34: Engraving of Justice Hall at the Old Bailey, from *The city ancient and modern* by Walter Thornbury, Cassell, 1880, Alan King engraving/Alamy Stock Photo

Page 59: Portrait of Lord John Hervey by John Fayram, c. 1737, ARTGEN/Alamy Stock Photo

Page 60: 'The Hervey Conversation Piece' by William Hogarth, c.1738–40, The History Collection/Alamy Stock Photo

Page 76: Mr Pulteney's Duel with Lord Hervey by Anon, mezzotint, c. 1731 © The Trustees of the British Museum

Page 80: © Anthony Delaney

Page 91: 'The Hervey Conversation Piece' by William Hogarth, c.1738–40, The History Collection/Alamy Stock Photo

Picture Acknowledgements

Page 104: 'Francis Whithed' (1719–51) by Rosalba Carriera (Venice 1673 – Venice 1757), c. 1741, © National Trust Images/John Hammond

Page 105: 'John Chute' (1701–76) (after Batoni) by Johann Heinrich Müntz, 1756, ARTGEN/Alamy Stock Photo

Page 110: 'British Gentlemen at Sir Horace Mann's Home in Florence' by Thomas Patch, c. 1763–65, Yale Center for British Art, Paul Mellon Collection

Page 130: Chevalier d'Eon ('The Trial of M. D'Eon by A Jury of Matrons') by Anonymous, published in Town and Country Magazine, 1 June 1771

Page 133: 'The Discovery or Female Free-Mason', Chevalier d'Eon dressed as a woman, published by S. Hooper, c. 1771, © The Trustees of the British Museum

Page 145: 'The Fencing-Match between the Chevalier de Saint-Georges and the Chevalier d'Eon' by Andre-Auguste Robineau, c. 1787, Royal Collection Trust/ © His Majesty King Charles III 2024

Page 156: © Anthony Delaney

Page 167: 'Mrs. Mary Carol' by W. Chester Crane, 1840, Llyfrgell Genedlaethol Cymru – The National Library of Wales

Page 171: Portrait of The Rt. Honble. Lady Eleanor Butler & Miss Ponsonby 'The Ladies of Llangollen' by James Henry Lynch, c. 1833–45, Maidun Collection/Alamy Stock Photo

Page 174: 'The East View of Powderham Castle in the County of Devon', 1734 (engraving) by Samuel Buck, from the British Library archive/ Bridgeman Images

Page 179: 'William Beckford' by Sir Joshua Reynolds, c. 1782, Album/Alamy Stock Photo

P 184: William Courtenay, the 9th Earl of Devon and 3rd Viscount Courtenay (1768–1835), c. 1790, engraving by Charles Turner, attributed to John Murphy, after Richard Cosway, Hulton Archive/Stringer via Getty Images

Page 187: 'Design for Fonthill Abbey' by James Wyatt, 1798, Yale Center for British Art, Paul Mellon Collection

Page 204: © Anthony Delaney

Picture Acknowledgements

Page 211: 'Plas Newydd' by Edwin Jacques (artist), W. L. Walton (engraver), 1840, Llyfrgell Genedlaethol Cymru – The National Library of Wales

Page 237: 'The American Packet Ship "Patrick Henry" Off The Cliffs of Dover' by Philip John Ouless, 1859, Bourgeault-Horan Antiquarians

Page 255: Lithograph depicting Mary Jones/Peter Sewally as 'The Man-Monster' by H. R. Robinson, Harry T. Peters 'America on Stone' Lithography Collection, courtesy of the Smithsonian National Museum of American History

Page 263: Grand Jury Indictment of Peter Sewally alias Mary Jones, 1836, NYDA Case Files, NYC Municipal Archives

Index

Figures in *italics* refer to illustrations.

Aboyne, Charles Gordon,
    4th Earl of 175
Addison, Joseph 129–30
ages of consent 191
AIDS 283
Ainsworth, Mr 221, 224–5
Albert, Prince Consort 107
Alexander, Sir William 241
Algarotti, Francesco 93–4, 96
Angelo, Domenico 136
Arnet, Richard 50–51

Baker, Thomas: *Tunbridge-Walks* 281
Baldick, Robert 152
Barron, Joseph: factory 242
Bateman, Mrs (actress) 146
Bath Chronicle and Weekly
    Gazette, The 124
BBC, the 121
Beckford, Alderman 175, 179
Beckford, Lady Margaret (*née* Gordon)
    174–5, 178–9, 180

Beckford, Susan Euphemia *see*
    Hamilton, Susan Hamilton,
    Duchess of
Beckford, William 179, 200, 285
    background 175, 179, 196–7
    and William 'Kitty' Courtenay 7,
        174–8, 180, 183–4, 185–6, 193, 282
    and death of his wife 180
    and Gregório Franchi 180, 181–2, 183,
        186–82, 196, 197, 198, 276–7, 281
    and Lord Loughborough
        176, 178–9
    sells Fonthill Abbey 196–8
Belcombe, Mariana *see* Lawton,
    Mariana
Belcombe, Dr Steph 222, 223, 224, 225
Belcombe, Dr William 223
Bell, Charles 38–9, 49
Belle Assemblée, La (magazine) 208
Bentley, Richard 116
Bertin, Marie-Jeanne 'Rose' 120, 121, 141
Billings, Thomas 44–5, 49

Index

Blakemore, Erin 10
Boswell, James 47–8, 142
Bow Street Runners 192
Bowyer, Constable 259–61, 262, 266, 267
Boyle, John 110–11
Bristol, Elizabeth Hervey (née Felton), Countess of 56
Bristol, George William Hervey, 2nd Earl of 66, 98, 99
Bristol, John Hervey, 1st Earl of 56, 65, 70, 83
Broglie, Charles de 127, 131, 132
Broglie, Victor François de Broglie, Mareschal 2nd duc de 148
Brontë, Charlotte: *Jane Eyre* 203
Buck, Samuel: *The East View of Powderham Castle in the County of Devon* 174
Buggery Act (1533) xi, 21, 240, 282
Burlington, Richard Boyle, 3rd Earl of 57, 79
Butler, Lady Eleanor Charlotte 171
  birth and background 6, 7, 157, 172
  death 171–2
  and Anne Lister's visit 155, 208–9, 210–13
  and Sarah Ponsonby 159, 160–70, 276
  settles at Llangollen 6–7, 170–71, 173, 209–10, 276
Butler, John 159
'Butler, Madam' (Eleanor de Montmorency Morres) 157, 164, 165, 166
Butler, Walter *see* Ormonde, 16th Earl of
Butlers of Ormonde 156
Byron, George Gordon Byron, 6th Baron 209

Caledonian Mercury, The 139
Cambrai, France 157
Caroline, Princess 210
Caroline of Ansbach, Queen 64, 72–3, 88, 95, 96
Carriera, Rosalba: *Francis Whithed* 104
Carryl, Mary 167, 167–8, 171
Chapman, Margaret 38, 39
Charles II 155
Charlotte, Queen 143, 149, 210
Chute, Anthony 103
Chute, Chaloner 112, 114
Chute, John 5, 105, 116, 118, 274, 280
  background 102–3, 112
  and Dr Antonio Cocchi 109, 110
  friendship with Horace Walpole 102, 103
  taxed under Marriage Duty Act 108
  and The Vyne 112–15, 118, 173, 189, 276, 281
  and Francis Whithed ('The Chutheds') 5, 103–7, 108, 278, 285
'Chutheds, The' *see* Chute, John; Whithed, Francis
Clack, Edward-Robert 194, 195
Clap, John 16, 17, 18
Clap, Margaret 'Mother' 4, 16, 17–18, 25, 26, 51–3, 285
  her Field Lane establishment 14, 15–17, 18, 19–22, 35, 49, 54, 61, 118, 275, 277–8, 279, 280, 282
  the 1726 raid xi, 19, 22–5, 32
  trial 32–41
Clark, Henry 267
Clark & Robinson: cotton mill 241
Cliffe Hill, West Yorkshire 217, 224, 225, 232
Cocchi, Dr Antonio 69, 109–12, 274, 280
  Del Matrimonio/The Grand Question, Is Marriage Fit For Literary Men? 69, 111

Index

Cole, Mary 149, 150
Conti, Louis François I, Prince de 122
Copeland, Thomas 151
Cosway, Richard: *William 3rd Viscount Courtenay in his coming-of-age masquerade attire* 184
'cotqueans' 2–4
Courtenay, Sir Philip: Powderham Castle 173
Courtenay, William Courtenay, 2nd Viscount 175, 176
Courtenay, William 'Kitty' *see* Devon, William Courtenay, 9th Earl of
Courtney, Edward 'Ned' 39–40, 42
Crane, William: *Mrs. Mary Carol* [sic] 167
Crow Nest, West Yorkshire 217, 218
Cummins, James 235, 236, 241–2
Cummins, Margaret 236
Cuvier, Baron Georges 216

Davis, Witney 186
Day, Robert 194
Derby Mercury, The 137, 139, 140
Derwin, Mr 17
Desaguliers, Reverend John Theophilus 92
DeSantis, Ron 283
Devon, Charles Courtenay, 19th Earl of 174, 199
Devon, Hugh Courtenay, 18th Earl of 199
Devon, William 'Kitty' Courtenay, 9th Earl of 184, 198–9,
 and William Beckford 7, 8, 174, 175–7, 180, 183–4, 185–6, 285
 his coming-of-age party 184–5
 death 198
 flees to America 192–6, 240, 282
Digby (*née* Fox), Charlotte 89
Donoghue, Emma: *Learned By Heart* 204

Dorset, John Sackville, 3rd Duke of 142
duelling 75–6, 76
Duncombe, Mr 110

Elizabeth, Empress of Russia 122
Éon, Charles de Beaumont, Chevalier d' xiii, 6, *133*, *145*
 background 121–2
 commanded by Louis XVI to appear at court as a woman (1777) 119–21, 282
 death and autopsy 150–52, 230
 negotiates Treaty of Paris (1763) 122–3
 publishes *Lettres, mémoires et négociations* ... 125–8, 129
 and Queen Charlotte 210
 recruited into *Secret du Roi* 122
 rumours regarding his sex 128–50, 152–3
 as spy in England 123–5
Éon de Beaumont, Françoise d' 121
Éon de Beaumont, Louis d' 121
Éon de Beaumont, Marguerite-Françoise 122
Éon de Beaumont, Théodore-André 122
Exeter Flying Post 195

Falkland, Lucius Cary, 7th Viscount 90
Farington, Joseph 193
Farquhar, John 197
Fayram, John: *The Right Honourable The Lord Hervey, PC* 59
Fielding, Henry 24
Fitzherbert, Maria 143
Fleet, River 25
Follett, Magistrate 194
Fonthill Abbey, Wiltshire 186–92, *187*, 196–8, 276–7, 281
'Fonthill Scandal' 180, 185, 193

Index

Fonthill Splendens, Wiltshire 177, 178, 186, 187
Foucault, Michel 273–4
Fownes, Lady Betty 158, 159–60, 161, 163–6, 167, 168–9
Fownes, Sir William 160, 161, 162, 163, 166, 168, 169, 170
Fox, Henry 55, 60, 76–7, 87–8, 92
Fox, Stephen 'Ste' (*later* Lord Ilchester) 60, 91
  background 59–60
  and John, Lord Hervey 5, 60–63, 67–9, 70, 75, 76, 79–80, 81–4, 86, 87, 90–91, 92–3, 94–5, 99–100, 110, 112, 199, 275–6, 285
  marriage 87–90, 93, 105, 278
Fox-Strangways, Elizabeth (*née* Strangways-Horner) 87–91, 93, 94, 96–8, 99, 105, 278
Fox-Strangways, Lady Frances Muriel 99
Fox-Strangways, Lady Susannah Sarah Louisa (Susan) 98
Franchi, Gregório Felipe Francisco 180
  and William Beckford 181–2, 183, 186, 187–92, 196–8, 276–7, 281, 285
  death 198
  marriage 182–3
Franchi, Loreto 181, 182
Franklin, Richard 74
Freeholder, The 130
Freeman's Journal, The 195
French National Assembly 144, 145–6
Fryer, Sir John, Lord Mayor of London 33
Fryer, William 194
Fuller, Thomas 38, 39, 49

General Evening Post, The 151–2
General Trades Union (of New York) 255–6

Gent, William 31
Gentleman Jack (TV series) 8, 202, 228, 233
George I 66
George II 70, 72, 73, 95
George III 143, 210
George IV: as Prince of Wales 142–4, 184
Girardi, Maria Prassede 181
Glasgow: cotton industry 235–6
Gloucester Journal, The 147–8
Goddard, Lucy 160, 161, 164, 165, 169, 170
Gordon, Lord Douglas 179
Grand Tour, the 57, 60, 63, 67
Gray, Thomas 102, 104, 106, 109, 114, 115–16, 118, 280, 281
Great Burlington Street, London: No. 31 79–83, *80*, 97–8
Greville, Charles 177
Griffin, William 39, 49, 275
Grombach, John V. 152
Guerchy, Claude Louis François Régnier, Comte de 124, 126, 127, 128
Gustav Adolph (ship) 196
Guthrie, James 42, 43, 44, 46, 49
  Ordinary's Accounts 42–3, 50

Halford, Diane 228–9
Hall, John 27
Hamilton, Caroline: *Reminiscences of Mrs Caroline Hamilton* 160
Hamilton, Charles 89, 251
Hamilton, Susan Euphemia Hamilton (*née* Beckford), Duchess of 180, 198
Hamilton, Sir William 177
Hardwicke's Marriage Act (1753) xi
Haslem, Robert 255, 256, 257, 258–9, 260, 261, 262, 263, 266
Hastings, Levi *see* Trujillo, Josh
Hayes, Catherine 44–5, 49
Hayes, John 44–5

Index

Hayes, Mr (surgeon) 138
Heffernan, Paul 111–12
Hellfire Club 115
Henley, Samuel 177
Henri II, of France 119
Henry VIII 21
Hepburn, John Newbolt 192
Hervey, Augustus John 66
Hervey, Lord Carr 56, 57
Hervey, Elizabeth 62
Hervey, Frederick 83
Hervey, George William *see* Bristol, 2nd Earl of
Hervey, John 'Jack', Lord 59, 91, 91–3
   background 56–8
   and Dr Antonio Cocchi 69, 110
   death 98
   and Ste Fox 5, 60–63, 67–9, 70, 79–80, 81–4, 86, 87, 88, 90–91, 94–5, 96, 99–100, 199, 278
   makes No. 31 Great Burlington Street home 79–80, 81–3, 84, 173, 189, 275–6, 285
   marble bust 100
   marriage and children 57, 63–4, 65–7, 68–9, 80–81, 83, 84, 98
   and Lady Mary Wortley Montagu 58–9, 93–4
   political life 58, 70–72, 95, 96
   and Alexander Pope 85–7
   and William Pulteney 55–6, 70–72, 73–7, 76, 84, 86
   relationship with Queen Caroline of Ansbach 73, 87, 88, 95
   Voltaire introduces to Francesco Algarotti 93–4, 96
   his will 98–9
Hervey, Lepell 66
Hervey, Mary 'Molly' (*née* Lepell), Lady 57, 63–7, 68–9, 80–81, 83, 84, 86, 98–9

Hervey, Mary (daughter) 66
Heworth Grange, Yorkshire 223
Hogarth (*née* Gibbons), Ann 91
Hogarth, Richard 91
Hogarth, William 91
   Lord Hervey and His Friends 90–3, 100
Holland House Papers 100
homosexuality 1–2, 9–11, 273–4
   and adult adoption 106
   and community 280–81
   and homes 275–7
   and the law xi, 282–4
   and marriage 277–9
   see also 'queer/queerness'; sodomites/sodomy
Hooper, S.: *The Discovery or Female Free-Mason* 133, 133–5
Hopson, Justice 250
Howe, William 194, 195
Hoxan, Henry 38, 39
Huntly, George Gordon, 9th Marquess of 179

Ickworth House, Suffolk 56, 58, 62, 63, 68, 70, 83–4, 98, 99
Ilchester, Giles Stephen Holland Fox-Strangways, 6th Earl of 100
Ipswich Journal 144
IRA (Irish Republican Army) 172
Irish Civil War (1922–3) 172
Irish Penal Laws 157, 158

Jackson, Augustus 269
Jacques, Monsieur (broker) 138, 139
James VI (of Scotland) and I (of England) 241
Jane (ship) 194
Jewit, Mary 215
João V, of Portugal 181
Johnson, Dr Samuel 48, 62, 109

Index

Jones, Mary (Peter Sewally) 8–9, 253–5, 255, 257–71, 282–3, 285
Jones, Suranne 202

Kandler, Frederick 112–13
Kedger, George 39–40, 42
Kent, William 57
Kertbeny, Károly Mária 1, 273
Kilkenny, County 6, 7, 155–6
   Inistioge 162, 172
   Kilkenny Castle 156, *156*, 159
   Woodstock 158, 159, 161–2, 163, 164, 165–6, 167–70, 171, 172
Kinsey, Albert 152

'Ladies of Llangollen' 6–7, 171, 285
   and Anne Lister's visit 7, 155, 208–9, 210–15
   see also Butler, Lady Eleanor *and* Ponsonby, Sarah
Lage, Bárbara Maria de Castelo de 183
Lage, Francisco de 183
Langley, Batty: *An Accurate Description of Newgate* 26, 27
Launay, Monsieur de (fencer) 149
Lawrence, Gabriel 4, 5, 14, 53–4
   at Mother Clap's Field Lane molly house 13–15, 17, 18, 21, 23, 275, 280, 282, 285
   in Newgate Prison 23–9, 31, 32, 41–4
   his trial 34, 35–9, 40–41, 107, 283
   Tyburn hanging 46, 49–51, 61
Laws Respecting Women, The 72
Lawton, Charles 207, 208, 214
Lawton, Mariana (*née* Belcombe) 206–9, 211, 212, 214–15, 217, 222
Leeds Mercury 231
Le Goux, Monsieur (surgeon) 138
Lemmey, Huy *see* Miller, Ben
Lepell, Mary (*née* Brooke) 64

Lepell, Brigadier-General Nicholas Wedig 64
Lidgate House, Yorkshire 218–19, 220, 221, 225, 226
Lister, Anne 7–8, 285
   birth and early life 203–5
   death and funeral 231–2
   as explorer 216
   inherits Shibden Hall 215–16
   and Mariana Lawton 206–9, 211, 212, 214–15, 217, 222
   her masculinity 205–6, 216, 275
   settles at Shibden Hall 230–31
   visits the Ladies of Llangollen 7, 155, 208–9, 210–14, 215, 276
   and Ann Walker 201–3, 217, 218–34, 278–9
Lister, Anne (Aunt Anne) 204, 208, 209, 211, 212
Lister, James 204, 215
Lister, Captain Jeremy 203
Lister, Jeremy (son) 203
Lister, John 203
Lister, Marian 203, 208, 231
Lister, Rebecca (*née* Battle) 203
Lister, Samuel 203
Llangollen, Wales 170–72, 208–9
   Plas Newydd 6, 155, 171, 173, 209–13, 214, *211*, 276
   see also 'Ladies of Llangollen'
London, 1746 map of (Rocque) 16
London Evening Post 130
London Journal, The 53
Lookup, Captain 237
Loughborough, Alexander Wedderburn, Baron (1st Earl of Rosslyn) 142, 176, 177, 178, 184
Louis XV, of France 120, 122, 123, 124–5, 126, 127–9, 135–6, 137, 142
Louis XVI, of France 119, 120, 121, 129, 136, 137, 140, 141, 145, 151

333

Index

Lowndes, Mr (magistrate) 245, 246, 247, 248, 249
Lynch, James Henry: *The Ladies of Llangollen* 171
Lyness, Joseph (John Williams) 267–70, 279

Mcfarlane, Reverend John 249
Mackenzie, James 218
Mackintosh, Martin ('Orange Deb') 15, 17, 21, 280
Male and The Female Husband, The (broadside) 215
Mandeville, Bernard de 47
Manion, Jen: *Female Husbands: A Trans History* 215, 239, 240
Mann, Sir Horace 102, 104, 106, 109, 110, 110, 111, 112, 118, 274, 280
Manor School, York 203, 223
Mansfield, William Murray, 1st Earl of 138, 139
Marcus, Sharon: *Between Women: Friendship, Desire, and Marriage in Victorian England* 107–8
Marie Antoinette, Queen of France 120, 141, 152
Marlborough, Charles Spencer, 3rd Duke of 92
Marriage Duty Act (1695) xi, 108
Martins, Sir George 17
Middleton, Reverend Conyers 92
Miller, Ben and Lemmey, Huw: *Bad Gays: A Homosexual History* 200
'mollies'/molly-houses xi, 4–5, 19–24, 31, 36–8, 39, 40, 42, 45, 51–2, 54, 59, 107, 118, 192, 274, 275, 277–8, 279
Montagu, George 102, 105, 106, 109, 114, 118
Montagu, John Montagu, 2nd Duke of 134

Montagu, Lady Mary Wortley 58, 59, 74, 86, 93–4
Moore, Mr (tutor) 175, 176, 177, 178
Morande, Monsieur de 138–9
Morning Herald 177, 180
Morning Post 136
Morrill, John A. 264
Morton, Dr William 273
Müntz, Johann Heinrich: *John Chute* 105

Naegle, Walter 106
Napoleonic Wars (1803–15) 217
New York
  Black community 258
  Claremont 195
  Forsyth Street 242–3
  Greene Street 258
  Pearl and Chatham Streets 243–4
  Sing Sing Prison 253–4, 256, 270
New York Herald, The 256, 257, 258–9, 262, 264, 268, 269–70
Newark Daily Advertiser 270
Newgate Prison 5, 24, 25, 26–9, 31, 34, 35, 41, 42, 43, 44, 45, 53, 192
Newton, Thomas 32–3, 36–7, 39, 41, 42, 43
Nivernais, Louis-Jules Mancini-Mazarini, duc de 123, 124, 138, 139
North, Senator William 10, 11
Northcliffe, Isabella 231

O'Grady, Paul (Lily Savage) ix
Old Bailey, the 29, 33–4, *34*
Old Burlington Street, London *see* Great Burlington Street, London
'Orange Deb' *see* Mackintosh, Martin
Orléans, Louis-Philippe, duc de 143
Ormonde, Walter Butler, 16th Earl of 157, 162, 163, 164, 165, 166, 169
Oxford Dictionary of National Biography 152
Oxford English Dictionary 193, 280

Park, Mr (solicitor) 169
Parke, Miss: school 158–9
Partridge, Mark 14, 17, 21, 23
Pasteur, Louis 273
Patch, Thomas: *British Gentlemen at Sir Horace Mann's Home in Florence* 110
Patrick Henry (packet ship) 237
Patterson, Mary 256–7
Pennant, Sir Samuel, Lord Mayor of London 35
Pennsylvanian, The 248, 249, 250
Phillips, Thomas 39, 275
Pictou, Nova Scotia 237, 241
pillorying 52–3
Pilot, The 151–2
Plas Newydd *see* Llangollen
Poitiers, Diane de 119
Ponsonby, Chambré Brabazon 158
Ponsonby, Louisa (*née* Lyons) 158
Ponsonby, Mary (*née* Barker) 158
Ponsonby, Sarah (Sally) 6–7, 158, *171*
   birth and background 6, 7, 158–60, 172
   and Lady Eleanor Butler 159, 160–70, 276
   death 172
   and Anne Lister's visit 155, 208–9, 210–13
   settles at Llangollen 6–7, 170–71, 173, 276
Ponsonby-Barker, Chambré Brabazon 158
Pope, Alexander 85–7
   Epistle to Dr Arbuthnot 86
Popery Act (1703) 157
Powderham Castle 173–6, *174*, 177–8, 183–5, 192, 199
'Powderham Scandal' 7, 174, 180
Priestley, Eliza 219–20, 221, 225, 226
Priestley, William 220, 221, 225, 226
Public Advertiser 185
Pullen, Samuel 38, 39

Pulteney, William 55–6, 70–72, 73, 76, 76–7, 86
   A Proper Reply to a Late Scurrilous Libel . . . 74–5, 76, 84, 86

Queensberry, William Douglas, 4th Duke of 149
'queer/queerness' xii, 1–2, 4, 5–6, 18, 107–8, 115, 117–18, 172, 173

Raine, Eliza 223
Reading Mercury, The 149
Redlynch, Somerset 59–60, 62, 94, 100
Reynolds, Sir Joshua: *William (Thomas) Beckford* 179
Richard of Chichester, St 203
Richardson, Messrs (publishers) 150
Richmond, Charles Lennox, 2nd Duke of 63, 67
Richmond, Sarah Lennox (*née* Cadogan), Duchess of 63, 67
'Rider, The' 129
Robineau, Alexandre-Auguste: *The Fencing-Match between the Chevalier de Saint-Georges and the Chevallier d'Éon* 145, *148*
Robinson, H. R.: *Peter Sewally* 254
Rocque, John: 1746 map of London 16
Rogister, J. M. J. 152
Rowe, Nicholas 64–5
Royal Vauxhall Tavern, London ix
Rundle, Sophie 202
Rustin, Bayard 106

Saint-Georges, Georges Bologne de 143
Saint-Georges, Joseph Bologne de 143–4
Salt, Sir Titus 232
Saltaire, West Yorkshire 232
Satan's Harvest Home (1749 pamphlet) 4, 67

Index

Savage, Lily *see* O'Grady, Paul
Scott, Sir Walter 209
Secret du Roi (secret service) 122, 123, 124–5, 126, 127, 128, 129, 136, 139
Sedgwick, Eve Kosofsky: *Tendencies* xii
Sellers, Joseph 23, 37, 54, 277
Sepulchre's, St, London 43, 46–7
Seven Years' War (1756–63) 122–3
Sewally, Peter *see* Jones, Mary
Seymar, William: *Marriage Asserted . . .* 109, 111
Seymour-Conway, Francis 150–51
Shelley, Percy Bysshe 209
Shibden Hall, Halifax 202, 203, 204, 204–5, 206, 208, 209, 213, 215–16, 127, 219, 221, 222, 227, 231, 232, 276
Slave Trade Act (1807) 197
Smith, John 251
Smith, Rear Admiral Sir Sidney 151
Smithfield, London: pillory 52, 53
Society for the Reformation of Manners 22–3, 32, 37, 277
sodomites/sodomy 5, 7, 17, 19, 20, 21, 22, 24, 27, 31–3, 35, 36, 38, 40, 55, 59, 67, 75–6, 84, 88, 111, 115, 192–3, 194, 275
    in America 240–41
Spiesen, Anna Sophia 129
Staffordshire Advertiser, The 147
Staples, Sir Robert 158
Stephens, Samuel 23, 37, 51–2, 54, 107, 277, 278
Steuben, Friedrich Wilhelm August Heinrich Ferdinand von 9–11
Stonewall (charity) 284
Stonewall riots, New York (1969) 1
Strangways-Horner, Susannah 87–9, 90, 96, 97
Strangways-Horner, Thomas 87, 88–9
Strawberry Hill House, Twickenham 102, 114, 186

Strype, John: *Survey of the Cities of London and Westminster* 15, 33–4
Sun, The (England) 151
Sun, The (New York) 262, 266
Sutherland, Elizabeth (*née* Walker) 217, 218, 221
Sutherland, Captain George Mackay 218, 221, 228
Sutherland-Walker, Evan Charles 232

Talochon, Marie-Vincent (Le Père Elysée) 151
Tatler, The 20–21
Taylor, John: 'The Description of Tyburn' 48
Test Acts 85
'Third Sex', the 59, 74
Thompson (packet ship) 237–9, 241
Toft, Mary 134
Tory Party 70, 86, 87, 89, 206
Town and Country Magazine: *The Trial of M. D'Eon By A Jury of Matrons* (anon.) 130, 130–31
Treaty of Paris (1763) 123
Trujillo, Josh and Hastings, Levi: *Washington's Gay General: The legends and Loves of Baron von Steuben* 9–10
Turner, Charles 151
Tyburn, London 5, 25, 28, 44, 45, 46, 48, 50, 61

Uganda: Anti-Homosexuality Act (2023) 284
Ulrichs, Karl Heinrich 1

Van Buren, President Martin 273
Van Dyck, Anthony 185
Vickery, Amanda: *Behind Closed Doors* 3, 275

Index

Victoria, Queen 107, 156, 273
Villeman, Reverend 89, 92
Voltaire 93
Vyne, The, Hampshire 5, 103, 112–15, 118, 276, 281

Wainwright, Sally: *Gentleman Jack* 7–8, 202
Walker, Ann
  background 217–18
  death 232
  and Anne Lister 201–3, 217, 218–34, 278–9
Walker, Aunt 224–5, 226, 232
Walker, Benjamin 10
Walker, Fanny (*née* Penfold) 218
Walker, John 217, 218
Walker, John (son) 217, 218
Walker, Mary (*née* Edwards) 217, 218
Walker, William 217
Walpole, Horace 101, 116, 118
  The Castle of Otranto 102
  and Dr Antonio Cocchi 109, 112
  and John Chute 102, 103–5, 106–7, 114–15, 116, 280–81
  political career 101–2
  and Strawberry Hill House 102, 114, 186
Walpole, Sir Robert 71, 72, 73, 74, 76, 86, 89, 95–6, 101
Walton, W. L.: *Plas Newydd* 211
Ward, Edward 'Ned': *The Secret History of Clubs* 19–20, 21, 107, 277, 278

Wedderburn, Alexander *see* Loughborough, Baron
Weekly Journal, The 31–2, 53
Whale, John 32
Whig Party 55, 70–71, 74, 86, 89, 92, 95, 96, 102
White, Thomas 192
White Swan, Vere Street, London xi, 192, 193, 282
Whithed, Francis 5, 103–7, *104*, 108, 109, 112, 118, 278, 280
Whytle, George 40–41
Williams, Constable 23, 32–3, 37
Willis, Constable 23, 32–3, 37
Wilson, Elizabeth (*née* Cummins) 235–9, 240, 241, 242, 245, 246–9, 250–51, 279
Wilson, George 8, 235–51, 266–7, 279, 282–3, 285
Wilson, Mr (professor of anatomy) 151
Winnington, Thomas 89, 92
Wolfenden Report (1957) 1
Wood, Thomas 45
Woods, George 194, 195
Woodward, Reverend Josiah 22
Wordsworth, William 209, 210
Wyatt, James: Fonthill Abbey 186–7, *187*
Wymms, Captain 163

Yard, Mr (apothecary) 193
Yonge, Sir William: *Sedition and Defamation Display'd* 74
York: Holy Trinity Church, Goodramgate 201–2, 227–8, 232–3

ABOUT THE AUTHOR

Dr Anthony Delaney has a PhD in history from the University of Exeter, where he is an Honorary Fellow, and presents the History Hit podcast *After Dark*. *Queer Georgians* is his first book.